RAISING ROGER'S CROSS

CHARLES KUNKEL

Let us raise the Cross together

Fr. Charlie

authorHOUSE™

1663 LIBERTY DRIVE, SUITE 200
BLOOMINGTON, INDIANA 47403
(800) 839-8640
WWW.AUTHORHOUSE.COM

First published by AuthorHouse: 11/16/2005

ISBN: 1-4208-7793-3 (sc)

Printed in the United States of America
Bloomington, Indiana

This book is printed on acid-free paper.

Photos:
Photo of Roger used with permission of his family.
Photo of Kitten Club used with permission of the Luedke family.
Photos and artwork of Paul Grella used with permission
Other photos by Charles Kunkel, OSC
Photo editing by Gene Plaisted, OSC

DEDICATION

For Carol Vaillancourt, who waited forty-eight years to hear why her son was killed.

Earlier she told her children, "I don't want flowers on my coffin when I die, only a large cross placed there. I have lived with the cross all my life."

CONTENTS

Introduction   ix

CHAPTER ONE
Tender in the Fires   1

CHAPTER TWO
Readiness for Life   5

CHAPTER THREE
At the Rainbow Café   10

CHAPTER FOUR
The Foley Youth   15

CHAPTER FIVE
Riding Hostage   39

CHAPTER SIX
At the Kitten Club   46

CHAPTER SEVEN
Into the Cornfield   68

CHAPTER EIGHT
Naked on the Cross   73

Chapter Nine
A Plan for the Body 80

Chapter Ten
Washing Away the Blood 95

Chapter Eleven
Weird Whisperings 104

Chapter Twelve
The Motives 123

Chapter Thirteen
The Secret Plan 132

Chapter Fourteen
Shy Investigators 144

Chapter Fifteen
Cover-Up Speculations 154

Chapter Sixteen
The Truth Behind the Cover-Up? 171

Chapter Seventeen
Knifing in the Soul 181

Epilogue 194

Appendix A
Kitten Club 195

Appendix B
Newspaper Articles 198

Appendix C
Official Documents 203

ACKNOWLEDGMENTS
AND THANKS TO:

Roger's mother and family who gave their blessing to the project;
Hundreds of storytellers who shared as well as they could;
Key risk-takers who shared beyond their comfort zone;
Local authorities who heard and waited for the right time;
Parishioners who tolerated a mysterious book project;
Crosier brothers who supported an absent-minded first-time author;
Expert critical readers who critiqued and cleaned up the text;
Writing coach, Paul Grella, who promised a "Pulitzer-in-the-making";
AuthorHouse publisher, Kevin King, and content editor, Lesley Bolton,
who added their genius to launch the book into higher orbit; and
Friends who prayed that the author and book would serve the Cross.

All mistakes in the final version of the story belong to the author.

INTRODUCTION

Three years ago I met a young man who had been sexually assaulted, stabbed, and then crushed under the wheels of a car. I could not shake him off and walk away. In my first meeting, this young man did not have a name; he was simply introduced as "that boy from Foley."

He appeared suddenly in a gathering of Crosiers,[1] as we were sharing memories and making plans. I told my religious brothers that I wanted to write a book about the Cross. My mission was to explore how a real story of suffering creates a community of suffering where the risen Lord as the crucified one offers healing. I needed to find a real story of the Cross.

One of the Crosiers in the group said, "When I was eight years old, my mother came home from Foley and said to us kids, 'It is a shame what they did to that boy from Foley. They pushed corncobs down his throat and up his rectum. They stabbed him. Then they threw him out of their car and ran over him.'" Without a moment's hesitation I said, "That's my story."

That "boy from Foley" was Roger Vaillancourt; he was seventeen years old when he was killed on October 6, 1957. While the parish Death Register reported the cause of death as "killed by a car on Highway 169,"

---

[1] The Crosiers, a Roman Catholic religious community, were founded in 1210 with a special mission for the Cross (www.crosier.org).

there seemed to be much more to the story. Two years of research and one year of writing followed.

During the first months of research, I tried to recover this story from a distance as an uninvolved observer. As a story of torture and murder began to emerge, I wanted to step back. But Roger's family and his many friends said, "You opened this door of painful memories; now you must take it all the way." I learned that writing a book about "reality Cross" meant living with a community of suffering and moving together from darkness into the light of truth and healing.

Roger's mother wanted to know the whole truth. When raw, disturbing stories were shared with her, Carol Vaillancourt said, "Keep on digging; I want to know all." She is eighty-seven years old and full of grace from a life filled with suffering. Before the research started, she told her kids, "I don't want flowers on my coffin when I die, only a large cross placed there. I have lived with the cross all of my life."

At least one hundred fifty storytellers helped to recover the story of Roger, which had become scattered during forty-eight years. Each storyteller held a precious fragment. No one knew the whole story. Searching for the truth, piece by piece, was like finding a hidden trail in the underbrush. When the trail faded away or divided, invariably someone's "hand on my shoulder" pointed me in the right direction. Roger himself was guiding the way.

The stories of rape, torture, castration, and murder appeared nowhere in newspaper articles, in the State Highway Accident Report, or in the Death Certificate. There were no reports of any investigations by the state patrol, by the Mille Lacs County sheriff, by the Benton County sheriff, or by the Foley police department. There were no records in the Princeton funeral home, where the body was taken first, and no records in the Foley funeral home, where it was prepared for viewing at two wake services. The gruesome stories, however, were flying around Foley and other area towns already on Sunday afternoon of the same day that Roger died at about 1:20 AM north of the Kitten Club.[2]

What happened to Roger? Why did it happen and who was involved? What happened to the investigation? Why did all the officials in two

---

[2] See Appendix A: Kitten Club.

counties and in two funeral homes, except for the state patrol officers, agree to cover up this story? Why did Roger's father participate in this cover up? Was the reality of castration so terrible that no one in authority could deal with it? What were the hidden issues of sexuality that motivated and caused the final sexual assault, castration, and murder?

There is a growing urgency to know the truth about the murder of Roger Vaillancourt. His mother, Carol, is holding on to dear life until she knows the full truth. She says that she is doing this for her other children. She wants them to receive healing for this gaping open wound. Anyone with any sense of justice wants to make it possible for Roger's mother to have flowers on her coffin when she dies, and not just a large cross placed there.

Hopefully **Raising Roger's Cross** will bring the rest of Roger's story out of darkness and into the light of truth. Risen life and flowers are waiting.

CHAPTER ONE

TENDER IN THE FIRES

It was two nights before the full moon—the harvest moon, or sometimes called the corn moon. On this bright night in the cornfield, Roger was naked at the center of his group. He felt Mack bracing his behind. He saw the seven wild ones leaning in to see. There was wildness and meanness in their eyes. Roger was displayed to the moon. He was worn out.

Mack took charge of the wild ones, knowing now that they were his pathetic accomplices. They had had their fun. He would do the rest. He told them to hold Roger up. He quickly cut away cornstalks, creating his circle. He cut one thin stalk six inches long. He gripped Roger's neck to open his mouth and shoved the cornstalk down his throat, silencing any scream, careful not to cut off his windpipe. Roger could make only muffled sounds; his bulging eyes looked around, searching for help. The Foley youth looked around at each other, amazed at the madman and stunned ...

Neither Mack nor any member of the wild group told the story of what happened to Roger in the cornfield that night. The story was recovered from a hundred different sources and then restored to wholeness. Pieces are still missing; gaps appear; and parts might be assembled in the wrong places.

It was a blessed experience to get to know Roger Vaillancourt through the treasured memories of family members, friends, classmates, Foley residents, and even through the guarded comments of those who were allegedly with Roger when he was mutilated and murdered, those referred to as the "Foley youth" in newspaper articles. At least one hundred fifty storytellers have shared their memories. Only a few turned away. All names have been changed or withheld out of respect for those still living with Roger's Cross and their brave act of telling his story.

Recalling their memories often allowed a deep simmering sadness to surface. Sharing the story of Roger meant telling the truth, which was usually a mixture of good and bad. This scattered story of a brutal murder came together through the memories of many.

Roger's mother, Carol, said that early on "Roger was such a good baby, almost never cried; a child always satisfied with everything; never complained." Roger was the eldest of five children at the time of his death. His mother loved him dearly, as did his two sisters and his two brothers. Roger's sister said, "We younger kids loved him to death. We liked it when Dad and Mom went some place, so that Roger could take care of us. He played hide-and-seek with us. He would make brown sugar sandwiches for us. He would take us on scooter rides."

Roger was more than the eldest child in his family. His father, Vern, was gone often as an over-the-road truck driver. When he was at home, Vern's untreated alcoholism exploded often as physical and sexual violence against his wife. Roger was aware of this terrible abuse of his mother and tried to remain unwavering in this stormy sea. He was an anchor of love for the family. His sister said, "Roger had a very close relationship with our mother. He was always there for Mom. He felt a kind of protective responsibility because of what our mother was suffering." A best friend reported, "Whenever his mother asked him to do something, Roger did not hesitate, but listened and respectfully proceeded to do the chores requested."

Roger too was "badly mistreated" by his father, according to a family member—berated in angry outbursts, belittled during drinking bouts, battered by the butt of a gun, cornered in a very small house by a wounded man. Roger was deeply impacted by the bond of suffering he shared with his mother. He was being toughened by these harsh realities. At the same time, he was still deeply compassionate and tender beyond his years. The sexuality around him was deeply connected with violence. Sexuality and violence were destined to be blood brothers within him, like twin tigers teasing and taunting him out of his tender lair.

Outside of his home, Roger had dozens of "best friends." These friends have treasured memories. Roger was an easy person to be with. He was smiling, friendly, and full of fun. He was well built, short, strong, and fast on his feet. He was feisty, gutsy, spunky, and loved a good risk. He played small-town pranks expected of a growing boy in Foley, Minnesota. One of his friends said, "We crawled to the top of every building in town, threw snowballs at cars and at buildings and other people and found rotten eggs and threw them at dogs." Roger played sports with friends and roughhoused in the neighborhood. He tried hunting, trapping, and chasing in the woods. Most friends felt that Roger's teenage years were wholesome and on the right course, in spite of his father's violence at home.

Even though he had many friends, Roger was not a joiner. In school, he did not try out for varsity or intramural sports. He did not join the band, chorus, or clubs. Socially, Roger did not mix with the A group, B group, or any other group of peers. But Roger was not a loner. He was simply tapping his toes to a different drumbeat. The Senior Class of 1958 dedicated their yearbook to Roger with a full-page picture. His classmates summed up the class memory: "He was well-liked and friendly."

Though he was eager to bring smiles to others, he was aware that he had to deal with some of the limitations in his life—poverty at home, a father withholding affection, his father's alcoholism, loose sexual boundaries around him, small-town aversion for his family, his tender side, his own preference to stand apart from groups, and his shyness with girls.

He attended St. John's Catholic Church regularly and received the sacraments. His faith reminded him that he did not walk by himself but that the Spirit of Jesus was with him, even when he could not feel that special presence. He was grounded and confident enough to maintain a joyful youthful spirit in spite of his growing-up troubles and heartaches.

Roger got a regular job at the Baskfield Shoe Shop in town, working there every day after school, except on Wednesday afternoons when the shop was closed. He also set pins at the bowling alley, keeping him up late at night and by design away from his father when he was at home. He found other odd jobs around town and outside of Foley. His friendly personality opened doors. Roger was diligent and determined to earn his own money and find his own way to get ahead in life. Many people remembered how impressed they were with Roger's initiative and hard work.

Roger's heart was set on owning a Cushman Eagle Scooter like four or five other boys in town. He gave some of his earnings each week to Don, a cousin, who was selling scooters at his gas station. It took awhile, but Roger got a yellow scooter of his own. Now he was no longer tied to home, to the neighborhood, or to small-town Foley. Roger was on the road. He took his friends, boys and girls, on rides to neighboring towns and even as far as St. Cloud. The yellow scooter meant life was good again for Roger. He liked the speed, the chance to share, riding close, and seeking higher ground to spark a smile from someone.

The yellow scooter also meant that Roger could test his ability to venture beyond his comfort zone. Roger was coy and a cut-up among his friends. He was also acutely curious about what was yet beyond his reach. He was no star in school, but he was open and searching for the lessons of life—how far to go, how to survive, how to find a balance, how to get around things, how to stay on course, how to relate, how to break through his walls of fear, and how to be tough and friendly at the same time. The yellow scooter was Roger's special partner, teaching him how to do this new kind of dancing. Roger was well poised to test his adventurous side with the Foley youth. Unfortunately for Roger, he would get much more than he bargained for.

A family member who grew up in Foley suggested, "Foley was such a boring town for a young man; there was nothing to do. Maybe Roger was looking for a change of scenery, some new ways to have fun, some change from this boring place. Roger could have seen in this wild group a chance to break out of his boring background and find a little fun. Of course he would have felt that he would not get too involved in the wild things and would be able to keep everything under control. But sometimes, other things take over, and the person who only intends to play around on the edges of this wildness gets sucked into the vortex and cannot back out of the trouble that is brewing."

CHAPTER TWO

READINESS FOR LIFE

In the summer before his murder, Roger put his adventurousness to a new test. Some of his friends said that Roger was drifting away from them and toward the wild Foley youth. His family did not notice or remember this change, but his friends remember it well. A best friend said, "I want to make it clear that I was not put out because Roger moved into another circle; sometimes an individual just has to find a different circle of friends."

Roger was following his deeper instincts. His friends saw it as drifting. Roger was drawn toward the Foley youth. His friends worried that Roger was naïve about their way of being "wild." But Roger felt a kinship with these fringe folks. He saw his mother being treated badly by his father, and his maturing heart leaned toward others who were being treated badly by the community. His friends feared that these Foley youth would use Roger for their own personal interests. The yellow scooter convinced Roger that he was free enough to take this ride and to bring a smile to the wild ones in town.

Roger was not on a mission to change the Foley youth. He was still an adolescent searching for his own truth and how to live that truth in his own life. He had received sufficient formation from his family, friends, church, school, local community, and some adult mentors. Now he faced a more solitary task: learning how to be tender like his mother, but in his own way, and tough like his father, but in his own way but without the violence. The Foley youth seemed like the right group with whom he could do his work of "coming of age." He was drawn to them as people struggling like himself. They could be his community. He felt sure that he could bring a smile to these folks on the fringe. With them, he could carve out a splendid readiness for life.

Most of the people who were aware of this change in Roger could not see the deeper story. They could see only what was happening on the surface, and what they saw did not make sense. One of Roger's best friends puzzled over it this way: "It is true that Roger drifted into this wilder group, but I never knew why he did. Roger had lots of good friends without belonging to that wilder group. I wondered if he had some need to move into the 'A' group or the 'in' group in school or town. But the problem with this was that the wild group was not the 'A' group or the 'in' group. The wild group was an 'in group unto itself.'"

Another classmate, who was part of the A group and a star athlete, took his own guess: "Roger was no athlete at all. It is possible that Roger had a 'small man syndrome,' which maybe he felt that he needed to overcome by getting into some older group or into some wilder group. On a scale of one to ten from loner to good mixer, I would place Roger at number four."

Roger's family could not explain why he took this turn. His mother, Carol, said, "I think Roger thought that they were his friends. And my kids had such a hard life; maybe he felt that he wanted to have a little fun."

Most of the townspeople in Foley knew about the Foley youth. One of them explained, "Foley was a small, conservative town at that time. The majority of the people wanted everything to follow the same, normal course of conduct and routines. The few people who stood out were called 'the wild crowd' back then. Today that wild crowd might be considered normal teenagers."

A classmate said that she knew about this group and who the key persons were. "They were definitely wild people. They smoked cigs long before other kids were smoking. They did big 'keggers' in the gravel pits. They went to one party after another. And most of them were sexually active, even though the guys were in their early to mid twenties and the girls were in their mid to late teens."

Roger was finding his way with this wild group, the Foley youth. It was a gradual process, as Roger tested the waters of the group and his own fears and desires. The group had its core members but was not otherwise highly organized. "Wildness" meant going with the flow, allowing others to come and go, letting newcomers test whether they could handle the "fast ride." Some interviewees said that they socialized occasionally with this group but wanted to make clear upfront that they were not always with them and not at the Kitten Club the night of Roger's death. But the spirit of wildness required recruiting others into their wild romps with tales of prowess and carousing. As with other previous challenges in life, likely Roger was not a slow learner in this new setting, but someone who welcomed the risks.

It was not really clear when Roger took the dive into the Foley youth. His mother's best guess was that it happened sometime during the summer of 1957, only a few months before his death in October of the same year. A friend of Roger, who found it difficult to imagine Roger going with any group, said that he "remembers something of a personality change in Roger in the last half-year of his life. Roger never did those kinds of things before; it just wasn't Roger." This friend was shocked to discover that Roger had been with the Foley youth at the Kitten Club when he was killed.

One student who knew Roger only in typing class in the month before his death shared her experience of Roger being different: "Roger must have had some kind of personality change during this time. He became a smart-mouthed kid with an attitude. Roger wanted to run with the fast crowd. Twice during September he was kicked out of typing class by the typing teacher because he mouthed off. He didn't care if he got kicked out." She added, "Roger became the kind of kid that made a young girl feel uncomfortable. It was like he was watching me sexually. His appearance was done up like Fonzi on the TV show, a too-cool kid with a leather jacket, slicked-back hair, the kind of kid that nice girls did not go out with. Roger had some personality change like the kind caused by using drugs. It was a very noticeable change in Roger at the beginning of his senior year. Other students noticed it too."

Did Roger get involved with illegal drugs with the Foley youth? The possibility of illegal drugs in Foley in the late 1950s was tested with many of those interviewed. Most said that they never heard of drugs at that time, only the misuse of beer and hard liquor. The town historian said, "Heavy rumors persisted that Roger's death was drug related. The Kitten Club was famous as a place where drugs could be obtained. If it were possible to identify who introduced drugs into the Foley area, it would be possible to find an answer about who killed Roger." This historian graduated from Foley High School in 1951. She said that she was seeing drugs in Foley in that year. An article in the *St. Cloud Times* reported hard drugs being peddled in the St. Cloud Reformatory in 1951. If there were drugs inside the prison, they could also be on the streets in small towns.

Hesitatingly, a classmate said, "There were some faint memories about drugs being considered as a possible cause for Roger's death, that Roger was buying or selling drugs or couldn't come up with the money. But these are just faint memories."

Another classmate said that he heard a rumor that at the Kitten Club the night of his murder, Roger had lots of money on him. Supposedly he was showing this around and attracted quite a crowd.

At this point in the search, however, it has to be said that there has been no clue at all that drugs played any role in the murder of Roger. It is more likely that the story of the alleged use of or dealing in drugs by Roger developed later as a possible reason for a story of mutilation and murder that had no explanation and no ending.

The story of Roger can be grounded in two realities that were at the core of the Foley youth. These two realities hold the secret to what was happening to Roger in the last months of his life and to the circumstances surrounding his murder. These two realities were alcohol and sex. It was critical to think of these two realities as closely connected in the story of Roger with the Foley youth. They were two sides of the same coin, two ingredients in the same stew, two partners in the same dance. If the focus remained only on one of the two, with the other put to the side, the heart of the story of Roger and the Foley youth would be missed. When someone in the story of Roger talked about alcohol, sex was hidden in the same story, even if it was still "untalkable."

A friend who knew Roger fairly well said, "Alcohol changed Roger's personality. He was a nice guy and very likeable until he was drinking.

Then Roger could become belligerent and cocky, very much unlike his normal self. Roger at the Kitten Club seemed like a natural development for Roger, who was drinking alcohol more and more."

On the other hand, Roger's drinking of alcohol should not be overplayed, even while asserting that it was playing a greater role in his young life. Roger's drinking was not always with the Foley youth. Some of his scooter rides with friends took them to bars in small towns where "if you were big enough to put a quarter on the bar, you could get a beer," as reported by one of them. Sometimes Roger's neighborhood group of friends would get a case of beer and drink it together. One of them said about those times, "When Roger was drinking alcohol, sometimes his French blood would get working. It was his 'French Connection.' But with alcohol, Roger could go either passive or argumentative." Some of his friends said that they had wondered if Roger was heading down the same path as his father, who suffered a serious alcohol addiction.

The story of Roger being drunk at the Kitten Club on the night that he was murdered is not unsupported. Alcohol was part of Roger's story, and it was definitely part of his connection with the Foley youth. When the members were interviewed, most of them felt free to tell that part of the story: Roger's being "wildly" drunk at the Kitten Club. They were not free to tell the remainder of the story, however. While the story of alcohol and Roger's drinking is clear, discovering the truth about the role the combination of alcohol and sex played in the story of the Foley youth has been a more challenging task.

CHAPTER THREE

AT THE RAINBOW CAFÉ

Was Roger sexually active? What was Roger's sexual experience during the last months of his life before he was sexually assaulted, castrated, and murdered in the cornfield? Many people around Foley at that time who heard about the cornstalk in his throat, corncob in his rectum, and castration assumed that there was a sexual element to this tragedy. Few could talk about it, and no one could make any sense of it.

Two factors about sexuality in the story of Roger have suggested a reasonable assumption. The first factor was that he gravitated toward the Foley youth, who were allegedly devoted to alcohol and sex and present at the Kitten Club on the night of his murder. The second factor was that the assault and murder involved sexual abuse with a corncob and sexual mutilation. A reasonable assumption was that Roger's association with the Foley youth included some form of sexual activity that led to this kind of brutal assault and death.

Someone who knew Roger and his new wild friends said, "I would have to assume that Roger was sexually active because of the crowd that he hung with; guilt by association. Maybe Roger wanted people to think that he was sexually active and attractive to the girls by hanging out with this wilder group, and maybe he was not sexually active at all. It could be true that Roger was as pure as white driven snow. Roger was a funny kid to read."

Most likely no one outside of the Foley youth knows the truth about this part of the story, and they are not willing to share. Even so, those members who shared their memories and their versions of Roger's death offered some subtle clues, unintentionally or otherwise. These memories are worth our consideration. The stories of the others are helpful too, as a mixture of memories involving some truth and a variety of speculations.

One memory that seems to hold true was that "Roger was not into girls," as one friend said. Roger had several good friends who were girls, but they themselves said that it was like a brother/sister friendship. One of these girls said, "I loved to be with Roger when I was younger as a teen. It was fun to be with him, even though he was quiet and not outgoing. It was necessary to go up to Roger and talk to him. Roger would not come up to others on his own. I remember giving Roger a few dollars to take me on a ride on his new scooter. We would ride to the Gilman pool hall and play the games. When I would say, 'Rog, let's go ridin',' he would never turn me down. Roger was not a girl-chasing guy. But he always had a smile for me, and he was very easy to be with. He was humble and did not pretend to be someone special."

A classmate shared a pleasant memory about Roger in their early high-school years. She said, "In our freshman and sophomore years, Roger and I had a kind of 'crush' on each other, but we never dated. We sat together in the back of the classroom. Roger was short, clean, well built, and had flashing black eyes that came from his French background. I was never allowed to date in those early years of high school. Roger and I never went out on a 'date date.' In fact, I never saw Roger with a girlfriend."

A male friend and classmate said, "He was a very, very close friend of mine, but Roger was not interested in girls. At one point in our freshman or sophomore year, Roger was hooked up with a date with a certain girl by another friend, Don. I don't know how this happened for Roger. But in any case, Roger came to me and asked me if I would want to go on a 'blind date with someone.' I took the chance and took that girl on that date. I ended up marrying her. Roger just did not want to go on a date."

Once Roger got his yellow Cushman Eagle Scooter, he was ready to take his friends on rides. This included friends who were girls and friends who were boys. From the stories shared about Roger and his yellow scooter, it appeared that he was all over the county, in all of the small towns, and into St. Cloud. One male friend has faint memories of Roger making a number of solo scooter trips to a St. Cloud drive-in, where Roger was interested in a girl working there. Another lady said that on a scooter ride with Roger back to Foley from Benton Beach on Little Rock Lake, Roger asked her for a date. She said that she declined because she was already going with someone.

Summing up these memories of Roger's friends, it seemed to them that Roger's attraction to girls was uncertain, slow in maturing, repressed, or absent. Roger had a number of friends who were girls, who enjoyed being with him as a humble and friendly and occasionally gutsy guy. But that special magic was still missing in Roger.

Was it possible that Roger's personality as more quiet, shy, and smiling included a delayed adolescent sexual development, still to be discovered? Was it possible that Roger's experience of his father's abuse of his mother caused a wall of fear within him, a psychological and emotional barrier that prevented his sexuality from emerging in his teen years, maybe creating confusion or a fear that someday he too might end up abusing a girl? Was it possible that Roger was at the early stages of discovering that he was attracted to guys instead of girls, or attracted in some degree to both, a confusing, hidden, and difficult sexual awareness to accept and with which to deal?

A cousin and friend shared how Roger shifted from his usual lightheartedness to sullenness after experiencing his father's abusive behavior. Roger would be very irate but only register a light complaint. He said, "Roger never really vented his deeper feelings. He would say, 'Dad is at it again,' and then clam up and never say what he was feeling. The same would happen with girls. Roger would hug them but never show his real feelings. It seemed that Roger had to live behind a defensive wall, where he would pull down the shade and hide his true feelings."

Sometime during his high-school junior year or during the summer between his junior and senior years and possibly somewhere out on the road, alone with his yellow scooter, Roger made a decision to come out from behind his "defensive wall" of fear, confusion, and repressed feelings. Roger was confronted with a choice: boldly claim his own young humanity or allow his hidden feelings to drag him into a deep dark pit. Roger made a deliberate decision to get connected with the Foley youth. Joining them seemed right to Roger. He was gutsy enough to enter their world. He was handsome enough to turn heads. He was curious enough to explore the connection between alcohol and sex. It was easy enough to make the move. Roger simply walked five business places north from the Baskfield Shoe Shop where he worked and walked into the Rainbow Café.

In the late 1950s, Foley had at least nine social gathering places with various clienteles and reputations. There was the Rainbow Café, serving beer and food; Ruth's Koffe Kup, serving food, especially for youth; Hodel's with beer; the pool hall with beer and sandwiches; Anne's Hotel and Café with a small bar; the Legion; the Municipal Liquor Store; Parkway's Dance Hall and Roller Rink, serving beer and set-ups; and Gus's, serving beer.

A young person of that era clarified the role of the Rainbow Café: "There were two places in Foley where the older kids could hang out. The Rainbow Café was the place where the wild group hung out. They served alcohol. The other place was Ruth's Koffe Kup, the place where the good kids hung out. They did not serve alcohol. If some kids were still at Ruth's at 10:00 at night, Ruthie made them call home. The Rainbow was a nice place too. It had the family café in the front room, and the bar in the back room. I worked for a little while at the Rainbow. But in terms of reputations, the Rainbow was favored by the wild group, and Ruth's was favored by the good kids. Roger was hanging out at the Rainbow at that time."

The Rainbow Café was a special place. It had a reputation for welcoming both regular folks and those on the fringe, who brought to the Rainbow that sense of being on the cutting edge of social change in a small town where change was not welcomed. When regular folks went to the Rainbow, they were looking for a safe way to play around just outside of their own comfort zones. It was the natural hangout for the Foley youth. From their perspective, it was their place in town. The regulars were their guests.

For Roger, the Rainbow Café would be his place of initiation where he could take one giant step into the adult world. Roger arrived at the Rainbow as the quiet, shy, hardworking kid around town, with his smiling face and his beautiful, flashing dark eyes. He arrived with a reputation of being innocent and untouched sexually and with a determination to get connected with the fringe group who claimed the Rainbow as their own. It took Roger only a short while to become "the sweetheart boy of the Rainbow Café."

The summer of 1957 set the stage for Roger's mutilation and murder, and the Rainbow Café was the wild gathering place where it may have been planned. After the murder, the Rainbow Café was no longer the Foley youth's special gathering place. They were not seen together very often. Each one tried to disappear. All but one left Foley as soon as they could. But they could not leave behind the story of Roger.

CHAPTER FOUR

THE FOLEY YOUTH

The group known as "the Foley youth" first appeared in newspaper articles reporting Roger's death. The *Mille Lacs County Times* (October 10, 1957) reported that "a group of Foley young people went to the Kitten Club to dance and when it came time to go home Roger refused to accompany them. The group left for home ..." The *St Cloud Times* (October 24, 1957) reported, "The youth [Roger] had been at the dance with a group of other youths and girls ranging in ages from 19 to 26." Two papers reported the connection of Roger with the Foley youth.[3] What were the deeper connections?

Gradually the names of the Foley youth became known from Roger's family and other storytellers. During interviews, members of the Foley youth contributed missing names. Many storytellers alleged that this group of Foley youth were connected with the death of Roger. It was said, "They took him into the cornfield to initiate him but something went wrong." The purpose of the research was not to delve into their personal histories but to explore how each one related to the group and how this relationship might have contributed to Roger's death.

From the very beginning, the scent in the air suggested that the whole group could have been involved. If only one in the group was

---

[3]   See Appendix B: Newspaper Articles.

totally responsible for everything done to Roger, it could be said that the others in the group, or at least one of them, would have made some effort to get the truth out. Total group silence caused a smell.

The Foley youth were wounded people, not unlike many other folks who lived in Small Town, USA, in the fifties. What made these wild ones special was their risky, reckless ways of sharing their wounds with others. They did not want to wait for a better day and did not want to keep their wounds to themselves.

The fifties are seen sometimes as the "good old days" before all hell broke loose in the sixties. But sociologists will say that the fifties were more like a dammed-up river of social changes generated by the upheavals of World War II. Changes of the sixties were already happening under the surface in the fifties. Many families were hard pressed to hold the line on traditional values and virtues.

The wounds of World War II and the wounds of hidden change were wreaking havoc. Alcoholism, domestic violence, and sexual violence at all levels were happening in the fifties without the understanding of addiction and the social means to intervene. Sexual mores were mutating without anyone being allowed to talk about sex. Sexual boundaries were loosening under the camouflage of alcohol. Social control of communities was held in check by a few authorities and influential families who were not yet accountable in the public arena. The wounds in many families were not yet visible and could not be shared. No one imagined yet that social change could be handled in a more healing way.

In a sense, the Foley youth were the scouts out in front checking the horizon, forging a trail, and testing danger zones for the folks in the rear. They were curious and daring enough to probe the edges of their social wilderness. However, living "wild" meant living with lots of extra suffering afterwards.

Several members admitted in their interviews that Roger's death changed their worlds. One member said, "Like most other teenagers, before the death of Roger, I was mostly self-absorbed, concerned about myself and my own future, and all of that self-centered stuff. After the death of Roger, my life focus changed."

Each wounded person in this story will always be precious. Each one has a valuable story to tell. All can write a stunning book of their own about their forty-eight years of dancing with Roger. But none can risk telling more at this time. Could it be that fear, shame, and trauma keep them from telling their own stories and from sharing their wounds in a way that would lead to healing?

The profiles of each member of the Foley youth are given here to help us understand the story of Roger, something these wild ones could have done a long time ago if they had talked. The profiles are presented in such a way that their personal identities will remain hidden behind pseudonyms. But the story of Roger is no longer theirs to hide or control. It is hoped that someday the Foley youth will choose to tell their own stories and bring their long days and long nights to a restful place of peace.

These profiles are simply sketches. Where possible, the profiles will identify the passion and the motivation that drove them to share their wounds with Roger. Hopefully this approach will explain how it was possible that the Foley youth could have ended up in the cornfield after midnight on October 6, 1957, participating in the mutilation and murder of Roger C. Vaillancourt.

MACK

Mack was the focus of more research than the others in the Foley youth. His own story would be worthy of a book. Numerous folks shared parts of his story. Many of them asked to be considered confidential sources as they feared for their lives if they were to be named. The threat to kill seems to have been a routine ploy for Mack to keep his own story of violence and sexual wildness undercover.

As research began, Mack did not have a name. Many people in Foley could not remember or would not say his name out loud. For them, he was simply "the man out west." Throughout the research, two images of him persisted: mysterious and violent. This man was able to keep everyone off balance and guessing what he was up to next. Some members of the Foley youth said that Mack was not part of their social group. They knew him but not well. They claimed to have been surprised that he was with them at the Kitten Club on the night that Roger was murdered. All of them are afraid of him to this day. One insisted that he could not remember him at all, even after being shown a picture of Mack from the *Benton County News*, though the two may have been close collaborators in what happened to Roger.

Mack grew up in a seemingly normal family and was baptized a child of God on August 23, 1936. There was no "family of origin" explanation for his strange life. During the two-hour interview at his home "out west," Mack said that he had never once thought about Roger after that first month following his death. He claimed no connection with the castration and murder of Roger by commenting, "It looks like I was carrying a cross for these past forty-eight years that I didn't know I was carrying." But another comment by him may have been closer to the truth: "God must have a sense of humor to save a man like me."

As a child he learned how to create a circle of fear around himself. According to stories, he was more than just a troubled child; he created trouble. He did this as a child, as a teen, for three years in the navy, and for the five months between his discharge and the murder of Roger. Then Mack's trail went north to a mining community of Minnesota, then to western states, then living in a mobile home traveling around the country before settling into his desert hideout as "the man out west."

A neighbor commented, "Mack was always a strange person. He was a rebel from the word *go*. I saw him as a disturbed person already as a child. Early on, I saw what he was capable of doing and that he was up to no good and that he could actually do any kind of harm without a second thought. I decided to stay my distance from him for the rest of my life. If he greeted me on the street, I would be cordial, but I would never engage in any kind of conversation with him, always keeping my distance. Mack was creepier than creep. He was always a bully, even as a little kid. Nothing would surprise me about what Mack could have done during his life of crime. All of those possibilities were evident to me in those early years."

Mack did not just play with guns and knives. When he was a youngster, his toys were real weapons, and his weapons were used as real threats to do harm. A neighbor remembered, "Mack was no ordinary bully. He was a bully always with a weapon; and that is a different kind of bully. You do not challenge a bully who is wielding a knife in your face. He wore a leather jacket and cowboy boots to add to his 'tough guy' image. He always carried a switchblade, one of those that flipped open when you pushed the button. As a young teen, Mack was a bully out of control. He bullied other kids all the time. He would pull out his switchblade and wave it in the face of another kid and say, 'If you don't do what I say, I will cut your nuts off.' Then he would twist the switchblade in your face as if he was carving off your nuts."

Other people shared stories about Mack that suggested a possible lifelong history of sexual violence. The early memories of this same neighbor indicate that Mack was fascinated with male genitals. If true, he protected himself from these attractions by a forceful repulsion expressed in threats of violence against the male genitals. The neighbor said, "Yes, it was Mack's standard threat: 'If you don't do what I say, I will cut your nuts off.' I heard him say that all the time. He used his knife to control others. It was true that he was also a 'loud mouth,' but primarily Mack's bully style of violence was focused on his knife and his threat to cut off someone's genitals."

One night in a deer hunter's tent, after a couple of drinks, Mack's father said to his hunting partner, "I don't know what will ever become of my son!" This hunting partner said that this father "often expressed his sadness, but never gave any details about Mack's behavior or the troubles that he caused. He would shake his head and say, 'I don't know what will ever become of him.'"

People around Foley do not have many memories of Mack as a high-school teenager. He was kicked out of school during his sophomore or junior year. He would have been free to roam and develop a special instinct for violence. Old-timers of Foley remember Mack hanging out with a hoodlum group who were not from the Foley area.

In the 1950s, *hoodlums* was the word for "gangs" or "gangsters." These hoodlums wore fancy belt buckles, leather jackets, and cowboy boots and looked like they belonged to another world. Mack allegedly had a need to find trouble to participate in or to create the trouble himself. But like all bullies, Mack would have needed his strong, fearless hoodlum group around him for protection.

Research has been unable to find anyone who was a fellow hoodlum with Mack or knew him well enough during these teenage years to know what kind of trouble he was supposedly causing. There are some stories about Mack bringing drugs into Foley. It is possible to surmise that Mack was trying to develop a market in the Foley area for drug peddling. Many locals believe that he had these kinds of connections and was the source of drugs in Foley during the summer of 1957. He could have introduced drugs to the Foley youth at the very same time that Roger was trying out this new social outlet.

However, if he were pushing drugs, he himself did not become a confirmed dope user. He never seemed to lose his sharp, devious mind for conniving and creating his forceful circle of fear, especially for other young men. There are other stories that at times the girls would swarm around this tall, handsome guy who could turn his sexual energies on or off with the greatest ease.

The unknown shadow world of Mack could have followed up on his boyhood tendencies to traumatize other people whenever possible and to occasionally threaten other young men with castration. If there were any actual crimes of sexual violence during his teenage years, they have remained the hidden stories of those individuals and families who would have been controlled by shame and fear.

One story of possible violence by Mack has been silenced for at least fifty years. If true, it happened in the same cornfield next to the Kitten Club several years before the sexual mutilation of Roger. Mack has threatened to kill the witness many times since that event. This event happened either before Mack entered the navy in the spring of 1954 or during one of his home leaves, possibly in the fall of 1955. It happened in the fall between August and November, when a cornfield provided the cover for Mack's alleged act of violence.

The witness arrived at the Kitten Club with two friends between 9:00 and 9:30 PM. The witness parked the car and got out of the driver's seat; two friends got out of the car on the other side. The witness never told the friends what was experienced. The witness and Mack knew each other. The witness offered this statement: "I saw Mack coming out of the cornfield wiping blood off his hunter's knife on the inside of his pant leg and on the inside of the shirttails of his red and black shirt. Mack noticed me witnessing this and gave me a dirty look. A short while later, Mack came into the Kitten Club, got a drink at the bar, and then pushed into the booth behind me. He leaned over and whispered into my ear, 'If you ever repeat what you saw, I will kill you.' After that event, Mack has threatened to kill me many times. The last threat was only five years ago when he was back in Minnesota visiting family."

Repeated researches of the archives of the four local newspapers from 1951 to 1956 for the months from August to November have produced no story of a body found in the cornfield. Neither was there any story about a castration victim. However, a castrated man could have crawled out of the cornfield, found a doctor to care for him, and lived his entire life in silence. Mack and the victim could have engaged in sexual activity, causing sufficient shame to enforce the silence. Could Mack have walked away feeling righteous before God that one more abomination had been removed from the earth?

A story of Mack walking out of a cornfield wiping off his knife on the inside of his shirttails by itself did not indicate that a violent crime had taken place. But the whispered threat several minutes later changed everything: "If you ever repeat what you saw, I will kill you." His repeated threat to kill the witness over the past fifty years seems to confirm a story of violence. The fact that no body was found has suggested that a murder did not take place. However, a different crime with a hunter's knife could have been committed. Mack's youthful fixation on regularly threatening other boys with a switchblade to "cut off your nuts" may suggest the violent crime of castration. An acquaintance of Mack said that "he has always been violently anti-gay in a fanatically religious way."

Mack was at a groom's party in Foley. Others attending the party reported that Mack was involved in a violent fistfight outside with Dennis Leason, Roger's cousin, before the party started. The argument continued off and on during the party.

At midnight, Dennis left for home, where he was staying with relatives southeast of Ronneby. He stopped at the café in Ronneby for a hamburger, which he took with him. About a half-mile away, his car ended up on the railing of the bridge over the St. Francis River. His body was found in the deep springtime swirling water hole south of the bridge about 4:00 PM on Sunday afternoon.

Sheriff Hewart Siemers decided that Dennis, probably drunk from the party, ran his car up on the railing. Instead of safely opening the car door on the driver's side over the road, the assumption was made that Dennis climbed out of a squashed car window on the passenger side over an embankment that fell off quickly into the river. Supposedly, he rolled into the water and drowned. An eyewitness on the scene the next day said, "This upward climb in the leaning car would have been very difficult for an intoxicated man. The car door on the driver's side was not damaged and easily opened."

Could Mack have finished his fight with Dennis Leason at the bridge southeast of Ronneby and forced Dennis's car on to the railing of the bridge? Old-timers in Foley remembered looking over this scene at the bridge and becoming convinced that this death had to have been the result of a crime. The same eyewitness reported that the gravel mess and footprints around the car indicated some kind of fight had happened. These old-timers have been convinced that Mack was the culprit in this death.

During months before Roger's death, Mack started to hang around the Foley youth as somewhat of a stranger. He might have considered these wild ones almost too tame to keep his interest. At this same time, Roger was making his debut with the group. For Mack, Roger may have presented a much more interesting target for his strange attractions and repulsions.

Ten months after the murder of Roger, Mack married and moved to northern Minnesota to find a job in the iron mines. He and his wife had four children, two boys and two girls. It seemed as though his tumultuous spirit continued to spawn violence within his home and family. Neighbors and coworkers alike knew about gun battles that flared between Mack and his wife, Mattie, right in their home. Their children learned to dodge and run for cover as bullets flew in all directions. Mack was in and out of jail but continued to recover from these setbacks to stay on the job. One of his coworkers said that Mack always kept the crew stirred up, and yet he served as the grievance man for the union.

Some of the old-timers who worked with Mack said that he continued to create fear around him. Since he could not threaten the tough mine workers, he developed his rage against religious and political groups. They said that he would fit into the category of a radical political fanatic, such as the white supremacists and the violently anti-gay hate groups, and that he could easily be considered a member of an American-type al Qaeda terrorist group, which would approve of torture and murder to support their hatred of others and love of violence.

People who were willing to speak about Mack's violent spirit spoke about it in the present tense, as if he were still around, still a threat. "Mack is a mean, violent, and vindictive person. He is not a dummy, but smart." "He is always working with a devious mind, trying to find a way to cheat someone else. Along with this, he has a very destructive temper." "If Mack were using drugs, he did not lose his sharp, devious mind for deceiving others." "He never quits in an argument, but drives it to some kind of violent result. He always blames someone else for whatever goes wrong. He always has an excuse for getting mad or for ending up in jail. He seems to be able to rationalize for himself that he can do no wrong because he has been 'saved.' He talks as if he is the best person in the world. He is a smooth talker, even in his fanatical faith. Mack likes to say: 'I am so saved by the Lord that I could kill someone and no one could do anything against me.'"

Currently, Mack and Mattie live out west in a desert ranch home, about seven miles away from the closest town. Both grew up Roman Catholic but now refer to that Church as "the Romans." They claim that they will have nothing to do with any established Christian church ever again. They gather with a small group of like-minded Christians to read the Bible about the end times, using only Revelation in the New Testament and parts of the Acts of the Apostles, which reaffirm their belief that Christ will return to the earth within the next five to ten years. They believe that after Christ has cleaned up the world, there will be one thousand years with Christ as the ruler of the world. Then Satan will be released, allowed one more try to unite the nations against Christ. Then Christ will conquer Satan. Then there will be the new heavens and the new earth promised in the book of Revelation.

During a lengthy interview in their home, both preached about their Christian beliefs as the true faith. They focused on the future, on the end times, on Christ coming in victory. They did not want to deal with past issues. Mattie reacted forcefully when I mentioned the murder of Roger: "None of that is true; none of that is true!" Later she seemed to grieve: "Why can't these people leave these terrible things of the past alone? Why do they have to bring this stuff up again and again?"

When the detail about the corncob forced into Roger's rectum was introduced, without the slightest inference that this could have been one of Mack's violently anti-gay activities, Mattie exploded with, "There were no 'queers' back then like we have today. There is no truth to that story. None of that is true. I never heard stories about those queers with the corncobs. I was a classmate of Roger, and I was very involved in activities in the school, but I never heard anything about those queer things with the corncobs." The echo of her anger vibrated in the air.

One of the Foley youth said, "Years later, we heard that Mack had gone to prison for rape. All of us in the group were greatly relieved." It would be helpful to know exactly what kind of sexual crime might have been involved in this case. It cannot be assumed that it was the normal kind of rape. Others have said that he had been in and out of prison and often involved with the law.

The chief of police of the town close to where Mack and Mattie live clarified the situation very simply. When he heard about the castration preceding the murder of Roger, he said, "Any act of violence that attacks the genitals usually reveals a personality profile of someone with a sexual aberration, someone with a very special kind of violence." The chief said that there is almost no exception to this rule.

Back in those days, society did not have the right psychological insight to think clearly about the unusual behavior of someone with such a "special kind of violence." Today, such a person would likely be identified as a "sociopath," a person without a conscience. There is no clear scientific explanation for this occasional phenomenon. It could be a DNA deficiency, a structural deficit in the brain, a lack of bonding attachment in early childhood, or some other random factor that creates such a person.

Persons without a conscience are those free to do whatever they want to do when they want to do it. They are not limited by normal codes of conduct that keep the rest within normal bounds. To others, it appears that the sociopath is acting impulsively, but that is not the sociopath's own experience. He imagines himself acting normally. He does not have a moral compass, conscience, to guide him.

These persons can be alert manipulators of others. They are usually bold, blunt, cold-hearted, with no feelings toward the ones they hurt, scare, or kill. They can control others by clever calculation or by raw instincts. They are practiced liars and are able to show whatever face is necessary. They do not carry a history of guilt for the terrible things they've done. Worst of all, a sociopath does not recognize that other people have an identity, feelings, spiritual reality, presence, or bonds of affection with others. For these reasons, such individuals can be terribly dangerous and often can manipulate their way through life.

This is not meant to be the great unmasking of Mack. But it is the unmasking of a false mystery that has controlled and prevented healing. The parting words of Mack at the end of the interview at his home in the desert indicated that now he might understand that the time has come to show his true colors.

Mack walked with me to the car, just the two of us. On the way to the car, he said, "I want you to know that I did not kill that boy." I did not have anything to say. Mack then pointed to the gun on his belt and said, "By the way, this was not meant for you. I was helping a neighbor clean some brush, and this is the best way to take care of rattlesnakes."

Then Mack said something strange that sounded like a sly threat: "You know, I have never found a Mojave here in these parts." He asked if I knew what a Mojave was. I said that I did not. He explained, "A Mojave is a rattlesnake that changes colors with the environment that it is in. So it is very difficult to see when a Mojave is present." Knowing some of the history of this man, a queasy and uneasy feeling surfaced in my being. Was he saying that I was a Mojave rattlesnake that changes colors to hide out and that the gun was really meant for me after all?

I thanked him for his hospitality. Then I asked him, "Can I call you in the future for some help with this story, if necessary, or if there is something that might be helpful to you?" He said, "By all means." I drove away, breathing a lot easier. I was very grateful that I was able to complete this part of the mission and wondered whether Mack was the true Mojave in this story and was indicating that he was ready to show his true colors.

Before leaving this desert town, many reflections surfaced about this unusual encounter with Mack and Mattie. Their intense belief in the imminent coming of Christ within the next five to ten years seemed to beg for some major relief from God within their foreseeable lifetime.

Their extreme faith was not a pretense; it seemed to be very real for them. They yearned for the end of the world as they knew it. Were they yearning for liberation from their own lives?

DEWEY

Dewey had quite a reputation around Foley. Parents struggled to keep their daughters and sons away from him, while he used his secret ways of captivating one after the other. Vern Vaillancourt tried his best to keep Roger away from Dewey. Vern lost; Dewey won. A friend who saw Roger drifting away from his neighborhood group said, "Dewey was one of Roger's better friends" in the summer of 1957. "People talked about Dewey and Roger being together; 'town kids' hanging out together, a strange relationship."

Dewey was five years older than Roger. It was said that he came from a home where there was sex without walls or boundaries. It seemed Dewey developed as a sexually wounded man, a sexual merry-go-round, a wild fire burning in all directions, a man addicted to venereal pleasures wherever possible. People said that he regularly pursued numerous girls at the same time.

Roger entered this circle of fire with his own sexual wound. Roger, still mostly uninitiated, felt a kinship with this wounded man. It can be said that Roger was enticed. But it can also be said that Roger walked into this circle of sexually wounded friends with a kind heart for other people on the fringe.

One of the waitresses at the Rainbow at this time said that "Dewey was not just an out-of-control lover who wanted too many women friends; he was a mean man, controlling others with his meanness." Dewey's meanness was a regular theme with Foley old-timers. One couple said, "We have always believed that Dewey was involved in causing the death of Roger. We do not know how it happened, but we believe that he was at the center of it. We have always been convinced that Dewey was capable of murder if he was in the right situation and with the right group. Dewey has always been a totally self-centered man."

CINDY

Cindy came out of the same turbulent whirlpool and sexually wounded family as Dewey. She found her own way through the wildness of her early years. It is speculated that Cindy had a single goal: marry an older man who had the financial means to lift her out of poverty and out of Foley. She supposedly focused all of her passions on this one purpose.

During her sexually active years in the Foley area, Cindy was as wild as she could be, dating numerous men at the same time, always looking for one more. One of her erstwhile girlfriends said, "Cindy did not have the best reputation in town. We were friends for a couple of years. She wanted to be on the 'wild side.' Cindy was scared of the guys whom she couldn't wait to date." That was a strange comment that rang the bell of truth. It suggested that Cindy was willing to toy with sex and the possibility of violence to reach her goal.

She was blond and petite and always wore high-heeled shoes, was usually well-dressed and ready for action. She wore a pink rainbow pin along with a winning smile. She found her dates, who were always older men, at the Rainbow Café, even if she had to sit in an empty bar for hours waiting for the one she wanted. It is said that Cindy, though petite and smiling, was not tolerant, tentative, or easily pushed aside; instead, she was focused, fierce, and forceful about her mission—anyone hampering her hunt would be dealt with.

At the time of Roger's death, one of Cindy's potential partners for life was Pete. His own profile and story will indicate that at that time there was no possibility he was going to settle down with a sixteen-year-old, hyperintense high-school girl. Pete lived in a much bigger world than Cindy. Could Roger have made a foolish mistake in breaking Cindy's stride and her concentration on her chosen prey, Pete—a foolish mistake that proved fatal?

Clearly, Cindy did not have eyes for Roger. Roger could never have met her standards. Roger was from a poor family; he would never have been able to take her out of poverty and out of Foley. Sexually, Roger was still at the starting gate, while Cindy had allegedly been around the track many times.

When the whole story of Roger's mutilation and murder was shared with her and Dewey at the latter's home, Cindy's closing comment was, "I do not feel any guilt about anything in regards to this past event; no guilt at all." Her comment could suggest that she never shed a single tear for Roger's death. She gave the impression that she had been too hardened by the wounds of wild sex in her own life to seek healing. Could Roger have been just an unlucky chilling misstep in her chase to the goal?

Pete

Pete died in 1999 and left behind a solid image in his family and community as a gentle, good man. All the storytellers could not say enough about his goodness. All said that it was impossible for him to ever hurt anyone, even an animal. It made no sense at all to them that Pete could have been involved in any way with the mutilation and murder of Roger. His story of goodness has remained intact. But there was a hidden story that also needed to be probed. He added his own wound to the story of Roger. The pieces of the puzzle come together to place him at the scene.

Pete was twenty-seven years old in 1957, ten years older than Roger. According to some of the storytellers, Pete was bisexual. Later in life, he married and was totally faithful to his wife and family, leaving behind those earlier suspicions. In the story of Roger, however, Pete was still open to the wider spectrum of sexual experiences.

Ann was one of the Foley youth. She worked for a while as a waitress at the Rainbow Café. At the same time, Pete worked in the bar section. The two sections of the café were visible to each other. Ann said that "Pete and Bill Fox were very good friends. They were always together." Everyone in the Foley area knew that Bill Fox (now deceased) was an openly gay man throughout his life. When Pete was working the bar, Bill was there. When Pete was not working the bar, he was often at the Rainbow with his good friend Bill. Ann said, "I often saw Pete and Bill rubbing shoulders and having their hands on each other's buttocks."

Bisexuality itself was not the issue. The issue was how Pete's bisexuality possibly contributed to the story of Roger. Pete offered normal friendships to all kinds of people. His sexual attraction to a wider spectrum was only one part of his life. His friends included the regular folks of Foley, the fringe folks from the country and town, the Foley youth, the more hidden bisexual group of men from the area, several openly gay men, and the younger high-school girls who hung out at the Rainbow. The innate kindness of Pete gathered around him many types who could use a little kindness in their lives.

"Pete was often one of the drivers who took others to socials and games," recalled one of the young women of that time who held him in highest regard. "Most youth did not have their own cars in those days. It was always a project to organize group transportation to events. Pete was a reliable friend for rides. He was not wild or full of vinegar. He would not swat a fly. He was a laid-back kind of guy, kind, slow, easy to be with, not the kind of person who would hurt anyone. He had an old yellow Buick that others piled into. We could always count on Pete."

Darlene was another of the Foley youth. She offered her own words about Pete: "He was like the guardian angel over us younger girls who were running with some older guys. He was very protective over us. We younger gals got to know the older guys through Pete. He was like a 'big, big brother' to us. He was a quiet, shy guy, but lots of fun, always knew what was going on, and when he was around, we knew it was going to be safe for us gals."

A clear image of Pete emerged. He was an effective social facilitator for the folks of Foley. He brought people together by means of his goodness. He helped others to find friends, dates, and good times. He was fatherly toward younger folks and calmed the wildness of social storms. He dropped off people at home when they were too drunk to drive. He was comfortable with the variety of sexual orientations in the group. Everyone had a friend in Pete.

Though separated by ten years, the personalities of Pete and Roger were similar. Both tended to be more quiet, less assertive, friendly, and easy to be with. Both were attractive to a wide spectrum of regular and fringe folks. There would have been a natural affinity between these two men. They would have liked each other immediately. If Roger were looking for a taste of wildness in the summer of 1957 at the Rainbow

Café, and if he were still uncomfortable in dating girls, Pete and Roger could have easily found a hidden place to park the old yellow Buick and share a few sexual intimacies. From their perspective, this would have been a comfortable, calming, minor event promising some valued support and friendship for the future.

Two quiet guys in a hidden place for a few sexual intimacies seemed harmless enough. But a small town kept no secrets. This rendezvous would have likely happened in a wooded spot out in the country before the gossip hit the streets of Foley within a day or two. The Rainbow would have been alive with talk—some approving, some jealous, others inflamed with hidden rage.

This sexual connection with Pete could have inflamed Cindy. This event might have propelled the Foley youth to move from the Rainbow Café to the Kitten Club. Could Pete have been caught up in something that was beyond his control and not known how to "facilitate" the growing turbulence?

His surviving spouse has accepted the possibilities of this story, even though it seemed so contrary to everything else she knew about her beloved Pete. Once married, there was never any inkling of any unfaithful activity. She said, "I am convinced that he would never do anything to hurt anyone. But also Pete did not share with me his deepest, darkest burden, that is, whatever he knew about the death of Roger. He carried that burden with him to the grave. Several years after the death of Roger, Pete had two surgeries to deal with stomach ulcers, something occasionally caused by stress. I never asked him about the death of Roger, even though I thought about it often. Both of us knew that it was a taboo topic in our relationship. I was probably afraid what I might find out, not that Pete had done something to hurt someone, but that he did not tell the authorities what he knew about that event. Now I regret never taking the initiative to ask him about what he knew."

Roger and Pete had a lot in common. But they differed about one important matter. Quiet, shy, non-assertive Roger, once confronted, never backed down. This could have been one of the contributing factors in his death. Pete, on the other hand, always looked for a nonconfrontational solution to a pending fight.

DARLENE

Darlene came from a large family that lived two blocks south of Roger's home on the same street. Until Roger's death, these two families intermingled. But mostly Roger hung out at Darlene's home. Her mother loved it when her house was full of everyone's kids. When Vern was storming around his own home, the children took refuge down the street.

Darlene's older brother was one of Roger's best friends. He was one year ahead of Roger and already in the marines. Roger had plans to join his friend in the marines as soon as he graduated from high school. Until then, Roger expected to spend a lot of his extra time at Darlene's home.

Roger and Darlene were good friends, like brother and sister, never romantically connected with each other, according to her own words. When Darlene's brother joined the marines, Roger became Darlene's big brother and protector. The three of them had an understanding, a pact. Roger would take her brother's place and look after Darlene. Roger took his role seriously.

It has remained a puzzle why Darlene was so different from the rest within her own family. She was a loner, kept to herself, did not confide in her mother or siblings, and was closer to her father. She was a drifter. She needed someone to watch out for her whenever she drifted away from her family and safe friends.

Darlene was no ordinary young girl on the streets of Foley. One gal gave her own peculiar assessment: "Darlene was ugly. Nobody would fight over her." But the guys interviewed had a different view. They unanimously agreed that she was "gorgeous, well endowed, and shapely, with the body of a goddess." Darlene was eye-catching and turned a lot of heads. Guys took special notice. Gals turned aside. Roger held his watchful, protective stance.

Darlene presented herself to the community and to the Foley youth as a loner in the family, a drifter on her own, a goddess who made men wild, a junior in high school who made older men jump to their feet, with Roger serving as her guardian protector. This setup suggested the wound that Darlene, knowingly or unknowingly, dragged into the story of Roger.

It was likely that Darlene was not aware of the danger that she was creating for Roger. She was portrayed as young and a chaser, running with the Foley youth to dance halls and parties, drinking, drunk or dizzy with hangovers, flighty and unreliable, saying one thing but then doing the opposite. As a drifter in her own family, she would have needed a new group to belong to. She would have needed the Foley youth. They were her new family. She could be loyal to them.

Roger took Darlene on scooter rides to bars and beaches around Foley. The goddess rode behind Roger and held on tightly. It was a good scene for a movie. But Roger was not drawn into this closeness. A friend said, "Roger knew her in a different way, as family. They lived so close." But Roger and Darlene as a strange pair were stirring up trouble below the surface of the wild pool at the Rainbow.

Darlene told her own story about Roger experiencing some danger during the summer of 1957. During interviews with others, this danger was called the "red alert factor." Every possible danger was tested to interpret her story. Did Roger witness some crime (drugs, illegal gambling, payoffs, sexual crimes, etc.) that put him in danger? Did Roger see some shady dealings between his father and Mack? Was it the bisexual relationship with Pete that Roger wanted to keep hidden from Darlene? The mystery remained until Roger's story better understood.

Darlene was asked if Roger was different during the summer of 1957. She said, "Roger was not different around me or my family. But during that period, something was happening to Roger. I think somebody was after him. We would be riding on his scooter, when Roger would see someone or something, and then he would take me home and tell me, 'Go into your house and stay there. Do not come downtown tonight. You cannot be around me in town.' Roger never explained to me what was going on with this red alert reaction to something in Foley. Roger never made it obvious to me about what was going on. This red alert started in the summer. It happened a couple of times, as far as I can remember. It is a very clear memory that I have often wondered about."

Several times, Darlene was asked to probe this experience. She explained it in this way: "Foley was a small town, and on weekends it became a busy town. Lots of people were hanging around, especially at the Rainbow Café. Lots of strangers. I have wondered if someone arrived in town that represented a danger to Roger and put him on the alert. I always felt that Roger had seen something or witnessed someone doing something that made him afraid for his life. I could feel that kind of fright in Roger's new and strange reactions. Roger was being very cautious about staying away from someone. Also, it seemed to me that Roger was being very protective of me, as he always was, especially after my brother left for the marines. Roger took on the responsibility from him of protecting me."

Summing up, Darlene said, "There definitely was a change in Roger for several months before his death. Roger saw something. 'They' were sure that Roger saw it. Roger knew that they were after him. Roger did not want me to be included in the danger that surrounded him. No names were ever mentioned to me as to who was a threat to Roger. He showed himself as a very protective person. Roger was exposed to something very dangerous. He would never tell me what it was about."

The "red alert" was a real threat to Roger. But what was the danger? Why the alert? After many interviews and speculations, the pieces fit together to reveal Darlene herself as the likely cause for the "red alert." Roger's need to protect her and her need for protection seemed to have become a real and growing threat faced by Roger. At this time, Darlene was one of Dewey's many special girlfriends. Would Dewey have tolerated any interference from innocent Roger? In his role as protector, Roger was likely sneered at as an untutored acolyte fiddling at the altar of the goddess. Roger could have been in the way of one, or many, guys who wanted to get Darlene. Roger, when confronted, would not back down.

The Foley youth continued to gather at the Rainbow to party and danced in every popular venue of the area throughout the summer of 1957, most of the time without Roger on the scene. Darlene was with the Foley youth, her new family. Her protector did not ride along. Did she hear or sense that there was a looming, menacing, mean message being whispered by the entire group? "Roger is a big problem." "Roger is disrupting our whole group." "Our whole group has become messed up since Roger arrived at the Rainbow." "Something has to be done about Roger."

A classmate reported, "After the death of Roger, Darlene cried and cried in school. No one could comfort her." Eventually she stopped crying and went on with her life, but no longer wearing the tiara of confidence befitting a young goddess.

ANN

Ann was a waitress at the Rainbow Café during the time of the Foley youth and was with them before the group disbanded at the Kitten Club on October 6, 1957. One of her friends said, "Ann and Dewey dated each other for a period of time before the death of Roger. But her parents did everything to break it up, calling Dewey 'a snake in the grass.'" Ann herself never admitted to being one of Dewey's many girlfriends.

Storytellers reported that Ann seemed to be a strong and grounded person. She was the same age as Roger, but she seemed older than she was. She would not doll up for the guys. She was just "plain Jane." She claimed, "If it is good enough for me, it better be good enough for them." She preferred to be upfront about herself, presenting herself without pretensions. She was self-confident and easygoing, and did not fuss over things.

It would seem that Ann did not fit the image of the Foley youth, deeply wounded and wildly reckless in sharing their wounds with each other and with others outside the group. It was possible that she was not one of the regulars with this fringe group as they partied and looked for creative ways to mix alcohol and sex. Ann said that she hung out with them because she liked to dance. This group went to many dances, even though most of them did not do a lot of dancing. They sat in the booth, drank, hung out, groused, and looked for their next pick-up. Ann said that she was almost always out on the dance floor.

It seems strange but possible that Ann did not stay on the Kitten Club dance floor, as she said she did, but tiptoed into the cornfield with the rest of the group for the sexual mutilation and murder of Roger as the theory proposes. Is it possible that she heard about the deadly plan taking shape at other meetings in the dark corners of the Rainbow Café? Was Ann still enthralled with Dewey's forceful sexual style? Did Ann let down her guard just once to allow her curiosity to drag her headlong into the darkness of the cornfield? Were the whispers of the Foley youth so titillating that Ann could not resist? Was this furtive fling worth all the trouble? With such a good memory of so many other details of the story, is it fair to ask how well Ann remembers Roger, this young wild one, stripped naked, receiving his lessons in wildness and fighting for his life?

She said that she was the first of the group to get out of Foley after Roger's death. She did not hesitate. She knew that Roger's death would never leave her alone but would cling to her like a desperate child. She admitted, "The experience of the death of Roger was a dramatic and traumatic turning point in my life."

Ann remembered being traumatized at the wake service for Roger. She had already filed past the coffin and was standing on the porch of the funeral home. She said, "While standing there, the mother of Roger, Carol Vaillancourt, came up to me. Carol's face was four inches from my face. Carol said to me, 'I hope you burn in hell for this.' This was a traumatic experience for me and affected me for a long time. I moved out of Foley as soon as I could and tried to put all of this behind me." This memory did not include any comment about the trauma experienced by Roger's mother. Also, this memory clearly suggested that at the time of Roger's wake service and funeral, the family knew that Ann was part of the Foley youth and thus might have had some responsibility for what happened to Roger.

It seems that Ann learned how to dance around the truth. If nothing else, the story of Roger taught her well how to do this tricky tango. Maybe others showed her the way. Ann shared this little story, which, if true, revealed how one of the authorities was dancing around the truth: "A cop came to our house on one of the days after the death of Roger. He talked to me through the front screen door, never came into the house. I told him that I didn't know anything. There was never any other police work done with me." Hopefully Ann still has enough spunk and self-confidence to share the whole story someday, as she knows it.

TERRIE

Terrie was one of the "three musketeers," as she described her connection with Cindy and Darlene. They were classmates and chums, and one year younger than Roger. These three girls were juniors in high school as members of the Foley youth. Terrie said, "I lived in the same neighborhood with Roger and sometimes walked to school with him, but he never hung out with me and my friends." She was younger than Roger but walked a quicker pace. "I remember Roger as a very quiet person."

In interviews with Terrie, she demonstrated a genuine kindness and openness. Her desire to be helpful in recovering the story of Roger seemed real. She seemed ready to share all that she could remember. She was the first of the group to be interviewed. Her memories and statements in her first interview could not be compared with others in the group or with other revealing stories still to come. Her story did not change in the second interview after hearing all that had been laid bare. Terrie's first response was, "I think too many people lost their minds in all of these stories." Later on, she said, "I will have to talk to others and try to remember." Sorry to say, it seems that only some of her memories are still credible; others appear to be invented, purposely left vague, or traumatically hidden.

The process of recovering the story of Roger gradually placed one group member after another at the scene of the mutilation and murder. At the very beginning, the story placed only Mack with Roger in the cornfield. Then storytellers placed Dewey and Cindy on the scene. Then Shirley. Then Ann. After these surprising revelations, it made more sense to put the other three (Pete, Darlene, and Terrie) in the cornfield too, unless research proved that they were exceptions and did not follow the rest into the darkness to share in the whole ordeal. Sorry to say, research could not establish any exceptions in the group. The story suggests that all three were at the scene, including Terrie.

Terrie shared her special wound in the story of Roger. Her wound was that she could not allow herself to see what she was looking at. The trauma of Roger's brutal death could have created this kind of wound in almost anyone, especially a sixteen-year-old high-school student. Who could keep his or her eyes focused on such a nightmarish incident for forty-eight years? Terrie's word for what she experienced was the *incident*. It was a word that revealed and concealed what lay behind it. The "incident," as shared by Terrie, was likely a mixture of her true memories, the Foley youth's invented story, and a comfortable scheme for holding the story of Roger at arm's length.

Terrie's version of the story was designed to keep her very far from the scene. When she claimed that she could not remember, she might have been saying that she did not want to look at what was there. However, her profile has contributed a most revealing way for seeing beyond the veil of the "incident." In her timid style, she pointed the way for seeing beyond the truthful tidbits and invented stories, to see how the Foley youth might have been able to sacrifice Roger for the survival of their group without seeing what they were actually doing.

For many months, Terrie's role in the story of Roger seemed to be minor. Gradually, her genuinely honest way of handling the story began to reveal how the group dealt with this memory. Terrie's role changed and became the guide for listening to the truth hidden behind the invented stories of the rest. The story of Roger lives on several levels of reality: the real story as experienced by Roger; the invented stories of the Foley youth; the mixture of memories, interpretations, and special language; and the story-myth that keeps the whole story in a safe place and makes it possible to talk about a truth that cannot be seen while looking directly at it.

Terrie said truthfully, "I am still struggling to remember." Concerning the end of that terrible night at the Kitten Club, she said, "I heard nothing more and remember nothing more until the next morning [Sunday] when I heard the news that Roger had been run over on the highway and killed. I remember the sadness that followed. Lots of people crying. I heard some story that maybe Roger had been killed before he was hit by a car on the road."

SHIRLEY

Shirley (now deceased) was the only one of the Foley youth to break the silence. She was such a wounded person that it was impossible for her to keep the silence. Thank God for Shirley and her wounds. Someday the rest of the Foley youth will thank her too.

None of the Foley youth mentioned her name or remembered her being at the Kitten Club that night. Other storytellers did not know about her existence. She almost disappeared from the story of Roger. It was a brother of Dewey and Cindy who remembered. Then a brother of

Shirley shared, "My sister was going with that idiot Dewey at the time of Roger's death." Then the search was on.

Shirley came from a troubled past, traveling a bumpy road from biological parents, adoptive parents, and foster parents. She was eighteen or nineteen years old when she entered Dewey's circle of girlfriends. She lived with Dewey on weekends in his mother's home. Shirley was always a needy kind of person, normally quite hyper, uneasy, a high-strung person, suffering some confusion about herself because of her poor background. Dewey and Cindy's mother always felt a special compassion for Shirley and was hoping that Dewey and Shirley would marry. The mutilation and murder of Roger closed that door for good.

Except for two statements, which will be shared later, she remained close mouthed, taking her secret to the grave in fear and trembling. However, she did say, "This horrible experience happened after the dancing." Maybe she got Roger on his feet that night and took him for one little turn around the floor. Roger was a shy dancer then.

CHAPTER FIVE

RIDING HOSTAGE

Many stories have circulated throughout Foley and the surrounding areas recounting what "really" happened to Roger on the night of his death. However, no one aside from those involved truly knows the course of events that led up to and followed Roger's murder and mutilation. Until one of those witnesses comes forward with the truth, we are left with speculation. In piecing together bits of interviews, official reports, heresay, and tales, a brand-new story has surfaced—one complete with details withheld from the legend and even from Roger's mother for forty-eight years.

Roger had gone to the Kitten Club with the Foley youth just once before his deadly night at the dance hall east of Long Siding. His family remembers that Roger was begging his father, Vern, to let him go with Dewey, whose noisy car was sputtering at the curb. Vern resisted; Roger insisted. Finally, Vern said, "Okay, only if you're back by midnight." Roger quickly went out to the car and came back with Dewey, who told Vern, "No problem. We'll have him back by midnight."

During this first night at the Kitten Club, Roger wanted to learn how to dance. Being rather shy, he thought that dancing would help him to better socialize with the opposite sex. But the Foley youth, wild with booze and sex, had other plans. They wanted to teach Roger a lesson on how to have sex with girls. However, the lesson wasn't delivered that night. That night, Roger came home safely from the Kitten Club. The lesson was postponed to a different date.

His second night at the Kitten Club was on Saturday, October 5, 1957. This time, Roger was allowed to go without argument or curfew. His mother remembers that Roger came home from work at the shoe shop, ate supper in haste, and then quickly changed clothes. Several uncles were at the family supper table that night. There was a lot of activity in the house, and Roger's departure for the Kitten Club happened in the middle of this family commotion. It was a small house and everything was noticed. But this night something was different. Roger's departure happened too easily. Roger was given a short ride to the gathering place, a quarter of a mile away. An uncle gave him the lift and reminded him to get to the early Mass the next morning, so they could go duck hunting as planned.

When Roger arrived at the gathering place, he saw in an instant his fateful misfortune unfolding as Mack held the car door open and told Roger to get in. Roger had been on the alert for Mack. Just a few weeks earlier, Roger and a friend stopped at the Parkway dance hall in Foley where they saw Mack. Walking past him, Roger whispered to his friend, "Please don't talk to him; say 'Hi' and keep walking." When asked how he interpreted Roger's reaction, the friend said, "It was a real fear about something that had been said to him by Mack; Roger was knowledgeable about something." Roger knew that getting into the front seat of that car next to Mack meant menacing danger.

Pete was in the driver's seat of his yellow buick. Roger would have felt some comfort sliding into the seat next to him and hoped that this good man on his left could partly offset the evil force on his right. Mack got in and shut the door.

Short, shy Roger was sitting between two older, tall men—one kind, the other mean. He was trapped. There was no way out but through the darkness that lay ahead. The story suggests that Dewey and Cindy could have promised to paint "Homo Roger" all over Foley if he did not succumb. Mack smiled to himself, tickled by everyone else's edginess.

Three or four cars of Foley youth went to the Kitten Club that night. The nine people named in Roger's story traveled in two cars. Unnamed classmates arrived in the other cars to see the action. Riding to the Kitten

Club on Saturday, October 5, 1957, was not just another trip from Foley to Long Siding for another night out.

Ann described the first car with great clarity regarding certain details. Like all stories told by the Foley youth, her story is part real and part invented. "There were three guys and three gals in the one car that went to the Kitten Club that night. The car belonged to Pete. Most guys did not have their own cars, and girls never had cars. So we had to travel in groups. On this night, the six people in the car were going as a group, not as couples. There was a connection between Pete and Cindy, but the basic atmosphere in the car was that the six were going to the dance as a group. The six people in the car were: Pete, Roger Vaillancourt, and Mack in the front seat; Cindy, Darlene, and myself in the back seat."

Ann placed all participants in "the one car that went to the Kitten Club that night." She was clear about who the six people were and that they arrived in one car. For some reason, she kept Shirley and Dewey off the scene. When asked about Dewey, she said, "I do not remember seeing him there that night." Was there a desire to protect Dewey, whom she had dated for a while? Or did she want to focus the whole story on what Mack did to Roger, hiding Dewey's involvement and, along with him, hiding the Foley youth's presence on the scene? Later in the interview, she slipped and added Dewey to the group at the club.

Cindy told a different story about how she got to the Kitten Club. She wanted to stay as far from the scene as possible. Apparently, she did not want to be in the same car with Mack. After hearing Ann's report, which placed her in Pete's car, she said, "I am almost certain that I rode to the Kitten Club in the car driven by Dewey. The reason I remember this is that I had a job babysitting that night. Somehow I got out of that job and was picked up by Dewey at the home where I was babysitting. I remember the babysitting, because I carried guilt for a number of years that I left my job and went to the party at the Kitten Club where Roger died. I felt for a long time that if I had stayed at my job, I would not have been part of that scene. Also, I think that Dewey's car was not full, not six people. There were just a few of us in his car, with Dewey driving."

Was Cindy sharing a real story or an invented story about how she arrived at the Kitten Club? Speculating that Cindy was on the scene where Roger was mutilated and murdered demanded a critical stance toward her little story. Babysitting provided a good diversion. She said she carried guilt because she left her job and went to the party "where Roger died." Cindy created a story to make it look as if she ended up at the Kitten Club that night by accident. At the last minute, she found a substitute for her job, jumped in Dewey's car, and expected an ordinary, uneventful party at the club.

It was more likely that Cindy insisted on riding in Pete's car, even though it seems that she had had a great falling out with him over Roger. She would have wanted to be a watchdog over the whole plan, keeping an eye on Roger and on her former lover.

Dewey said again and again that he could not remember very much about that night at the Kitten Club. What he remembered about the drive to the Kitten Club has a strange twist. He said, "I remember that I drove my mother's car to the Kitten Club that night, because I remember the state patrol officers and maybe Foley Chief of Police Jack Lloyd coming to our home on Sunday to talk to me and to check out my car."

In two separate interviews, Dewey jumped ahead of the conversation to make the urgent announcement that his mother's car, which he used that night, was declared to be "all clean." This was the only memory that Dewey was willing to share about his drive to the Kitten Club.

Terrie gave a blank report on her car ride: "I do not remember how I got to the Kitten Club that night or how I got home, that is, whose car and who did the driving. I know that Roger was not in the car that I was in, coming to the Kitten Club. I do not know how Roger got there."

In her lost memory or equivocation about this forty-eight-year-old story, Terrie provided some clarity about the relationships within the Foley youth. She remembered the close connection between Cindy and Pete, but did not know/remember or was covering up the brouhaha of these two over Roger. She fondly remembered Pete and another older man who provided transportation for youth who were without cars or not old enough to drive. She said, "I am surprised that I would not be in the car with Pete." She also said, "I do not understand why Darlene would not be in the car with Dewey, whom she was dating at the time."

It was possible that Terrie was bumped from Pete's car, with whom she normally rode to parties, to make room for someone else, Darlene or Mack. Also, she clarified that Darlene should have been in Dewey's car, as one of his dates. But on this trip to the Kitten Club, could Darlene have shifted from riding with Dewey to being close to Roger to prepare herself for Roger's lesson or to keep an eye on Mack, to whom she had tossed her own indecent, unacceptable task?

Ann placed Mack in the front seat of Pete's car, escorting Roger to the Kitten Club. The girls in the back seat confirmed Mack's presence in the front seat of the car that they were in. Cindy said, "Mack's presence in Pete's car that night and at the Kitten Club with our group does not make sense to me, according to my best memory of things." With her statement, Cindy was confirming the presence of Mack in the car and at the club, but his presence with them did not make sense to her. Darlene started her interview unable to remember anything about Mack, but gradually gained confidence to add, "I do not know why I cannot visualize Mack. But as we talked about the story of Roger, Mack's involvement came back to me more and more. I can even faintly see Pete, Roger, and Mack in the front seat of the car on the way to the Kitten Club."

Mack is sixty-eight years old. In his older years, it seems he has lost some of his cleverness. The story that he told about riding to the Kitten Club was not worthy of his reputation for deception. According to his story, he arrived at and departed from the Kitten Club in his own car, a new but already battered 1957 red Chevrolet sedan. He had his own date, and his friend who worked with him in the mines in northern Minnesota had Mattie, later Mack's wife, as his date.

Mack told it this way: "I and Mattie were at the Kitten Club that night when Roger died. My friend, Dick Orpin [Mack inserted that he was unsure of the spelling of his name or if Dick were alive and if so, where he would be living] was Mattie's date for that night. At that time, Dick Orpin worked for the iron mines along with me. The two of us had driven down earlier that Saturday morning, arriving in the Foley area about noon. I had had an all-night job the night before, and so I was riding in the passenger side, sleeping, and Dick was driving my car for the long trip from northern Minnesota to the Foley area.

"I had a date problem that night—namely, I had promised too many girls that I would be their date. I think one of the girls was Jane Roski, but I am not sure about that. I had met Roger one time before that night at the Kitten Club, but I do not remember exactly the circumstances. I am quite sure it was some festive party event."

Later in the interview, Mack returned to this story to clarify several points. He wanted to establish distance from the story of Roger. He said, "Only once did Dick Orpin drive with me to Foley. It was that night when Roger died. We arrived early in the day, or about noon. Later in the early evening, Dick and I picked up the girls. Like I said earlier, I had too many dates."

It was not clear why it was important to Mack's story that Dick Orpin drove with him "only once" to Foley. It was likely that his concern was not about Dick Orpin as a traveling buddy at all, but rather his trailing comment with which he reiterated "I had too many dates" for that night, clarifying his self-image as a strong, sexually straight man.

Mack's invented story has at least three false claims. One of the former bosses of the mining company, who remembered Mack, responded to the inquiry about Dick Orpin in this way: "He made up that name. I never heard of such a name around here." Jane Roski, whom Mack remembered as one of his dates for that night, responded, "I never dated that man and never would have considered it." And Mattie, who upheld her husband's lie that she was at the Kitten Club that night as Dick Orpin's date, was actually at her parents' home, waiting for Mack.

Mack also lied about meeting Roger only "one time before that night at the Kitten Club." Roger the protector had confronted Mack early in the summer of 1957, warning him not to harm his cousin in any way, whom he was dating for a short while. After that, Mack seems to have pursued his nervy nemesis until Darlene and the rest of the Foley youth offered him a convenient ride to the Kitten Club on the night of October 5, 1957.

The ride to the Kitten Club seems to have become a revealing story. One can imagine that Roger rode along as a humiliated hostage and was the center of attention for the eight people in these two cars. Did Roger know that he was in serious trouble, that something awful was going to happen to him? Perhaps he had no other option but to go along for the ride.

It was a half-hour ride from Foley to Long Siding. The Kitten Club, located on the northeast corner of the intersection of Highway 169 and County Road 13, was open and waiting for the dancing and drinking crowd on a Saturday night. It was built in the early 1930s to be a dance hall out of town, four and a half miles north of Princeton, where the noise and naughtiness would not attract notice.

The Kitten Club was a large, low, one-story building, with exterior walls bleached white and covered with stucco. The bar was on the south side along with the living quarters for the owners. Two main entrances to the bar and the ballroom were on the west side facing the highway. There was one rear exit door facing east. The mammoth dance hall was on the north side. It was usually a packed house on Saturday nights, with many folks from Foley. The parking lot was too small, resulting in cars parked up and down County Road 13. In October, tall standing corn shrouded the north and east sides.

Local bands and other famous bands from around the state played good dancing music from 9:30 at night to 1:00 in the morning, with a different band every Saturday night. The Kitten Club did not have a license to sell hard liquor. People had to bring their own bottles of booze to the club. Underage drinking was common and easily available with the help of older friends or relatives. Drinking alcohol dominated the social culture of the fifties and sixties until other drugs arrived on the scene.

The Kitten Club had a good reputation for great dancing music and great crowds and the promise of finding a date. More conservative folks shied away from the spot. Many said they avoided the Kitten Club because alcohol and fighting combined to create a risky roughhousing atmosphere that was more than they could handle. Others were drawn there like flies to a fire. The Foley youth with Roger and Mack arrived there in the early hours of the night.

CHAPTER SIX

At the Kitten Club

When these nine people from Foley arrived at the Kitten Club, dancers were already out on the floor. Some were finding the flow; some struggling; some strutting their stuff. A few were dancing quite well. These few flowed easily with the music, one letting the other lead, with gentle cues, a nudge to the back, or pressing lightly in one direction or another. The fine dancers were like one body in beautiful motion, yielding, attentive, and gentle to the soul of the other. Roger smiled and was comforted by this vision.

The research included stories that have suggested in a slightly sleazy way that Roger caused his own mutilation and death by his excessive use of alcohol. But could this assumption have been used with malicious intent to hide the truth that a group used alcohol to play roughshod with Roger's passions and sexually assault him?

THE DRUNK ROGER STORY

The pretense of this story was that everyone and everything else was normal that night except for "drunk Roger." In the stories of the Foley youth, they remembered with great clarity and unabashed exaggeration "drunk Roger." Often the rest of the story was driven out with anxious foreboding: "I can't remember."

If the Foley youth were indeed present at the Kitten Club to give Roger a lesson in sex, then the story of Roger had to have troubled them from the start. They would have been ready to give Roger his lesson, but they would not have been clear on how to make it happen at the Kitten Club, no less with a huge crowd of people hanging around and dancing their hearts out. Having failed to deliver on Roger's first night out with them, they would have wanted desperately to breach their wall of fear during this second night. They were sexually experienced and sexually connected with each other. Together they would have had to find a way to bring Roger into their wildness. Perhaps they counted on alcohol to get them over their edginess.

Mack would have worried the wild ones. Their usual confidence would have been kicked off balance by his steely cold presence in their circle. His calm and collected presence with his "don't give a damn" grin would have rankled and riled the rest of them.

Heavy use of alcohol at parties in the fifties was a given. Alcohol and the Foley youth were natural companions. Alcohol eased them into the wildness of easy sex. Roger and alcohol had become clumsy friends in the previous months. But on this special night, in the hands of the Foley youth, alcohol became something more, an anesthetic, a tranquilizer for Roger. It was not an accident that Roger became drunk.

Each member of the group started the story of Roger at the Kitten Club in the very same way, with "drunk Roger." As the stories were told, it became obvious that "drunk Roger" was not really the issue. The hidden truth was their need to avoid looking at what happened to Roger by exaggerating the story of Roger's drunkenness. In this way, they were able to blame the chaos on one person—namely, "drunk Roger."

The interviews with the Foley youth reported that Roger arrived at the Kitten Club "probably drunk." Roger might have understood that he would be forced to have sex that night. In addition, sitting next to Mack for a half-hour ride might have given Roger ample time to feel the enormity of the impending violence overtaking him. "Probably drunk" was one way for Roger to prepare for the worst.

Ann started the story, "Yes, we were drinking alcohol in the car on the way to the Kitten Club. The beer or booze was provided by Mack. This was the first time that I met Mack; I never saw him before that night. It was not so strange to have alcohol in the car on the way to a dance at that time. I knew Roger beforehand, but had not really talked to him or spent any time with him. Roger seemed out of place in the car and with this group. He was a kind of naïve, shy, sweet boy, and had no experience with drinking. He was probably drunk by the time we arrived at the Kitten Club."

Roger's mother heard "back then" that it was Pete who brought the bottle of booze with him in the car for the trip to the Kitten Club. But the bigger truth most likely was that the trunk of the car was stashed with enough booze to cover the entire evening ordeal. What Ann saw and reported was the first bottle of booze of the night being passed around in the car by Mack. The rest was for the action at the club.

Cindy found it hard to accept that Roger was drunk: "That doesn't make sense, that Roger would be drunk, when it took only a half-hour to drive to the Kitten Club from Foley. That seems wrong."

Darlene related her own version: "I remember that Roger very quickly at the Kitten Club went from sober to obnoxiously drunk. I had wondered if there were other reasons for this happening, such as someone putting some drugs into Roger's drinks. But I have not heard anything like this. I do not know why Roger was at the Kitten Club that night. He was a very gentle, sweet young man, who became so totally different that night." After forty-eight years, it seemed as though Darlene still feared Mack as a threat to her life. It was a great risk for her to speak her inner thoughts about what might have caused Roger's disarray. Therefore, she took precautions in her comments: That "someone" in her story could have been Mack. Even though she said that she had "not heard anything like this," the whisper in her words reported what she may have actually seen from the back seat of the car.

This story was strange coming from someone who lived two blocks from Roger's home, who rode with Roger on his scooter, who knew Roger as a good friend, "like sister and brother," she said. More than that, Roger tried his best to protect Darlene as she chased around, stirring up the passions of Foley men. She professed that she didn't know why he was there that night. But could this statement have been made to hide the fact that Dewey had given her the nod for having sex with Roger that night and that she had put this mortifying lesson in the bully lap of Mack?

Her exaggerated language exposed her twisting of the story: "This very gentle, sweet young man [became] obnoxiously drunk." It seemed that between these two exaggerations, she tucked a hidden, invented story of her not knowing why he was there. Was Darlene right there at the center of what happened to Roger? If so, she would have had to cover up what she and the Foley youth did to him in the hours before his sexual mutilation and murder in the cornfield.

Darlene attempted to create a great chasm between herself and Roger. In so many words, Darlene said that she no longer knew this person called Roger. Something had gone dramatically wrong with him, something that he did to himself. She was decisive in trying to create a wall between the real story and her invented story. This wall of separation would have been necessary if she had to explain to herself how she jumped from being Roger's good friend to being connected with his castration and murder. The exaggerated language about Roger's being drunk would have blanked out her involvement with what happened in between friendship and murder—namely, the sexual assault of Roger.

Terrie shared her version of Roger's drunkenness: "I have a very clear memory of Roger being very intoxicated and very belligerent and riled up. He would not allow any of the other Foley youth to settle him down. I think that all of us tried to talk Roger into settling down. Roger had drunk far too much liquor. I remember some kind of fighting words, threats, and some pushing and shoving. Roger became very upset and ran out of the Kitten Club very angry and very drunk."

At first, the stories of "drunk Roger" seemed straight, reliable narratives of a true happening. After hearing the story about the plan to teach Roger a lesson in sex, the stories changed colors and began to reveal a story hidden behind these clear memories. Again the exaggeration in Terrie's words about Roger's intoxication became suspicious for covering up another story about the group's sexual activity with Roger.

Before they arrived at the Kitten Club that night, Roger was the focus of everyone in the group. Roger was not an unexpected guest. One story claims that the Foley youth went to the Kitten Club that night to "fix Roger." If this is true, all their counterclaims clang with phony hollowness. Terrie pretended otherwise: "I believe that that night was the first time for Roger at the Kitten Club. I remember being somewhat

49

surprised that he was actually there. I never hung out with Roger." The statement that this was Roger's first visit could have allowed Terrie to create distance between herself and what happened to Roger.

Dewey has insisted that he has blocked out almost everything that happened that night at the Kitten Club, or he has refused to remember and share. But about "drunk Roger," Dewey's memory was like a wake-up bell in the silent and shady darkness. Dewey said, "I remember that Roger was really out of control at the Kitten Club and was fighting and belligerent." Quiet, shy Roger. Like all the others, Dewey tenaciously placed the whole burden of that night on "drunk Roger." In other words, he was setting up the story that if anything terrible happened to Roger, his drunkenness caused it.

But the simple narrative about "drunk Roger" told in various versions has become more and more untenable. If Dewey made sure that Roger got drunk and stayed drunk, making sure combative Roger was under his control, then Dewey would have had good reasons for blanking out his memory of that night and denying any violence.

Cindy was not as belligerent as the others in relating Roger's drunkenness. She told her story with less exaggeration. She said, "I remember that Roger was quite inebriated. Recently, I heard this from Terrie, but I also remember it myself. She told me about the fighting. I remember Roger having a difficult time walking and staying on his feet." Cindy told her version of the story as the madam in charge. Her preferred self-image was that she saw it all, kept her distance, and presumably made sure that no one got hurt in the ensuing fracas.

Cindy danced around the truth in her memory, unintentionally telling a hidden story. She said that she remembered Roger inebriated, heard it from Terrie, but also remembered it herself. This three-step dance about "drunk Roger" exposed what she was trying not to trip over. In telling the story, she wanted to share without indicating anything more incriminating. If Cindy were the madam in charge of the sexual lesson for Roger, it would make sense that she was ever so careful about what she remembered; she would have had to tiptoe around it.

Mack chimed in with his own version: "Roger was loaded and drunk. Totally intoxicated." Mack reported this fact as if he was surprised. He had sat next to Roger in the car and pushed booze at him during the half-hour drive from Foley to the Kitten Club. Darlene witnessed this from the back seat. The bigger truth could be that Mack did not care if Roger was wildly drunk or shy and sober. Perhaps Mack had a different agenda for Roger than the Foley youth.

Roger was not oblivious to what was happening to him. He certainly knew that he was quite drunk, with his mind spinning, his feelings rushing in circles, with an urge to prance and brag, getting louder, floating above the floor, losing ground. Roger was carried along by this volatile current, staying afloat, trying to hold his own. A wild stream was flowing around him, trying to take him under. Roger was being prepped for his lesson. He felt his group surrounding him with too much attention, glancing and staring at him, making him feel awkward and shook up. He knew that a lesson in sex was on its way. He did not know what or how it would come.

The exaggerations about "drunk Roger" were not Roger's personal experience. That was the work of others in creating a good cover story. The fact that Roger had drunk too much alcohol was a different story altogether from "drunk Roger." Again, the real story and the invented story became embarrassingly entwined. It was true that Roger drank too much alcohol that night. It was certainly true that the combination of Roger and alcohol did not beget a passive puppy, prepped for tender cuddling. Just the opposite happened. Alcohol hid his shyness and sparked a sudden readiness for combat. Roger became combative with the Foley youth. These two forces—angry Roger and the predatory wild ones—shaped the story that was hidden in their shared stories.

THE FIGHTING ROGER STORY

The stories reported by the Foley youth provided only pieces of the puzzle. Roger was drunk, unstable, under the booth. Roger was angry, fighting, wild, out of control. The group was in two booths, trying to help or control Roger. There were conflicting stories about Roger fighting with different guys over different girls. There was the appearance of a weapon, a gun or a knife, in the booth used by Mack. There were conflicting stories about when the knife appeared, before or after the ordeal in the cornfield. There was the cautious pointing of the finger at one or several culprits for what eventually happened to Roger in the cornfield. There was the careful dance of words to avoid any hint of sexual assault.

If the stories are to be believed, then perhaps behind all these stories was their palpable fear that Mack could terrorize and destroy them as they experienced firsthand what he did to Roger.

Terrie's Story

Terrie focused her whole story on what she called "the basic incident of Roger and Dewey wanting to be with Darlene." She said that both wanted Darlene as their girlfriend. She reported, "Roger had drunk far too much liquor. I remember some kind of fighting words, threats, and some pushing and shoving. Roger became very upset and ran out of the Kitten Club very angry and very drunk. I remember seeing some weapon for a split second, maybe a gun or a knife, lying on the booth across from me, but I am not absolutely sure what it was. I remember being very scared; it scared the devil out of me. Definitely the Foley youth were in booths right across the aisle from each other. That is how I saw some kind of weapon for a split second on the other booth."

When pressed to share the names of others involved with the fighting event in the dance hall, she repeated, "It was strictly a fight between Roger and Dewey over Darlene. Roger got so angry; he just bolted out of the place. I think that Roger maybe dated Darlene once or twice, but that she preferred to stay with Dewey."

She said that the fight was simply the result of Roger's drunken condition; nothing else was a factor. The trouble ended when Roger "bolted" out of the Kitten Club, never to be seen alive again. By limiting the "basic incident" to three people in a lover's quarrel, Terrie could have been trying to hide the fact that the whole group engaged not only in a fight with Roger, but also in a sadistic ordeal.

Terrie claimed significant memory lapses about many details, reasonable for experiences forty-eight years old. However, a medical doctor said that trauma of the magnitude indicated in the story of Roger normally would not allow individuals involved to forget. Terrie's story was stripped of vital elements and anything implicating her in the group's trauma or in the violence against Roger.

On the helpful side, Terrie confirmed the pivotal role of Darlene in shaping the story of Roger at the Kitten Club. As Dewey's girlfriend, Darlene would have been set up to play the temptress in Roger's lesson. As one of the "three musketeers," Darlene could have enticed the other two, Terrie and Cindy, to help her in stimulating Roger as they took turns under the booth.

Terrie also introduced a weapon into the story. Her "split second" glimpse of the weapon suggested that "fighting Roger" had gotten so far out of control that a weapon was needed. Was she trying to reveal that the weapon used to mutilate and murder Roger was out in the open for the Foley youth to see? It was on the booth, and it was in full view.

Ann's story clarified that the weapon was a knife. When Terrie pointed to the knife in her story, was she directing attention away from the sexual violence in the Kitten Club to the more terrible violence of sexual mutilation and murder in the cornfield? But the weapon could be seen as the connecting link between the two stories of violence against Roger: the weapon could have been used in the club as a warning to "fighting Roger" to submit to his lesson, and after the so-called lesson, the same weapon was used to take the fight out of Roger.

Terrie wanted her story to be kept very simple. The "basic incident" was "strictly a fight between Roger and Dewey over Darlene." If we are to believe that all members of the group joined Mack in the cornfield for the final act, then it has to be assumed that all were involved in some manner in the sexual assault during the earlier hours of the night. No other rationale explains why everyone would have followed Mack into the cornfield. Terrie tried to extricate herself from the final scene: "I do not have any memory of Mack, and I wonder why I cannot remember him."

Ann's Story

Ann provided a unique focus to the story of Roger. She wanted to share something about the trauma of that night. She built her story around the presence and action of Mack. The story of "fighting Roger" and the sexual lesson became almost invisible. This story was submerged in her story about Mack. For Ann, the group was innocently standing by, gazing at the stars while Mack was mutilating and murdering Roger in the nearby cornfield.

The story of "fighting Roger" was difficult to identify in the invented story of Ann, but it was not totally absent. It seemed she had four special agendas: keep the group on the sidelines, keep Dewey totally off the scene, keep the focus on Mack, and keep the cornfield violence hidden. Ann told a story that did not include the alleged chief planner of the lesson in sex: her wild boyfriend, Dewey.

When she heard that Terrie had tied Dewey to a conflict with Roger in the Kitten Club over Darlene, Ann reluctantly accepted the fact that Dewey was there. But she wanted to keep her own story basically intact. She found an explanation: "The account of Dewey and Roger fighting over Darlene could have happened at another table in the Kitten Club that night. It was a very large dance hall, and there was always a large crowd on Saturday nights. But I saw no evidence at all of any confrontation between Roger and Dewey over Darlene." Then she added, "In fact, I saw no effort on Roger's part to pair up with Darlene."

Ann wanted it known that she danced away from all the bad stuff that happened to Roger inside the Kitten Club. She returned to the booth "occasionally." Once, she noticed beer bottles on the booth and "Roger on the floor under the booth." She returned to the dance floor. She came back to the booth again, and Roger was gone. She asked, "Where is Roger?" In her story, Roger became almost a nonentity. Hers was a story about Mack, even though the interview was about Roger. For Ann, Roger became the unintended, unfortunate, unequal, disappearing rival of Mack. Her whole story begged the question, "Where is Roger?"

Ann might have been a whirling dervish on the dance floor that night, but could she have also danced into the cornfield after the midnight hour? If so, that meant that she participated in the sex lesson with Roger, which ended up dragging her dancing shoes gracelessly into the darkness and onto the final scene in the cornfield.

On the helpful side, Ann provided many details about the dirty work of Mack. In providing this help, she was wily and vigilant about keeping herself away from any connection with the violence against Roger. In several ways, she pulled the curtains shut to protect herself: "I had no sense that Mack was setting up Roger for this violent result."

Ann's story about Mack set him up perfectly as the murderer of Roger. After she asked where Roger was, she said that "both Cindy and

Darlene said that they took Roger out to the car to sleep it off." She returned to the dance floor and came back, she said, "at closing time, at 1:00 AM." On this last visit to the booth, she found the following: "I definitely saw a knife at the counter after Mack had gone out to find Roger in the car or in the cornfield. Mack had some kind of hunting knife lying on the booth. Standing there and looking at it were Mack, Dewey, Pete, and Cindy."

Ann provided valuable details, organizing them into her own story and dancing away from the truth. She said that she was surprised that "naïve, shy, sweet" Roger was in the car, going to the dance. She seemed to want to explain that sexual activity was an important part of what happened to Roger at the Kitten Club, but she wanted to spell this out indirectly. Twice she brought up the bisexuality of Pete, saying that he was a good friend of Bill Fox. This piece of information was meant to set the stage. Then she shifted the hidden story of sexuality to "domineering" Mack. Ann divulged her curiosity about the sexual activity underway in the booth by carefully numbering her "occasional" visits. However, the story leads us to believe she was not totally unaware or uninvolved.

The setup of Mack took clear shape with the presence of the hunting knife lying in the booth. In her story, the knife belonged to Mack. In the hidden story, the knife belonged to the whole group, using it to keep Roger silent and submissive. The knife represented all of the missing action in her story of the alleged sexual violence directed against Roger.

Ann was skilled in creating the story of Roger's disappearance. Two girls of the group said that they took Roger to the car. Then Mack left for a time. He came back and put his hunting knife in the booth. In her story, Ann deliberately pointed her finger at four people: Mack, Dewey, Pete, and Cindy. Was she naming the individuals in the group who were more at fault for the sexual assault and murder of Roger than the rest, perhaps trying to liberate herself from the trauma that had plagued her life?

Ann constructed her story so that the knife was seen only after Mack took his solo journey to "find Roger." Terrie saw the knife earlier in the evening. It could be assumed that everyone saw the knife during the ordeal in the Kitten Club. The knife could have been used in various ways to threaten and control Roger, to work up his fear and his anger, to make a young man sweat for his life, to keep everyone on edge and excited about the darkest possibilities, to open the door for the malevolent powers that would take possession of the group and make them do the unimaginable.

DARLENE'S STORY

Darlene was blunt and boorish in her telling of "fighting Roger." The primary agenda for Darlene's story was to say that he was strangely out of control, no longer the person she had known. Later in the story, when the girls took him out to the car, she described his drunken state as "like a wild bear." She spoke of Roger's drunkenness as if he had "the snakes," implying that he was in the condition whereby a drunken person becomes almost superhuman in strength and no one can hold him down.

Darlene wanted her story to convey an extraordinary image of Roger. In his drunkenness, he had become a superhuman small man. He was no longer the same special friend who regularly hung out in her family's home, who had taken her on scooter rides, who had been her protector for the summer after her brother joined the marines, who was otherwise a "very gentle, sweet young man." Roger "had become totally different that night at the KC." He was so superhuman that he was picking fights with her boyfriend, Dewey, who could be, as stories told, one of the meanest men in Foley.

Darlene seemed to lose control in her storytelling. Her story about "fighting Roger" became a gross overstatement, a deliberate effort to force all attention on Roger. He was the great catastrophe of the whole affair at the Kitten Club. Overstatement became a standard technique of the Foley youth to redirect the story of Roger away from their dark corner. The story suggests that Darlene allegedly played a central role in the lesson for Roger, but she stepped into the shadows on the sidelines by pushing Roger into the limelight.

CINDY'S STORY

Cindy was careful about what she was willing to remember or share about the story of Roger at the Kitten Club. She listened to the stories of others and then said that she could see how they might come to such a conclusion. She was not willing to take a stand. She relied on her own version of the Fifth Amendment to protect herself against self-incrimination. Cindy did a lot of dancing around the truth.

With the help of forty-eight years, she spoke kindly about Roger. "I liked him as a friend. I saw him as a soft, fun kind of guy." She said that she was concerned about his level of drinking before that night at the Kitten Club. "He hung around our family home but not too much." Mostly she "bumped into him in downtown Foley."

Cindy understood the reason for the fighting: "I am quite sure that there had been some conflict between Dewey and Mack, and I think that that happened before their night at the Kitten Club, but I do not remember what the conflict was about. I remember Mack as being some kind of oddball guy who created fear around him." If the stories are true, she knew well that this conflict was about her own agenda for Roger and which bully would end up in charge of Roger's lesson. But Cindy kept her secrets well.

None of these memories revealed anything about Cindy's role at the Kitten Club. She offered nothing on her own. Darlene was willing to point the finger: "Cindy might have known more about what happened than the rest of us, being the sister of Dewey, but she never said anything." Was Cindy a disinterested, dimwitted cheerleader on the sidelines in the dance hall, or was she the mistress of the madness who took possession of the Foley youth to transform shy Roger into one of their own kind, her fiery anger keeping her group charged up for a series of sexual assaults until all of them arrived stupidly in the cornfield for just one more chance to "fix" what she called "hurting Roger"?

DEWEY'S STORY

Dewey started his own story remembering Roger and the four girls at the Kitten Club that night. When the door was squeaked open for a little peek at the Foley youth's actions, Dewey slammed it shut with a nervous shaking of his whole body. He stammered, "I cannot remember anything that happened in the dance hall that night." He has continued to refuse to share anything about that night of violence.

In quick harmony with the rest of his accomplices, Dewey blamed Roger himself for all that happened to him. He easily remembered that "Roger was really out of control at the Kitten Club and was fighting and belligerent." However, when the story of Mack showing off a knife in the booth was shared, Dewey reverted to, "I cannot remember anything that happened in the dance hall that night."

When pushed to admit even the existence of Mack, Dewey glared and flared, "I do not remember any Mack. I cannot remember anything about a Mack." Then he softened a bit. "Maybe if I saw a picture of him, I might remember something, but I cannot remember anything now." Later when a picture was presented, Dewey shook his head and said, "I never saw that man before."

The door of violence against Roger at the Kitten Club could not be pried open with any help from Dewey. He put all his weight against that door. Had he been so centrally involved in that violence that any slight admission could topple his precarious house of cards played with all these years?

As a result of his own obstruction about what happened to Roger in the Kitten Club, Dewey has left himself vulnerable. Many in the Foley community remembered Dewey as the one who killed Roger. The memories and stories of others have been waiting for Dewey to come clean. Roger's mother said, "If it were not for Dewey, Roger would be here today." Roger's father, who died six years after Roger, had said, "Before I die, I will have to kill Dewey."

PETE'S STORY

Pete is deceased. Only the Foley youth know what Pete knew about the sexual assault against Roger, followed by castration and murder. He was not allowed to exempt himself from the scene and this violent action. His earlier sexual experience with Roger may have set the violent tsunami in motion.

Even though Pete never divulged anything himself, someone in the past shared a version of "fighting Roger" with his family. The source of this story was not remembered. They heard that "Roger was making moves on Cindy, which got Dewey very angry. This seemed to fly in the face of the fact that Dewey and Roger were supposed to have been good buddies. We heard that lots of people had a great deal to do with the death of Roger." Pete's family had assumed all along that the Foley youth and maybe others had joined together to cause Roger's death, but they did not know all the pieces or how they came together.

They had no fear of Mack, because they had no memory of him at all. They said, "We have no knowledge about Mack; if we knew him once, we cannot remember him now. The girls who went to the Kitten Club were the wild, wild bunch in town who liked to party, and they did just that. As high-school juniors and seniors, they were seen as trash in town. On the way home from the Kitten Club that night, there was some speculation about what could have happened to Roger that he got that way. Cindy was connected to Pete in some way at that time. And Roger was trying to hit on Cindy before that night and at the Kitten Club, which caused some serious problems."

When Cindy was presented with this story, she repelled it with a shaking of her whole body. She denied any kind of special connection with "hurting Roger."

Pete's family knew at that time about the special relationship between him and Cindy. But they had no clue about a possible explosion in that relationship because of a possible sexual connection between Pete and Roger. Because Pete never shared his personal experience, the story of Roger held too many complexities for his family to unravel. Nonetheless, his family remembered a version of the story from years ago. He did not take everything with him to the grave.

MACK'S STORY

Mack used his flair as a storyteller to dress up his posturing about "fighting Roger." He told his story as if it were the final act in a tragic comedy. The discrepancy in the face-off between peewee Roger and brawny Mack was made to look like a sad ending in a silly drama. Of course, his story was not the final act at all. Much greater violence against Roger was just minutes away.

Earlier in the day, Mack had driven four hours to Foley, apparently having begged his boss to grant him another unprecedented weekend off. He had been on the job for only six weeks and had taken several already. He would have claimed he needed to wrap up important business back home in Foley.

Could this important business have been settling an old score with Roger? Silencing this young man who had brought him, the mighty Mack, to his knees in an unguarded moment of weakness? It seemed as though Mack loved the taste of violence. In his storytelling, he loved to walk on the cutting edge of a memory to relive it with all of its saltiness. This instinct was at work when he told his little story about what he called his one previous meeting with Roger. He said, "I met Roger one time before that night at the Kitten Club, but I do not remember exactly the circumstances. I am quite sure it was some festive party event."

His personal profile and his own storytelling suggested that Mack could have been referring to a single homosexual encounter with Roger, which he described as "some festive party event." Such an event would have caused Mack to go to any extreme to deal with leftover "business" in the Foley area. His physical prowess could have been undermined by that stronger force within, an attraction to male genitals. A sexual connection between Mack and Roger would offer one more reason for the castration and murder of Roger.

Mack went on with his story with his notorious "don't give a damn" grin: "Roger was picking arguments and fights with several other people in the dance hall. I was not sure what he was stirred up about. He just wanted to pick fights. Roger came over to the booth where I was sitting and wanted to fight with me. It was strange to me to see this short, thin, good-looking young guy wanting to fight with me, who was six foot two and strong and able to handle anything. [Mack inserted an aside that he was not quite that tall any more after back surgery.] So I got up and said, 'Let's go outside.' Well, Roger walked ahead of me and was already outside, about twenty-five steps ahead of me. Before my foot could hit the dirt outside of the door of the Kitten Club, Roger ran for the cornfield, never looking back."

With his cunning mind, Mack added witnesses to his story. He said, "There were three or four guys drinking beer right outside of the door who saw this whole thing. It was about midnight when Roger ran into the cornfield."

This was a cautious, calculating story. With precision, he ridiculed the differences between Roger and himself, giving exact details. He even measured exactly how many steps he stayed back from this tactless upstart: twenty-five. Exact deception would have been standard fare for Mack's cock-and-bull stories.

Roger did fight that night. He had to fight for his self-respect and for his life. Roger's fighting was a defensive battle, not an unprovoked, aggressive drunken attack. Roger was being prodded and probed, stripped and stimulated, violently forced and violated.

According to the stories of the Foley youth and the scattered stories of others, "drunk Roger" became "fighting Roger" at the Kitten Club. If all of their stories were true as told, Roger would have spent most of the night fighting. But it seems as though these stories were again invented, using pieces of the real story. The issue was not whether Roger did some fighting that night, but rather how the Foley youth might have used this story to hide what really happened. The stories of "fighting Roger" need to be brought into the light, so the hidden story can be discovered.

The "fighting Roger" story took its lead from the invented story given to the authorities and to the newspapers right after the mutilation and murder of Roger. That story reported that Roger was the loser in a "beating" at the Kitten Club. This "beating" implied that Roger stupidly tangled with the wrong person or with a tougher group, as young men drinking too much at a party are inclined to do, and ended up as the loser. Together, the Foley youth created this story, and many people thought it was the truth.

The pieces of the puzzle come together to reveal that the likely mission of the Foley youth at the Kitten Club that night was to teach Roger a lesson in sex. This was hidden behind the story of "fighting Roger." Before reaching the cornfield, the group was in charge of what happened to Roger in the dance hall and in the parking lot. On the surface, "fighting Roger" was a story about Roger fighting with one or more persons. Below the surface, this became a story allegedly about how the group tried to free Roger from his fears about sex by goading and arousing him into sexual activity with the girls.

Interviews with the Foley youth suggested that their trauma gave them the excuse to hide what they did to Roger on their own. None was liberated sufficiently from his or her own fears to freely share his or her part of the tragedy. Their stories portrayed only one person getting out of line: Roger. The rest claimed that they were present to dance, party, meet friends, and have a good time.

The true story has been well-guarded. During the interviews, the Foley youth never hinted at the possibility that they could have engaged in sexual activity with Roger for their own noble reason of "teaching him a lesson." According to them, "fighting Roger" was the result of "drunk Roger." Their stories were blatantly misleading. The way they told their stories made it necessary to think suspiciously about everything else they shared. Their stories seemed to be told in a way to distract and sidetrack others from the possible story of their engaging sexually with Roger, which caused him to react forcefully. Roger was the one on the receiving end of sexual violence. At some point, Roger had to fight back as strongly as he could, even though he was under the control of the group, alcohol, and possibly drugs.

The nine people were crowded into two booths right across from each other. They were squeezed together, body to body. All of them were fully aware of each other and had their eyes fixed on Roger. Roger was alert and tensed, wondering what was coming and whether he would be able to hand himself over.

Did any in the group do any dancing that night? Ann declared, rather defensively, that she spent almost the whole night on the dance floor. In this way, she tried to remove herself from whatever the rest of the group was doing to Roger. By playing up her absence from the group and implying that no one else of the group did any dancing, it can be assumed that Ann was trying to report that the rest of the group was sexually involved with Roger in the booth. But by overstating her own all-night dancing, she also created the impression that she could have been in the booth more than she cared to remember.

Ann shared other carefully selected bits of information about what she observed on her "occasional" visits to the booths. She described a volatile, violent man doing his thing: "Mack was forceful and domineering and very forward with others. I do not remember seeing him dance at all that night. Maybe Pete did not dance either. Roger probably did not dance either, because he was in pretty tough shape by the time we arrived at the Kitten Club."

Her words could have been describing some kind of camouflaged action. Unintentionally, she seemed to explain the story of "fighting Roger." "Forceful" Mack could mean that Roger was being forced to defend himself. Crowded into a booth for a lesson in sex, the word *domineering* could mean that Mack and the rest were doing what was necessary to dominate Roger sexually. "Very forward" could mean that Mack and the rest were engaged in sexual activity of some kind.

Mack was mentioned first by Ann to suggest that he was leading the assault team, even though the story leads us to believe this role belonged to Dewey. Strangely, Dewey was missing in her story. As one of his girlfriends at that time, she tried her best during the interview to keep him off the scene. As the interview advanced, Ann forgot about protecting Dewey and casually included him with the others.

The story of Roger suggested that earlier Cindy had lured Dewey into fathering the plan for the sexual lesson. If true, he would have copyrighted this lesson plan, and he would have intended to play the lead role. Cindy talked about some conflict between Dewey and Mack. This conflict could have been imprinted during the actual assault against Roger in the booth. In this scenario, Dewey would have tried to hold his competitor in check and to take charge. In the ensuing chaos, both men would have shared a role in restraining Roger sitting between them, both silencing his sad growls and groans, both holding Roger sternly in their arms while the girls under the booth pulled down his pants and underwear and began to provide their royal favors. Roger would have been frozen with fear and lifeless with shame.

Ann's story included two other side comments. After stating that Mack definitely did not dance, she said, "Maybe Pete did not dance either." She wanted to include him on the scene, but her light comment tried to give him a pass with the sexual assault underway. Her second comment implied that Roger's condition was totally the result of too much alcohol or possibly drugs. But her report could have been indirectly about the sexual excitement happening under the booth, witnessed on one of her "occasional" visits. Roger slumped and saddled was in "pretty tough shape."

After his first sexual lesson, Roger could have been pushed to the floor under the booth, shamed and exhausted. He would have struggled to pull up his underwear and trousers. The guys and girls would have held him down with their feet, doing their own little dance on Roger's body. Roger would have felt the full weight of this dirty, grimy indignity. Pete could not watch this scene and took a walk.

Ann told her story about Roger lying under the booth with a different slant and with the Foley youth's self-serving purposes. She presented Roger, abandoned and alone, under a booth, too drunk to stand, sit, dance, or go to the bathroom. Roger was down and out because he was too reckless with his booze. "Drunk Roger" had become an embarrassment to the Foley youth. Everyone got fed up and walked away from Roger.

The details shared by Ann were simple and terrible: "I remember seeing beer bottles on the booth counter on one of my visits and Roger on the floor under the booth." These details were shared calmly as just another piece of her wild story. But these were ghastly details that seemed to be screaming for someone to notice them as part of the sickening scene. Was she indifferently describing Roger on the floor and beer bottles on the booth as the laughable leftovers of a group orgy?

Beneath her words, the sad reality was suggested. Roger was lying under the booth, spent and dispirited. He had been kicked around by his group and left behind. Roger had to be kept out of sight for a while, until his group could get up and stretch their legs and have another round of drinks.

Darlene, Cindy, Terrie, and Shirley liked to think of themselves as light-footed dancers and fun-loving friends. Were these friends loaded with belittling wildness, tromping together on Roger? They would have known why he was too ashamed and scared to come out from under the booth and face the mockery of the guys, the gals, and the classmate gawkers.

Eventually, Roger crawled out of this abyss. He needed fresh air. He needed to break out of this slimy pit. He needed help, if he were going to come out of this alive. He was not too stable on his feet. The story suggests that he might have stumbled over Dewey's feet, was bear-hugged by Mack, who brazenly banged his groin into Roger's buttocks, and then shoved him away with a loud laugh. Roger stumbled but got up again. He would have staggered over to Darlene, desperately clinging to the thought that she was the only one who could help him.

If Roger had already endured one sexual lesson, he would have sensed there would be more. The wild fun had just begun. What possibly happened at some point was a plunge from "teaching Roger a lesson" as an apparently reasonable, though outrageous, service for him to "teaching Roger a lesson" as an outburst of extreme anger or hatred for Roger as the enemy. The shift in the "lesson" could have been predictable as a plunge from wild sex to sadistic sex. The story of Roger suggests that at some point the Foley youth themselves turned from wildness to meanness. It was like a school of piranhas in a feeding frenzy, driven by a little taste to devouring Roger himself.

Roger would have been scared and desperate when he got to Darlene. His dark eyes would have looked deeply into hers, pleading. He would have begged her to help him out of this place, holding out his hands. Would she have stepped back? He would have reached out and put his arm around her shoulder. He would have whispered into her ear, promising to be a good friend. His eyes would have filled with tears, his heart breaking. Darlene would not have been able to think clearly. She was Dewey's girlfriend. She was everyone's date. She would have wanted to help her special friend, but there was nothing else to do but go with the flow. Darlene would have promised Roger that everything would work out just fine.

The stories of "fighting Roger" got wilder with each telling. After forty-eight years, the Foley youth recounted Roger fighting with untold numbers of people at the Kitten Club. The stories multiplied and became confusing. According to the stories, Roger was like the local tough guy at a county fair taking on all-comers in the boxing ring. Yet Roger was unable to stand on his feet, too drunk to navigate, too beat to hold his own.

And the likely story continues: Roger's famous fights in the Kitten Club arena got underway. Dewey stepped into the ring. He battered

Roger with a mixture of mean blows and sparring simulations. He played with Roger's fears. He threw a feint and a dodge. He slapped Roger hard, then tickled his tender spot. It was a sham barroom brawl. Dewey made a scene about Roger making a move on Darlene. Roger resented it and took up the pugilistic scrap in earnest. He lunged at Dewey but lost his balance. He took some swings but ended up in a hold, with Dewey fingering him boorishly below the belt. Roger was not afraid to fight. He was confused about his opponent's intentions to stand tough or toy with his feelings. No one stepped in to stop the fight or send it outdoors. Observers chuckled and squirmed at the crude banter. In the scuffle, Roger's energy and focus were partially restored. Roger felt again his instincts for never backing down in any kind of conflict.

The story switches to Mack. Mack would have stepped into the fracas, wanting to take his turn with the little guy. Like a ridiculous tag team of heavy wrestling hunks, Mack pushed Dewey aside. The taste of finality shivered through Roger's body with Mack standing over him. The fact that he stood six feet two inches tall against Roger at five feet eight inches made everyone around feel awkward. Mack grabbed Roger in a tight hold and whispered in his ear that his days of protecting Darlene were coming to an end. Mack backed away. Roger jumped and punched him in the jaw. Roger was then slammed with a quick one-two and staggered back against the booth, dizzy and bloodied.

Mack squeezes into the booth next to Darlene and made a big show of flirting and doing as he pleased. Dewey's ire was inflamed for his girl. But he was intimidated and only glared at the scene. The two bullies were bent on battling. The madam of the house, Cindy, stepped between them. She scolded them like naughty children. She reminded them of their mission for the night. Roger's lesson was not wrapped up to her liking. Her control of these fighting giants was magic. Again they would have turned their meanness on Roger.

They looked at each other and wondered what could be next. Dewey was still the master of this part of the program. The two of them grabbed hold of Roger. With suggestive signals, they gathered a crowd around the booth, creating a tight circle. Classmates and strangers were staring with nervous excitement. They had heard about the big lesson and wanted to see some action. They moved in and surrounded Roger. The two bullies held Roger while others pulled down his trousers and underwear. Girls in the crowd took turns tickling and teasing his tenderness. Good sports in the gang pushed money into Roger's shirt pockets, urging him on. The crowd, the money, and the girls left Roger limp, lost, and alone. They pulled up Roger's pants; the crowd dispersed; and the money disappeared.

It was time to take Roger to the car. Had that been the plan all along? It would have been necessary to get Roger ready for the real stuff. Pete had been pacing around, holding back, unable to say or do anything, feeling the guilt of the Foley youth gone mad, with Cindy leading the pack. Finally he stepped forward forcefully and yelled, "Not in my car!" Roger was taken to the car belonging to the mother of Dewey and Cindy. Allegedly Dewey had used this car on many nights with many girls. It would be a good place for Roger to learn his lesson.

CHAPTER SEVEN

INTO THE CORNFIELD

The parking lot at the Kitten Club was packed on Saturday nights. Dancers and drinkers spilled into the lot, hung out, smoked, found fresh air, and looked for a private place to be away from others. The cornfield on the east and north sides of the parking lot set boundaries for the cars, but not for the guys and gals who occasionally trekked along the corn rows to a hidden place in the darkness. The music and the lights of the Kitten Club provided a beacon guiding them back to safety.

Were the Foley youth there that night for dancing and hanging out in the parking lot, or did they have other business on their minds, with Roger in their crosshairs? Shortly after midnight, Roger's story relocates from the two booths in the Kitten Club to a backstage area in the parking lot to the back seat of the car belonging to the mother of Dewey and Cindy.

The story was told by several people that Roger was escorted to the car. After being held down in the car, Roger broke away from them and ran into the cornfield. Mack told a different story. He said that Roger ran directly from the Kitten Club into the cornfield, never looking back and never to be seen alive again. "Running Roger" was the next episode in the stories of the Foley youth.

They told of "fighting Roger" being "out of control" inside the Kitten Club. However, this contradicts the story that Roger was under the control of the group the whole night through. If the latter is true, the

Foley youth would never have allowed Roger to get too far out of their reach or control. It can be assumed that they forcibly escorted Roger to the car at about the midnight hour. But what happened next? Did they strip and stretch him out, holding him tightly so the girls could take their turns arousing him?

The story of Roger being escorted to the car did not appear in the stories of the wider community. Perhaps when the group was inventing their tales, they sensed that having Roger in the back seat of a car would have raised eyebrows and suspicions. When the Foley youth shared this story more recently, perhaps they felt the safety provided by the passage of forty-eight years.

Cindy tiptoed around the story of Roger in the car in her deliberately careful style. She said, "I remember seeing Roger in the car and several of them trying to keep him in the car. I do not know which car they put Roger into. But then Roger ran off, but I did not see that happen. I remember calling for him on the edge of the cornfield. I remember that someone went out to look for him, but I do not remember who that was. There was considerable talk about not being able to find Roger. We started to think that he hitched a ride with someone else and was already on his way back home to Foley. I do not remember seeing a knife on the booth countertop."

She told her story as if she were standing at a long distance from the car. She saw Roger in the car and others holding him down. She had no idea whose car it was, when most likely it was her own mother's car, driven by Dewey. She said that she knew that Roger ran off, but she saw nothing. Then she joined the search party to call for him from the edge of the cornfield. In her pretense of compassion for Roger, she said, "There was considerable talk about not being able to find him."

The purpose of Cindy's convoluted story was to make Roger simply disappear by running into the cornfield. She wanted to make clear that she did not touch or do anything to him. Others might have held on to him in the car, but not Cindy. She stayed far away from the car. She said that Roger ran off and she did not see a thing. Perhaps in her memory, the alleged shameful treatment of Roger in the car had to disappear and the last sight of the alleged messy, smelly, slashed, bloodied, naked body of Roger in the cornfield had to vanish and be no more.

According to Ann, uncontrollable Roger left the Kitten Club under the control of Cindy and Darlene. She continued, "Sometime after that, apparently Mack went out to the car to do whatever he was planning to do. He came back to the booth and told others that the car door was open and there was no Roger. When it was getting close to closing time at 1:00 AM, I returned to the booth and found Mack, Dewey, Pete, and Cindy. Mack had a knife lying on the booth. He said, 'Roger woke up and was going to walk home, but I showed Roger that he was not going to walk home.' When the evening ended, all of us went out to the car. We found the back seat empty, and the door was open, and there was no Roger."

Finally, Ann went out to the car with the rest and found it just as Mack had said it would be, the back seat empty, the door open, and no Roger. "Running Roger" had disappeared from her story. As Ann told it, Mack made it unnecessary for Roger to run from the car. Mack had saved her the trouble of thinking about what happened to Roger in the back seat of the car.

Darlene confirmed part of Ann's story. She said, "We girls made the effort to get Roger out to the car so that he could sleep it off. But we had a hard time keeping him in the car; he did not want to stay there. He was like a wild bear. He kept getting out of the car. For a while, we held him against the car, but we couldn't hold him. Someone went to the Kitten Club for help. But Roger ran away from us and into the cornfield." Unlike Cindy, Darlene wanted to assert very clearly, "I saw Roger run into the cornfield, but I do not remember Mack being out by the car when Roger ran into the cornfield." Darlene fashioned her story so that there could be no hint of sexual activity with Roger in the car.

Darlene added interesting details to her story. She spelled out her great concern and mission to find Roger: "We girls, Cindy, Terrie, and myself, walked up and down along the cornfield calling for Roger; we even walked a little ways into the cornfield and yelled for him. Then we went back into the dance hall. I think that the three of us came out several times to see if Roger was showing up or if the guys had found him. But Roger did not respond or show up. The guys went into the cornfield to look for Roger. I cannot visualize who the guys were; it must have included Pete and Dewey, but who else, I cannot remember. I do not remember Mack at all, except his presence there comes back to me as we talked further about him. I think that the guys were not out in the cornfield very long, but I cannot remember."

The cornfield was presented as a threatening, stormy ocean abyss that swallowed up people like Roger. The gals were also afraid of being swallowed up. It was past midnight, and as a man from Milaca remembered, "it was a cold, cold night." The story of "running Roger" was a relief for Darlene. On his own, supposedly, Roger ran away into the cornfield. At that point, he was no longer her problem. When he ran away naked into the cold cornfield, he ran out of her shivering memories about the back seat of the car.

Dewey said many times that he could not remember anything that happened at the Kitten Club that night. But suddenly he remembered this: "I think I helped take Roger out to the car to get him to sleep it off, but Roger would not stay there and ran off into the cornfield. I remember walking alongside of the cornfield and shouting for Roger and waiting around for him but eventually left for home without Roger. I do not remember going into the cornfield by myself or with anyone else to look for Roger. I remember leaving the Kitten Club without Roger, driving home, and going to bed not knowing what happened to Roger. Later on that Sunday morning, I heard the news that Roger had been hit by one or more cars and killed on the highway."

Was this story created to reassure Dewey that it was not his meanness that changed "drunk Roger" into "fighting Roger," who fled into the cornfield? Roger himself refused Dewey's help "to get him to sleep it off" in the car. However, Dewey was crafty enough not to get too involved in the story. He did not step into the dark cornfield abyss but only walked alongside of the cornfield, shouting for Roger. Darlene had said that two guys went into the cornfield to look for Roger. Dewey did not want to be one of them.

In his story about "running Roger," Mack did not wait around for what happened in the back seat of the car. In his story, he drove around this car scene and sent Roger directly into the cornfield. Mack claimed that "it was about midnight when Roger ran into the cornfield. When we left the Kitten Club about forty-five minutes later, there were flashing lights on Highway 169 about one-eighth to one-fourth mile north of the club entrance. We drove north on the highway, but we were directed by the police to drive on the far left side of the road, going around the police cars. There were two or three police cars with lights flashing. There was no ambulance there, as far as I can remember. And I never saw a body."

Did Roger actually run from the door of the Kitten Club, or from Dewey's car, or from some other point of origin? Did Roger make a run for it to save himself from more sexual assault or to save his life? Was there any truth to the stories of "running Roger"?

There are several possibilities, two of which are explored here. First, Roger did not run, and there was no chasing after him. After the group had finished their lesson in the back seat of the car, they followed Mack's mandate to escort Roger into the cornfield. In this story the Foley youth, carried away by wildness and meanness, dragged kicking Roger into the cornfield abyss. Second, Roger broke away from Mack and Dewey, who were holding him in the car for the girls. In this case, Roger ran away from all of them naked. Running naked into the cornfield was the least of Roger's concerns after all that he had endured that night. Then the group took off running after Roger, charged up about catching their runaway prey. Naked Roger was at their mercy. This second possibility seems to be the most likely scenario.

CHAPTER EIGHT

NAKED ON THE CROSS

If Roger were chased into the cornfield, away from public view and into the secluded darkness, what happened next? Foley residents have shared several theories, but since an eyewitness has yet to come forward, that's all they are—theories. In dissecting each of these stories and combining these bits with the facts of the case, the following story has emerged as a light in the darkness.

It was two nights before the full moon—the harvest moon, or sometimes called the corn moon. On this bright night in the cornfield, Roger was naked at the center of his group. He felt Mack bracing his behind. He saw the seven wild ones leaning in to see. There was wildness and meanness in their eyes. Roger was displayed to the moon. He was worn out.

The earth was spinning calmly on its predictable axis. The Cold War held the two superpowers temporarily at bay. *Sputnik 1*, launched into orbit just hours before, was offering the Great Powers a finer competition in outer space. Integration of the Little Rock schools in Arkansas was simmering with the help of federal troops. The Milwaukee Braves were humbling the great Yankees in the World Series. Buddy Holly & the Crickets were singing their new hit "That'll Be the Day." Some farmer in the distance was hustling to harvest his corn in the moonlight hours. The band had announced its final set of slower numbers for the tired dancers. Mack and the Foley youth looked at each other and stared down at their struggling prey.

The world around them was humming along in a testy balance, trying to hold itself together. This group, however, was poised on a scary slope, inching forward to the edge of an unfamiliar precipice. They had rallied around a maniac who was holding the naked Roger. Strange powers controlled them. The wild ones were raring to go. The grim reaper, gripping his prize, grinned at their panting and prancing around. Unnaturally they wanted more of Roger.

Dewey and Pete joined the smirking madman in lifting Roger's naked body out of the shadows and offering it to the light of the moon. Cindy, Darlene, Ann, Terrie, and Shirley took turns stimulating Roger's penis. Roger was surprised that he was no longer resisting, fearful, or holding back. He was riding along on his yellow scooter, shy no longer and free. The girls picked up their pace. His scooter climbed to a rise in the road where he could see a wide vista unfolding before him. He was carried away to the far reaches of a breathless adventure. He paused to take it all in. Then he coasted to the bottom of the hill. The Foley youth looked at each other and smiled. Mack ordered, "Everyone, stay put."

No one hinted in any report that there had been such a gathering, such a moment, such a satisfying lull in this otherwise hellish ritual. Remembering the lull would have meant remembering the rest. The moment anesthetized the group into a mindless stupor. They were bonded forever with a deep secret. No one has broken the secret code of what they did behind the veil. Their vow has been kept impeccably.

Mack took charge of the wild ones, knowing now that they were his pathetic accomplices. They had had their fun. He would do the rest. He told them to hold Roger up. He quickly cut away cornstalks, creating his circle. He cut one thin stalk six inches long. He gripped Roger's neck to open his mouth and shoved the cornstalk down his throat, silencing any scream, careful not to cut off his windpipe. Roger could make only muffled sounds; his bulging eyes looked around, searching for help. The Foley youth looked around at each other, amazed at the madman and stunned.

Mack was agitated and aroused. He had an overwhelming urge to turn Roger over and plunge into him. He was angry that he was cut off from doing it. There were too many eyes. His anger pushed the others to grip Roger tighter. Frantically, he grabbed Roger's testicles and twisted them as far as he could. Roger could not scream for the pain. Irritably, Mack snapped off a large ear of corn from its stalk and stripped off its husk. He pushed on the kernels and rubbed them away till his hand was sore. Finally, he had in his powerful hands something to use to make Roger squirm.

The wild ones knew that they were considered strange around Foley. Here they saw a man who seemed to be from a scarier planet. They were too frightened to do anything but hold on to Roger. Mack jammed kernels of corn into Roger's ears and nostrils and into his mouth. He seemed feverish to get inside Roger and to tear him apart. He grabbed Roger's genitals again and twisted them, and Roger rolled over. Everyone changed their grip.

Mack pushed Roger's legs apart. He gripped Roger's genitals from behind with one hand. With the other, he pried and pushed the corncob through Roger's anus and into his rectum. He heaved and groaned as he shoved the corncob in and out. He cursed Roger with his vile repertoire. His thrusting became vigorous. He could not stop himself. Roger moaned and tried to move with the cutting pain. The Foley youth surveyed the moon. They felt hypnotically suspended. Mack slowed for a deep breath. He shoved the corncob deep into Roger and left it there. He pitched himself against Roger's buttocks and clung to his hips with both hands. Mack gasped and groaned as everything foul and polluted gushed out of him and hung in the air.

Everyone stopped breathing for a long moment except Roger. He needed to howl with pain, but he could make only a whimper. Pete stepped back and said that he was going to the car to get Roger's clothes. His move brought Mack to life with a forceful holler, "Everyone, stay put!" A few in the group wanted to be done for the night. They were running on empty. They considered Roger's lesson finished. Mack's corncob sex was not their thing. They were ready to wash their hands and have a nightcap. Pete fell in line to hold Roger tightly and in the air.

Roger could not speak, but he could see the truth. He could see more clearly than everyone else, including Mack. The rest were blinded, clouded over, seeing something different than a victim at the center of a group's violence. They no longer saw Roger as naked. The cornstalk in his throat and the corncob in his rectum were forgotten. Roger's pain did not exist. The group no longer felt fear for the madman. They were caught up with his cravings for Roger's genitals. The harvest moon shed no light in their sad souls.

Mack shook himself and ordered the group to turn Roger over and hold him higher. Mack grabbed Roger's genitals in his left hand and jerked them back and forth. He made everyone look at them. He mocked them as the toys of a freak and a faggot. He scolded the group for wanting to have sex with such a weird animal and jeered at them for their four-letter foolishness all night long. He grabbed the hair of one of the girls and forced her face at Roger's penis and barked at her to do it again. Mack spit on Roger's naked body.

Then Mack commanded everyone to bend low and fix their eyes on Roger's genitals, and keep them there. Stupidly, they stared. Stealthily, he gripped his hunting knife. Smoothly, he moved his hidden hand. All were entranced with Roger's body. In the light of the harvest moon, they felt the phantom presence of a great knife swiping swiftly under Roger's genitals. They were not sure if they saw what happened. Mack lifted the genitals up and away. Blood shot out and sprayed in all directions. The group dropped Roger and backed up, wiping blood off of their faces. Roger lay on the ground, contorted and curled in pain beyond his knowing. Mack snarled, "Everyone, stay where you're at!" All of them froze.

Roger, writhing in excruciating pain on the ground, was unable to think any longer about what was happening. The rest of the violence still to come would be even more heinous and deadly. For Roger, it was progressive murder, with one devastating shock after another. For Mack, it was just an unfortunate, tasteless follow-through after he had satisfied his real passion in castrating Roger. As for the rest of the group, they were set free from all remaining inhibitions. The girls took turns dancing with their high heels on Roger's naked back. After their last dance, they took off their high heels and pounded them into Roger's back. They shoved their high heels into Roger's rectum, pushing the corncob deeper. For the girls, there was nothing more that they could do. They were exhausted.

Pete backed away and said he was getting Roger's clothes from the car. Roger's squirming and thrashing on the ground annoyed Mack. He and Dewey lifted Roger off the ground. Suddenly, Mack began thrusting his hunting knife into Roger's chest again and again. Roger's arms were swinging and flailing. In the stirring and stabbing turmoil, Roger's left ear and two fingers were cut off. In the final struggle, Roger was stabbed at least once in the back. Then the two bullies dropped Roger into his own pool of blood. They were sure that Roger was dead or dying. When the clothes arrived, Mack ordered everyone to dress Roger.

Roger's blood got on everyone. All had been sprayed in the face at the moment of castration. Trying to wipe the blood away only spread it around. Roger was still bleeding badly from all the stab wounds. Getting his bleeding body into his clothes was a nauseating chore. It was not obvious to them if Roger was alive or dead. They worked together to get it done and to get away. Finally, Roger looked more like himself. They wanted to turn off the light, but the moon would not take a bow and leave. They could not get away from the blood. They were not yet free to leave.

Mack mellowed some and got the exhausted group together. He explained how all of them would tell the same story for the rest of their lives about Roger getting drunk and fighting and running off into the cornfield and disappearing. Then he leveled his threat: "If any of you ever say anything about this, I will kill you." He repeated his words to each of the seven in the circle, looking directly into the eyes of each one as he drove the message into each one's soul. He instructed Dewey to bring his car around on Highway 169 a short distance north of the Kitten Club and wait for him. Then he allowed the rest to leave the cornfield. He told them to find some water and wash up because they looked like a mess.

FORTY-EIGHT YEARS LATER

Cindy was asked if the Foley youth made a "pact" to keep the real story of Roger's death a secret. Numerous townspeople had made this claim. Cindy flatly denied it: "I cannot remember anything about a pact." She probably told the truth. She and her group never went through the steps of actually creating an invented story, signing off on the final wording, shaking hands, and promising never to break the secret code about Roger's bloody death. However, the pact may have been created by their alleged shared experiences that were too terrible to tell. Extra code words were not needed to what was deeply imprinted on their minds and souls.

Five of the seven members of the group are still living. Each one agreed to meet and share something about his or her experience. Mack and his wife, Mattie, also agreed to participate in an interview. This willingness to share something revealed the presence of redeeming grace, even though no one shared anything about the cornfield ordeal. All shared what they could, even if it was only a pretense that they could not remember anything. Some shared more than they had planned. All, except Mack, unintentionally revealed the trauma of living alone for forty-eight years with the knifing of Roger.

This psychic pain had to be taken into account when asking members of the Foley youth to remember and to share their stories of what happened to Roger. The psychic pain of Roger's family and friends must not be overlooked either. Psychic pain sharpens the memory of a personal connection with violence, especially involving a weapon, such as a knife. Along with sharpening the memory, psychic pain blocks the person from facing the pain directly and remembering clearly how it became an irremovable part of his or her life experience. This is the standard understanding of posttraumatic stress disorder (PTSD).

This psychic disorder is at work when an actual experience of something from the past is re-experienced as present in a new way. Anything can trigger this new experience of the past traumatic event. This new assault takes over consciousness and causes adverse psychic and chemical activity that damages the ability to think and feel and handle life normally. Each person who was present and witnessed the knifing of Roger has been dealing with some kind of PTSD.

It was difficult for many to believe that the Foley youth could have kept their secret for forty-eight years. If they were involved, then their cornfield closet was padlocked securely. The story of Roger, with its mysterious sexual elements, was thrashed and branded as unclean, dirty, and unspeakable. Others could not talk about Roger's death in a normal way. Roger was deprived of both his life and his story, a ruthless deprivation.

If this story is true, what propelled these foolish Foley youth, the two adults and five young adults, to go into the cornfield with Mack, chasing Roger as he fled naked from the car? What kept them on the scene from start to finish? Did they still believe in the value of their sexual lesson for Roger? Were they in too deep to back out at that late hour? Were they still carried away with drunken, wild sexual desires? Did "group thinking" have such power over them?

What compelled these furious Foley youth? Were they afraid that their earlier reckless sexual assault would get them into serious trouble with the law? Were they desperate enough to threaten Roger to keep this assault secret? Was Mack's control over them so powerful and so complete? Did they imagine or actually know ahead of time about Mack's alleged intentions to castrate and murder Roger? How much did they allow themselves to be carried along by Mack's violence? Did they plunge from their normal level of wildness to a crueler level of meanness as some stories indicated? Did they get caught up and carried away with the excitement and participation in the mutilation and murder?

Too many storytellers told about the girls in the group using their high heels to inflict additional suffering on Roger. One of Roger's relatives said that she heard that Terrie danced on Roger's back with her high heels when he was on the ground. Another relative said that the high heels were used to hammer Roger and as a sexual instrument. These stories implied that, as the ordeal unfolded, the members of the group became more than gullible bystanders, caught off-guard by the violence of Mack.

CHAPTER NINE

A PLAN FOR THE BODY

Assuming the events in the cornfield took place as storytellers claim, then the story cannot stop there. Roger was found that night lying on the road.[4] So, how was he moved from the cornfield to Highway 169? The following offers one possible explanation.

The blood bath in the cornfield had shattered the group. They were stunned into silence. They stumbled around, dazed under the harvest moon. They hung on the edges of the cornfield. They wanted to run and get far away from dead Roger, but they were wearing his blood. One of them got a bucket of water. Mack wiped his bloody knife on the inside of his shirttails and dragged Roger through the field to a safe spot north of the club's parking lot. He waited in the shadows for Dewey's car to appear. Roger was still groaning, spoiling Mack's high.

Mack, thinking ahead, had parked his bright red Chevrolet sedan in Foley for the night. No blood would be splattered on his car! Dewey was told to bring his car around. He was slow to do so, bewildered but submissive to the force of the madman. He parked on the side of the road for long minutes. Finally, Mack rushed out of the standing corn carrying his bundle, timing himself in between headlights on the two-lane highway. He threw the body of Roger into the back seat and got in

---

[4]   See Appendix C: Official Documents.

beside it. Roger reeked with wretched smells, was bleeding and making a mess. Dewey wanted to panic about the condition of his car. He was told to drive north until ordered to slow down. Both watched for a break in the line of traffic.

Around midnight, the group had raced into the cornfield after naked Roger. About one hour later, Dewey was driving his car north on Highway 169 with a murderer and a dying young man in the back seat. About one mile north of the Kitten Club, as the road rises on a small incline, Dewey was ordered to slow and edge to the center of the road. When the road was clear of other traffic, Mack opened the right back door and threw Roger to the pavement. Dewey was told to drive back and forth over Roger. Mack then ordered Dewey to find a place to turn around and return to the Kitten Club. During the turn-around, Mack found one of Roger's socks in the car. He flung it out the window with disgust. His perfect plan for Roger was complete.

There were two cars involved in what happened to Roger on the road. The first car was used as a weapon of death. The second car was actually a godsend, sent to protect Roger and, after hours of terror, to offer some moments of kindness before his death. Dewey's car was car #1, which ran over Roger numerous times to kill, disfigure, and finally disguise the sexual mutilation and stab wounds. In crushing Roger, car #1 created a long streak of blood on the highway.

After this murderous act, car #1 drove north to find a turn-around spot. Car #1 drove back to the Kitten Club parking lot, where the rest of the group was waiting in panic to get home and out of sight. They were still covered in blood, muddied, and too messed up to be seen. They split up into the two cars driven by Dewey and Pete. They rushed back to Foley, taking back roads. Dewey's car was bloodied inside and under the car. Both cars were spattered by the bloodied passengers. Both cars would need a thorough cleaning before dawn.

At about 1:10 AM, car #2 arrived where Roger, still alive and groaning, was lying on the right side of the road, at a northeast to southwest angle, with his head off the road and his waist approximately where the white line mark would be, with his feet in the roadway, but on the far right side. Car #2 was driven by Norman Sebeck, who, according to his nighttime driving custom, was hugging the right side of the road to avoid oncoming cars and to protect his family.

Car #2 was a 1951 Chevrolet Sport Coupe, with both seats crowded— Mr. and Mrs. Sebeck and their fifteen-year-old son in the front seat and three children curled up under a blanket asleep in the back seat. In the trunk were three rolls of mica roofing paper, which weighted down the rear end of the car. Mr. Sebeck was traveling about 45 miles per hour as he passed the Kitten Club. About a mile north of the club, seeing an object on the road, which he thought was an animal, he slowed down.

In the last seconds, in his car's headlight, Mr. Sebeck saw black and white clothing on the object. He swerved left, crossing slightly into the other lane of oncoming traffic. As he went past the object, he heard a bump-bump. His son in the front seat was awake. He heard the same sound but had not seen the object before the bump-bump. The son reported, "After the bump-bump, Dad said, 'I think I ran over someone.'" Car #2 had run over the two legs of Roger. Roger was lying at the north end of the streak of blood, which already had been smeared on the pavement before car #2 arrived on the scene.

After driving over Roger's legs, Mr. Sebeck pulled to the side of the road just north of where Roger was lying. He told his family to stay in the car. He came back and found that the "object" was indeed a young man who was still alive. He began to flag down traffic. Many cars went by without slowing down. Finally, one car stopped with three young people inside. This group returned to the Kitten Club to call the authorities. They never returned to the scene. Mr. Sebeck said that he often wondered who they were and what they imagined happened there. A second car stopped with three young adult men who had been at the club. They stayed and helped redirect traffic away from Roger.

After a comparison of data in the police report, the written notes of Mr. Sebeck, and other sources, the sequence of events can be approximated. The crushing by car #1 happened at about 1:00 AM or slightly before. Car #2, with Norman Sebeck, ran over Roger's legs at about 1:10 AM. At about 1:15 AM, Sebeck was able to flag down a car with three young adults who agreed to go back to the Kitten Club to call the authorities. They did their duty but never came back.

At about 1:20 AM, another car with three young adult men stopped. They helped Mr. Sebeck with traffic control, to keep other cars from hitting Roger. They remained at the scene and later signed the state patrol officer's report as witnesses. One of them reported that while he and his friends were looking down at the boy lying face down in a pool of blood, he saw him take several breaths and then stop breathing. Roger died at approximately 1:30 AM lying on the road. The Certificate of Death on record confirmed 1:30 AM as the time of death.

State Patrol Officer Philip Dahlberg arrived at about 1:45 AM and took charge of what appeared to be a traffic accident fatality with strange twists. While on the scene that night, he couldn't figure out what really happened. A retired patrol officer said about such a patrol situation, "The primary task is to take care of the victim, make a quick and accurate assessment of what happened, and clear the scene so that traffic can return to normal."

From the trooper's report, the following can be established: Roger C. Vaillancourt died while lying on the road at about 1:30 AM, about fifteen minutes before the trooper arrived; the young man who witnessed the dying breath of Roger was still there; and the nature and extent of injuries included a "broken leg, 2 broken hips, broken neck, brain concussion." A thirty- to forty-foot streak of blood on the highway proved that Roger had been run over and dragged under a car, causing massive injuries to the entire body. Officer Dahlberg was not aware that Roger had been sexually mutilated.

Norman Sebeck reported to the trooper his conviction that he had run over only the legs of Roger, nothing else. Nonetheless, Officer Dahlberg described the accident scene and wrote up his report as if Norman Sebeck's car was the only car involved. His inaccurate, ambivalent report created the receptive environment with the newspapers and with the public for the Foley youth's story—namely, that Roger had run away into the cornfield after a beating at the Kitten Club; he wandered on to the road and was run over and dragged by the Sebeck car; and maybe he was glanced by a hit-and-run first car, which possibly disoriented Roger while stumbling along on the road.

Dahlberg wrote, partially quoting and misrepresenting Sebeck, "Vehicle 1 was driving north on Highway 169. Met a group of cars coming toward me, as the last one past [sic] saw something in the road direct in front of me swerved to avoid hitting it but ran over object. Stopped car immediately past object. Ran back and found a person.

Drove vehicle 1 off the highway and stopped another car to go call an ambulance and Highway Patrol."

From the very beginning of his involvement with the story of Roger, Mr. Sebeck was convinced that he had run over only the legs of Roger. Officer Dahlberg chose not to believe Mr. Sebeck that night on the scene. He reported that "vehicle 1 ... ran over object," without any clarification. Most likely, Sebeck's car was not "vehicle 1" but "vehicle 2." Also, Sebeck's car did not "[run] over the object" but ran over the legs of Roger. During the ensuing investigation on the following days, Dahlberg changed his mind. But the mistake had already caused irreparable harm to Mr. Sebeck and his family and would control the public perception of the story of Roger for forty-eight years.

The information about when the ambulance arrived to pick up the body of Roger was not clear in the record. Mr. Sebeck's own account written the day after the accident reported that the ambulance arrived before the state patrol officer. His written account said, "We waited for the ambulance and the highway patrol. The ambulance came and took the boy, then later the highway patrol came."

During a recent interview, Mr. Sebeck reported that he might have been mistaken about this piece of the story. In his memory, he thinks now that the highway patrol arrived before the ambulance. However, if the ambulance picked up the body of Roger before Dahlberg arrived, Dahlberg got his information about the condition of the body later from the Princeton Hospital or, more likely, from the director of the Scheffel Funeral Home in Princeton, Orville T. Scheffel, who was also the deputy coroner who signed the Certificate of Death.

If Dahlberg got this information later from one of these sources, then most likely he also heard from them that Roger had been castrated. If Dahlberg had this information and chose not to adjust his accident scene report, he was negligent in a serious matter. In any case, by Monday, the day after the death, Officer Dahlberg was giving signals to Sebeck that he now believed Sebeck's account that he ran over the legs of Roger and nothing more. Someone else had crushed Roger on the road. Dahlberg did not have enough information to explain his suspicions and new convictions about what happened on the state highway. What happened off the road, in the cornfield, was the responsibility of the local sheriff.

If Roger died at 1:30 AM, it was unlikely that the ambulance driver would have picked up the body and taken it away before the highway patrol arrived fifteen minutes later. If the ambulance arrived during this interim of time, and Roger was already dead, they would have waited for the officer. Three newspapers, the *St. Cloud Times*, the *Benton County News*, and the *Mille Lacs County Times* reported that Roger died en route to the Princeton Hospital. A retired patrol officer explained recently that it was standard practice in those days to make it appear that a violent death or a traffic fatality happened en route to some other location. No authority or institution wanted such a death to happen under its care or on their premises. So be it. Roger died at 1:30 AM, lying on Highway 169 one mile north of the Kitten Club.

The wife of Mille Lacs County Sheriff Bruce Milton recently shared that her husband received an emergency call shortly after Roger's accident. He got up and rushed from his Onamia home to the accident scene thirty-one miles away. He probably arrived between 2:15 and 2:30 AM, after the body had been taken away. Patrol Officer Dahlberg was still making his drawings and writing his report. The Sebeck family had left already; they arrived at their home in Foreston at 2:45 AM. The sheriff would have explained to Dahlberg that Roger's father was his first cousin and that he himself was a very close friend of Roger's father. At that hour, neither officer knew about the castration of Roger and the other atrocities.

Roger's parents also came to the accident scene after receiving a personal visit by a police officer. Sheriff Milton was gone before the Vaillancourts arrived. Carol told her story: "The police came to our house about 2:00 AM that Sunday morning. The police told us to stay at home, but Vern and I took off in the car, taking back roads to Long Siding. Vern didn't say anything all the way to the Kitten Club, but that was kind of normal for him not to say anything to me. Maybe he was in shock.

"We came to that spot on Highway 169 where Roger's body had been dragged by the car from Foreston. [For forty-eight years, Carol Vaillancourt had understood that the Sebeck car had dragged Roger's body.] We saw a big streak of blood going a long way down the road. The second car that hit Roger had a trunk loaded with something so that Roger's body got caught under the car, and it was dragged a long way before it got stopped. The second car, owned by Sebeck of Foreston, had no insurance on the car. Mr. Sebeck lost his driver's license for one year for this accident.

"The body of Roger was already gone. There were several police cars there, but one of the officers left for Milaca to get gas for his car. I thought that he was too nervous to be there with us and needed to get away. He did not want to see the parents of this young man. We got no report from the police at the scene of the accident. Vern and I went to the Long Siding Café and had a cup of coffee. We left for home. Once again, Vern said nothing all the way; no talking between us all the way home. I think that we sat up for the next few hours before Sunday Mass."

That "big streak of blood going a long way down the road" had a long-lasting impact on Carol. The image of Roger's blood spread on the highway kept reappearing in her mind. When asked why it had been so difficult for her to talk to her family about Roger's death and to search for better answers, she said, "I felt too bad. Every time I had to travel on the roads, I would see in my mind that scene on Highway 169. But I have to travel on the road." Flashbacks, psychic pain, PTSD permeated the story of Roger and plagued his mother.

Several months after Roger's funeral, Vern and Carol Vaillancourt visited the Sebeck home and brought a gift for them. They talked about how Roger's death brought them together. All understood that there was something very wrong in the way the death was investigated and reported. But even after that gracious act of hospitality and kindness, Carol still understood that the Sebeck car had dragged Roger to his death on the highway. There was no other helpful explanation. Only recently, after forty-eight years, was that story put to the test. She knows now that there is another explanation.

Carol said that at the scene one of the officers left for Milaca. This officer would have been Sheriff Bruce Milton, cousin of Vern Vaillancourt, who had arrived on the scene a short while before. When he saw his relatives approaching, he could not handle it. He got in his car and drove away. Carol has no memory of Sheriff Milton being there. She said that she would have easily remembered him if he had been present, because of the family connection.

The incident on Highway 169 seriously disrupted the lives of Norman Sebeck and his family, causing the long-term unjust wounding of this kind man and his family. Mr. Sebeck did not have the funds to defend himself legally. He was forced to suffer the indignities of public accusation and threats by authorities.

On Sunday morning, October 6, 1957, CBS's radio affiliate WCCO's news anchorman Cedric Adams, "the voice of truth in Minnesota," reported the story of Roger's death on the road and mistakenly referred to Mr. Sebeck as the "hit-and-run" driver who killed Roger. That error added a great wound to the injuries piling up against Sebeck. The *Princeton Union* newspaper took the most aggressive stance against Sebeck in its article of October 10, 1957, in effect accusing him of Roger's death, when they did not have any more accurate information than the other local newspapers. In addition, on Monday, October 7, 1957, one of the newspaper reporters of the *Princeton Union* threatened Sebeck. Mr. Sebeck recalled, "He accused me of killing Roger and promised me that he would prove it someday."

The third trauma came from one of the state patrol officers stationed in Milaca, Larry Cornelius (deceased). His name was not included on the police report of Roger's death signed by Officer Dahlberg. Officer Cornelius may have been on the scene that night or simply heard about it. On Monday, October 7, 1957, Officer Cornelius confronted Mr. Sebeck with a threat that traumatized him for life. He said, "I say you killed him. And someday you will say the wrong word, and then we got you."

Dahlberg and Cornelius are remembered as decent and upright law officers who would never have done anything contrary to fair play. If this were unusual behavior for Officer Cornelius, at least his threat implied that the state patrol was not involved in how the local police were handling this death. If this was the case, then the state patrol was not given the information that another force had caused deadly harm to Roger before Sebeck arrived on the scene.

The family of Norman Sebeck said that before this series of events, their father "had been someone who always would go out of his way to help others. Trauma severely challenged his instinct for doing good. Eventually he overcame this trauma, but it took a lot of grace and stamina." That night, at 1:10 AM on Highway 169, Norman Sebeck's presence was a blessing that Roger needed. Driving over Roger's legs was a minor extra that could not have been avoided. It added very little to the massive trauma already inflicted on Roger. Finally, a person of goodness and kindness was available to stand guard over Roger during the last twenty minutes of his life.

Sebeck's son who was in the front seat offered these memories: "Dad got out of the car and told the rest of us to stay in the car. I remember seeing the body of Roger, maybe because of the headlights of oncoming cars. After Dad looked at the body, he came back to the car; Dad was shaking like a leaf in a big storm. The blanket which was over the kids in the back seat was wrapped around Dad; he must have been in a state of shock. There was a cold chill that night, but it wasn't that cold. It was shock that shook Dad so quickly. After a little time, Dad placed the blanket over Roger to keep him warm until the ambulance arrived."

During those few minutes before Roger died, Sebeck said that "Roger was groaning or moaning and making some strange, funny sounds." When I explained about the cornstalk in Roger's throat, he said, "That might be the reason why his groaning sounded so strange." While Sebeck and others were guarding Roger from other traffic and waiting for the ambulance, "someone asked if he was still alive. At this time, the boy rolled his head back and forth twice. Someone pulled his shirt back and blood was coming from his mouth." Sebeck said, "I did not see the face of Roger; he remained face down until the ambulance driver picked him up. There was blood where he was lying."

The eyewitness who signed the police report recalled, "The fellow was still breathing. While we were standing there watching him, the fellow took some deep breaths and then stopped breathing. I believe that the fellow died at the moment. After that moment, there was no movement, nothing. I remember that he was lying partially on his side and partially on his stomach. There was blood around his head and around his mouth, but not a lot of blood."

After Mr. Sebeck heard the gruesome details suffered by Roger in the cornfield and about the car crushing before he arrived on the scene, his whole body shuddered with disgust, and he said with anger, "That is cannibalism, what they did to that boy." He understood now why Roger was lying on the road in the path of his car. In his memory, he looked south down the road and then said, "I was able to stand there in front of the boy and see the Kitten Club in the night. It seemed so close." He forgot that it was almost a full moon that night. His wife remembered that on the way home from the accident scene, her husband said, "That poor fellow. He must have been hitchhiking and someone came along and hit him."

During the next couple of days, Mr. Sebeck and his car were investigated thoroughly by the state patrol officers. The family was allowed to drive their car home. Mr. Sebeck said, "On Monday they came and took the car to a garage for inspection. The cops told me that they were looking for blood under my car and for some sharp object under my car that would have caused the deep puncture hole in Roger's back. I told the cops, 'If my car had gone over the top of Roger, and if there was a sharp object under my car that was supposed to cause that puncture hole, then that boy's whole back would have been torn wide open.'"

Mr. Sebeck continued, "The cops could find no blood under my car. They also put the three rolls of roofing paper back in the trunk and then measured how far the car was off the ground and said to me, 'That car could not have driven over Roger, because if it had, Roger's body would have been a mangled mess.' Also, when they were checking out my car, the cops told me that they had found blood on cornstalks in the cornfield earlier."

Mr. Sebeck suffered a lot of setbacks in his life because he came along the highway at that moment. Eventually, he sold his car because he did not want it around reminding him of that night. He had insurance on his car, contrary to the report that made the rounds. But someone decided that he did not have enough insurance for the kind of fatality accident that he was involved in. For that reason, his driver's license was suspended for thirteen months. During that time, one of his sons had to drive him to and from work each day. As soon as he could manage it, he sold his small farm and moved away from Foreston and started a new home and a bakery business, which supported his family of seven. He could not live and raise his family in a community where it was reported that he was a hit-and-run driver who killed Roger.

The son who was fifteen years old at the time of Roger's death and was sitting in the front seat of their car shared this story: "On Monday, the day after the death of Roger, I was attending a sophomore class in Milaca High School. It was one of those classes where each student had to stand up and share some personal story. I remember getting up and telling the story of the accident that happened early Sunday morning. The rest of the kids were very silent, and none of them ever made fun of me or my family for being involved in this incident. But later on Sunday, the radio report of the accident was saying that Mr. Sebeck was a hit-and-run driver who killed Roger. That was very upsetting to my dad and to our family." He went on to say, "This story had never been discussed within our family for these past forty-eight years, since the first month or so after the accident."

At the beginning of the interview, Mr. Sebeck had been paralyzed with fear that after all of these years of suffering he was going to be arrested and put in jail for Roger's death. After calming his nerves and hearing the story of his innocence, he was told, "You are to be thanked for your goodness and compassion to Roger that night on the road, after he had suffered so much earlier in the evening. As you blanketed Roger with some of God's goodness right before he died, you gave a gift to him that you can treasure for the rest of your days. Roger's family wants you to know how grateful they are for your great kindness."

RETURNING TO THE KITTEN CLUB

According to popular theory, there were two people involved in crushing Roger with a car. Mack and Dewey have denied any connection to the story. If they were involved, they drove away from the scene, leaving Roger with "every bone in his body ... broken" but still alive.

If this story is true, then their round trip would have lasted fifteen to twenty minutes, and for some unknown reason, the whole group waited for Dewey to return with his car. Pete waited to leave, because it is known that Mack rode back to Foley in the yellow Buick. Both cars left the Kitten Club together.

Years later, Darlene remembered this experience of waiting for Dewey's car to return. Darlene's older brother, one of Roger's best friends, said, "Years ago, Darlene told me something about the death of Roger, but it was only a little piece of the story. Darlene said that she thought

Roger was thrown out on the road and that Dewey was involved in this matter. Darlene never said anything more about this story."

In her interview, Darlene had a tendency to point the finger at others, never saying anything that would implicate herself. What she shared with her brother was "only a little piece of the story," but it was an important little piece. It is likely she shared more than she had planned to share with him. She thought it was a safe piece. The little story implicated Dewey, not herself. Darlene did not say anything about Mack being involved in this matter. She would have been too afraid of him to use his name, even with her brother.

Another witness confirmed this story. A family member of Pete said, "I have always heard that Roger was pushed from a vehicle and run over several times. Dewey's name has been brought up quite frequently as being involved in this matter."

Other people in the Foley area have heard that Roger was run over by the car of one of the Foley youth at the Kitten Club that night. These folks assumed that it was not an accidental happening but an intentional effort to kill Roger. Most people never knew, forgot, or didn't ask who drove the cars to the Kitten Club that night.

The group members knew that there were only two cars. In their interviews, most said that Pete would never hurt a flea, was a guardian angel for the girls, a good man who could not intentionally harm anyone. In their careful, hidden way, they may have been asserting that Pete's car was not the one that crushed Roger in the final act of murder on that fateful night.

According to Dewey, "On Sunday morning, a state patrol officer and Foley Chief of Police Jack Lloyd came to our house to check out the car that I had driven to the Kitten Club. They checked it out and found nothing wrong, no blood on the car, and left satisfied, as far as I understood." It was possible that Chief of Police Jack Lloyd found evidence of blood in the car and Roger's blood, skin, and bones under the car. This information could have been kept by the police for later use. However, on Sunday, the local authorities were already questioning what to do with the gruesome story that was emerging. Also it was possible that no evidence of blood or of the brutal killing was found under the car. Dewey would have had time to take the car to a garage and raise it up on a car hoist and hose it down completely. Some garage operator in the neighborhood or in a nearby town could have made this possible. The blood and mess in the back seat could also have been scoured out. The car could have been parked and ready for inspection on Sunday morning.

One problem has remained with Dewey's account of his clean car. In each account, he mentions a state patrol officer inspecting his car along with Foley Chief of Police Jack Lloyd. It has seemed evident all along that the state patrol at no time participated in how the local authorities were handling this case. The state patrol certainly suspected that Roger was victimized by other violence off the road, and Officer Dahlberg indicated to Mr. Sebeck that someone else's car was involved in causing the long streak of blood on the highway. The apparently casual treatment of Dewey's car by the state patrol has seemed to be out of sync with their professional diligence. On the other hand, the very fact that they were checking out someone else's car other than Mr. Sebeck's indicated that they were not satisfied with the story that was told to them.

Mack's alleged participation in the car crushing of Roger on Highway 169 appeared unexpectedly in an interview with the wife of Sheriff Bruce Milton, who was the sheriff of Mille Lacs County at the time of Roger's death and a first cousin to Roger's father.

The wife of the sheriff started her interview with a clear declaration: "Roger was murdered." She said that in addition to her husband at the accident scene, "Sheriff Siemers was there, as well as a state patrol officer. Bruce told me that all three were there. When Bruce came home that night after taking care of this tragic accident, he was very upset about the experience. Bruce told me that Roger Vaillancourt had been run over twice by two different cars. Bruce said that the first car was a hit-and-run driver."

She said that she understood her husband to say that "the first car intentionally ran over Roger, and the second car accidentally ran over him. The second car was driven by a man from Foreston. In any case, Roger was run over twice by cars. The state patrol took care of this case because it happened on a state highway." Then she stated, "I know the scoundrel who ran over Roger to kill him."

The wife of the sheriff had operated the Milton Home and Care Center in the town of Onamia for twenty-four years, from 1961 to 1985.

One of her residents was Joe O'Konek, known as Old Joe, who lived in her center for a number of years. She said, "I do not remember how many years, nor when he died. The bank in Foley paid me each month for taking care of Joe. Old Joe was a bachelor, never married. He was too much of an alcoholic to ever get married, a lifelong alcoholic. He died one morning about 5:00 AM in my arms, from a heart attack."

The story about "the scoundrel" who killed Roger was part of a very small conversation one day at the Milton Home and Care Center. It was a mysterious utterance by Old Joe that seemed to come out of nowhere. It was never pursued by the wife of the sheriff. Thankfully, it was remembered.

She shared the story: "One day, while I was taking care of some task in my senior care center, Joe, who apparently knew that Roger and I were relatives, said to me, 'I know who killed your cousin. My nephew killed him. He threw him on the road and ran over him with his car. And no one better mess with my nephew because no one else will win.' Joe said this with a strange laugh and a very unsettling grin on his face. I told him, 'I don't want to hear any more.' So Joe never said anything else about this, and I never brought it up to him again. Hearing him say that made me sick to my core, and I disliked him from that day on until he died."

After hearing this, the hunt was on to track down this nephew of Old Joe O'Konek. Many inquiries were made. Finally, a member of the O'Konek family was able to make the right connection. She checked through the entire list of nephews and grandnephews of Old Joe who would have been seventeen to thirty years old in October 1957, who could have been in the local area at that time, and who would have had the inclination toward that kind of violence. No nephew or grandnephew fit the description. Finally, she was able to remember that the O'Konek family was related to Mack's family in some way. She said, "We are second or third cousins, but I do not know how this relationship works."

It is possible that Old Joe did not know the exact family connection with his relative Mack, so he used the simple and traditional formula for referring to a relative in the next generation down. His "nephew" could have actually been a cousin, which was close enough for Old Joe.

Questions were raised: How did Old Joe find out about Mack throwing Roger out of a car and crushing him on the road? Did Mack whisper his secret in the ear of his cousin who was fifty-nine years older than himself? Was this one of those family secrets within the O'Konek family that no one was supposed to talk about? Did Mack one night have too many drinks with Old Joe, who was a lifelong alcoholic, according to the wife of the sheriff? Did a bragging competition between the old and young cousins get out of hand, so that Mack shared more than he planned to say?

Another possibility has poked its head into the open. Some of the old-timers in the Gilman and Oak Park areas have remembered that Old Joe O'Konek was castrated at some point in his life. The story was told that it happened one night on the local reservation where Old Joe was making a pass at someone's wife. Supposedly, a broken beer bottle was used to cut away Old Joe's testicles to teach him a hard lesson.

Old Joe could have shared his secret of castration with Mack at some family affair or at some bar. In this shared moment, Mack could have told his cousin how he castrated Roger and threw him on the road and drove over him with a car. Knowing that story, Old Joe would have been able to say with personal conviction, "No one better mess with my nephew because no one else will win."

The wife of the sheriff said that she had to help some of her older and weaker clients to get into the bathtub and to get their bath started. Old Joe always wore long underwear and never allowed her to help him in this way. So, she was unable to verify the story of Joe's castration.

Mack has been known for his sharp mind. He thinks ahead. If Mack were involved in Roger's mutilation and murder, he would have had a plan in mind to deal with Roger's body before he even left his home on Saturday morning, October 5, 1957.

CHAPTER TEN

Washing Away
the Blood

If the Foley youth experienced the traumatic event in the cornfield, it's likely that they were no longer a group by the time they reached the Kitten Club. Even so, they would have been forced to huddle and hang together. They might have carried buckets of water from the club into the cornfield to wash away Roger's blood. They may have washed their hands and faces over and over. They wouldn't have known what to do with his blood in their hair and on their clothes.

When the parking lot had thinned out, they could have crept out into the open, bloodied and muddied and anxious to get back to Foley and home, longing for something normal. No one would have wanted to get into the back seat of Dewey's car. It would have been messy and smelled of Roger. Of course, no one would have wanted to ride in the same car with Mack either. He would have been considered too scary and the bloodiest of all. One mile north, Roger was taking his last deep breaths.

As the story goes, when they left in their two cars a few minutes later, they looked north up Highway 169 and saw the flashing lights of police cars. They drove straight west through Long Siding, a seventeen-mile trip on back roads, to Foley, arriving just after 2:00 AM. Supposedly, the plan was for both cars to stop at the family home of Dewey and Cindy to clean up. Mack did not want anything more to do with this group and their plans. He wanted to be dropped off by his car.

DARLENE

Darlene shared her story: "Both cars left at the same time. We drove along the cornfield for a little ways to look for evidence of Roger. Then we saw the cops and the flashing lights on the road, but the cops would not tell us anything. So we left for Foley, looking for Roger along the way, possibly hitchhiking back to Foley. Pete was driving one car. Dewey was driving his car that night."

ANN

Ann's story about leaving the Kitten Club focused on Mack's guilt. She said, "When we got away from the Kitten Club, Mack said, 'I left Roger dead in the cornfield.' Mack was riding on the passenger side next to Pete, who was driving; the three girls were in the back seat. Mack said that he believed he left Roger dead and he said, 'If anyone of you opens your mouth, you will get the same thing.'"

Ann continued, "We saw a number of police cars, with lights flashing, stopping traffic. So we drove straight ahead through Long Siding to take back roads home to Foley." She identified Pete as the driver and Mack as being in the front passenger seat. She said there were three girls in the back seat.

Two of the three girls in Pete's car were Ann and Darlene. In her interview, Darlene said, "Pete left me off at my home." But their stories about where Roger was conflict. Ann said that very soon after leaving the Kitten Club, Mack said that he left Roger dead in the cornfield. Darlene, on the other hand, used the group's story of Roger hitchhiking back to Foley.

TERRIE

The third girl riding in the back seat of Pete's car had to have been Terrie. She said that she couldn't remember who drove her home. She was sure she was not in Pete's car on the way to the Kitten Club, which seemed correct. Ann, Darlene, and Cindy rode together in the back seat of that car on the way to the club. Most likely, Terrie was in Dewey's car earlier in the evening. But on the way home, she most likely rode in Pete's car. Cindy would have agreed to ride home in Dewey's car.

CINDY

Cindy gave the impression that she calmly took the ride home: "We started to think that he [Roger] hitched a ride with someone else and was already on the way back home to Foley." Then she switched her story to knowing somehow that Roger was wounded, dying, or dead on the road: "I remember seeing the flashing lights on the road where the police were tending to Roger."

After hearing Ann's story about Mack's threat in the car, Cindy concluded, "I do not remember at all any statement by Mack that he left Roger dead in the cornfield. Nor do I remember him making a threat that the same thing would happen to anyone who opened her mouth. If I had heard that threat, I certainly would have remembered that all of these years. So I must have been riding in Dewey's car on the way home and not in Pete's car, if in fact this is an accurate memory by Ann."

DEWEY

Dewey approached both interviews with his lifelong rehearsal of denial and lies. He remembered almost nothing, only those things that made Roger look bad and ridiculous. He said, "I remember leaving the Kitten Club without Roger and driving home and going to bed not knowing what happened to him. Later on that Sunday morning, I heard the news that Roger had been hit by one or more cars and killed on the highway."

MACK

If this story is to be believed, the bloodiest of all would have been Mack. He might have stashed a clean set of clothes in the trunk of Pete's car, along with the extra booze. That would have been natural for Mack's cunning mind. If this forethought had not happened, he might have had clean clothes in his new red Chevrolet sedan parked somewhere in Foley as part of his getaway plan. His presence would not have been wanted by the Foley youth, and he wouldn't have wanted anything to do with them. It would have been mutual disgust but one-sided fear and terror.

Mack claimed that he left in his own car, driving north on Highway 169, edging past police cars and flashing lights, leaving behind the Foley youth, the Kitten Club, and everything else that happened. He finished his little story about driving away from it all with, "And I never saw a body."

The truth was that Mack was a rider in Pete's car, as reported by several of the girls in the group. Pete's car drove directly west through Long Siding, not north on Highway 169. If Mack did murder Roger, it would make sense that he wanted to play around on the sharp edges of the murder scene, relishing what he created. In his imagination during the interview, he would have wanted to drive right by and look again at Roger lying there crumpled up, being just a few feet away from the puzzled police. In reality, Mack was not close enough to see an ambulance, much less the body of Roger. Pete's car, carrying Mack, drove straight west through Long Siding. But after supposedly enjoying it in his imagination for a brief moment, he proclaimed that the body was no longer there.

BATHING AND LAUNDERING

The story about the Foley youth bathing and laundering at the home of Dewey and Cindy came from within their own family. When Dewey and Cindy heard this revealing story in the second interview, both protested that none of it could be true. But neither one addressed the facts in the story. They ducked away and distracted themselves from the truth. This story was told a long time ago by Dewey and Cindy's mother to friends of hers, who told it to their children, who shared it for the sake of Roger's story. The mother and her friends are deceased.

This was the mother's story. The group arrived home at about 2:00 AM. They were making a lot of noise in the house. The mother got up and found all of them crowded into her house. They woke up everyone else. They were terribly shook up about something. They were doing their laundry and washing their hair and scrubbing themselves. They were not in very good shape, and their clothes were soiled with mud and blood. They were laundering their clothes to get the blood out and washing their hair and themselves to get rid of the blood.

The mother's story spoke of the one car bringing Dewey, Cindy, and Shirley to her home in this messy, shaken condition. But it also told of the whole group being there, specifically mentioning the name of Darlene. Mack would have insisted on being dropped off first where his car was parked in Foley, which would have taken a few minutes. The second carload with Pete, Ann, Darlene, and Terrie arrived a few minutes after the first car.

According to this story the Foley youth were shedding bloody clothes and borrowing clean ones. They needed more sinks, tubs, places to wash themselves. Waiting in line to wash out the blood created tension. It had to be gone right away. They were edgy and in each other's way.

In the crowded commotion, no one noticed that Shirley was sidelined, unable to hold her own. Finally, she shrieked a shrill cry for help. Her shriek put into words what the rest of the group would still not say out loud. Her shriek about Roger's blood in her hair would have worried the group for forty-eight years. Later that day, the news about Roger's death confirmed the truth of Shirley's words. The mother of Cindy and Dewey knew for sure that it was Roger's blood that had been washed down her sink.

The mother's story continued. Shirley was Dewey's girlfriend at the time. She was eighteen or nineteen years old. She was hysterical that night from the trauma and because she could not get the blood out of her hair. She screamed for help. She was normally an uneasy, high-strung person, and that night she became unglued. She screamed for someone to hurry up and help get Roger's blood out of her hair, and Dewey and Cindy's mother helped her.

Shirley's shrieks probably pushed the other carload to pick up their bags of bloody clothes and head for the door. Their plan to get everyone cleaned up in one place was not working. But they were clean enough to sneak into their own homes and finish the washing in their own bathrooms. Pete took Darlene, Ann, and Terrie to their homes. Then he drove slowly to his own place to supposedly scrub down his car, to burn his clothes, and to bury his heart in a hidden hollow that no one else would ever find.

Darlene said that Pete dropped her off at home. This would have happened between 2:15 and 2:30 AM. She said, "Just at the time Pete was dropping me off, Vern came flying down the road in his car like a crazy man, like he was going to run over everyone." That would have been Vern and Carol leaving their home to visit the scene where their son had been killed on the highway.

As she was bringing her story to an end, Darlene said, "Pete talked about driving back to the Kitten Club to see if he could find Roger walking along the road back to Foley." After this story, she said, "Anyhow, I went to bed. On Sunday morning after the first Mass, my mother came upstairs and woke me up and told me what had been announced at the first Mass—namely, that Roger had been run over on the road by the Kitten Club and was dead."

Terrie was dropped off at her home. She would have had work to do before she could go to bed and pretend to sleep away the unspeakable experiences of that night. In her story, she cleaned up her memories at the same time: "I heard nothing more and remembered nothing more until the next morning [Sunday] when I heard the news that Roger had been run over on the highway and killed."

Ann's story was given through her father's comments to a friend: "I don't know if I will ever get over seeing my girl that night washing her hair over and over and bathing to get the blood out." He had found her in their bathroom in the middle of the night trying to clean away the blood, the blood in her hair, the blood on her body, the blood that would not disappear. The father kept this secret for his daughter's sake, kept it away from the rest of the family, and took it to his death, except for one deep sigh with a friend.

Cindy and Dewey's mother lived silently with many painful personal and family wounds. At least once, she shared her motherly pain with some friends, a husband and a wife, about how the bloody laundering and washing away of Roger's blood happened in her home on that terrible night. She also told this same couple that her own children, Dewey and Cindy, were in the cornfield where Roger was killed.

No other story has emerged to reveal how this mother must have felt about Roger's murder and how her children and the others allegedly brought his blood into her home. No one would say a word. Only Shirley screeched once that it was Roger's blood in her hair. It had been a heavy and dark night.

If this story is true, Dewey and Cindy might have taken on the task of scrubbing out the family car. First they would have soaped down the back seat, using strong stuff to clean out the blood stains and sweet-smelling stuff to camouflage the odors. Then they would have taken the hose to the underside of the car. Discovering that this effort was futile, they would have taken the car to a garage in the neighborhood or in a neighboring town, where they had connections, to use the car hoist and water hose. They would have disturbed someone about 3:00 AM that Sunday morning to get the work done. Someone may remember this story.

When Dewey was asked to share his experience about that night, he singled out one event that summed it up for him. For him, one fact cleared away Roger's blood. During separate interviews, he jumped to this one fact that proved his innocence: His car was declared "all clean" by state patrol officers and Foley Police Chief Jack Lloyd. Nothing else mattered to Dewey. Nothing else was true.

Cindy distracted herself in another direction: "If there was such a noise in our home at 2:00 AM on Sunday morning, the neighbors would have noticed it and would have said something." Then Cindy tried to list the neighbors who lived around their home back then. She got lost in creating her list. But the distraction was effective. Laundering and washing away Roger's blood was no longer in the air causing a threat.

MACK ON THE RUN

Mack told a story: "I was walking in the woods one day with my three cats, Mister, Prince, and Tequila. I found a flyer about tithing, which I read, but remained untouched. As I finished my walk, I came upon eight guys standing together and talking about tithing. Ever since that event, I have felt closer to the Lord." Then Mack said, with a spirit of desperation, "I am running the race to gain the prize."

Mack has done a lot of running in his life. His biblical quote about "running the race to gain the prize" seemed out of step with his reality.

On the night of Roger's murder, the parents of Mattie were at their farm home two miles north of Jakeville, playing cards with another daughter and her husband. That daughter and her parents, Grandpa and Grandma, are deceased. However, her husband has vivid memories of that night.

Mattie's brother-in-law told the story: "Mack arrived at the home of Grandpa and Grandma very late. He flew into the yard in his car; the house was about a block from the road. He drove in like a maniac. He came in the front door of the house, which opened into the kitchen area where Grandpa and Grandma, my wife, and myself were still playing cards. Mack went around the table, going behind me, and went right into the living room, grabbing Mattie and taking her along. She had been standing around with only a housecoat on, and with nothing else underneath. She had come in to say good night and go to bed.

"Then Mack arrives, grabs Mattie, and takes her into the living room, which was right on the other side of the wall from the kitchen and with no door between. So everyone in the kitchen heard everything that he said to her in the living room. Mack said to Mattie, 'If anyone asks if I was here all night with you, you say yes.' We folks in the kitchen were not aware yet of Roger's death and what happened at the Kitten Club. But still we looked at each other and wondered, 'What the hell was Mack involved in now?'

"Next, Mack took Mattie, still dressed only in her housecoat and nothing else, and took her through the kitchen and out of the front door past the card players. They were gone about an hour. During this time, Grandpa asked the rest of us, 'What the hell was Mack talking about being here all night when all of us know that he was not here? What the hell has he gotten into now?' Mack came back and dropped off Mattie about an hour later and then sped off to some other place. She went straight upstairs to bed.

"After the death of Roger was reported to our families on Sunday morning, all of us figured that there was something wrong in the way Mack came home earlier that night and told everyone to lie for him, that he was at home all night, when everyone knew that he was not. Grandpa said to me, 'I just know that Mack had something to do with the death of Roger.'

"For years, Grandpa often talked about Mack coming into his home late that night when Roger was killed telling us to lie for him. Grandpa kept saying, 'What the hell is wrong with that man? How can he say that he was here all night when all of us knew that that was not true?' Our family has always felt that Mack had something to do with the death of Roger Vaillancourt. We never had any detailed understanding about what happened and what he might have done. No one seemed to know anything for sure. I cannot remember having any further conversation with anyone else in the family about this middle-of-the-night effort by Mack to establish an alibi for himself."

Both Mack and Mattie lied during their interview when they claimed that she was at the Kitten Club that night as the date of a man named Dick Orpin. According to research efforts, Dick Orpin never existed, and Mattie was at home with her folks. Her brother-in-law remembered Mattie as the girlfriend of Mack at that time. Why the two of them felt it necessary to falsify this part of the story might now become clear.

Later on Sunday, Mack drove back to the mining community some two hundred miles from Foley. It was a four-hour drive one way. He must have found a place to sleep after 3:30 AM and before that long drive. Maybe he slept in his car parked safely outside of Foley. Was he anxious to get out of town? Had he accomplished his mission, his reason for the long drive to Foley on Saturday?

CHAPTER ELEVEN

WEIRD WHISPERINGS

The story of Roger's death got a very bad start in Foley on Sunday morning through Father John Kroll (now deceased), pastor of St. John's Catholic Church. His words added greatly to the suffering of Roger's mother and to the reason why the Foley community turned away from the truth. In the early hours of Sunday morning, neither Vern nor Father Kroll knew about the gruesome details. They understood that Roger was killed on the road by one or two cars after a night at the Kitten Club. Father Kroll was angry at the Vaillancourts for not observing the bishop's rule about no Saturday night dances and for not being more careful as parents.

Carol Vaillancourt told her story: "On Sunday morning, after coming home from the death scene, we sat up for several hours. We went to see Father John Kroll before the 6:00 AM Mass. When we told the priest that our son was killed on the highway near the Kitten Club dance hall, Father Kroll responded, 'Parents should be more careful about whom their kids mix with.' Father Kroll scolded us for letting our son go to a dance hall on Saturday night, contrary to Catholic custom at that time, and for letting our son run with the wild crowd in town associated with Dewey. His condemning statement at that time has been one of the most painful memories of my life that was almost too much to bear."

Carol added, "Normally Vern did not go to church with me and with the children. But this morning, he went to church with us, going to the 8:00 AM Mass. Our usual place in the church was about halfway up on the side. When Father John Kroll announced at the beginning of this 8:00 AM Mass that Roger had been killed on the highway next to the Kitten Club, he added, 'Parents need to watch who their children associate with.' Once again, it felt like Father Kroll was giving us a public scolding for allowing our son to go to a dance on Saturday night."

The young associate pastor reported that he was still sleeping upstairs in the rectory when the Vaillancourts came to see Father Kroll about Roger's death. He was scheduled for the later Masses and was sleeping in. He was awakened by the loud scolding that the parents were receiving from Father Kroll. He said that he felt very badly for the parents, but he could do nothing at that moment.

On his doctor's orders, Father Kroll, who had been sickly, had planned a vacation trip to Yellowstone National Park, starting on Monday morning, using his new Rambler car. He took his vacation as planned and left everything in the hands of his new associate, a newly ordained priest. This was his first funeral. This priest reported that he knew only that Roger had been run over by a car on Highway 169. The funeral was in the church, not in the high-school gym, as some reported. The associate pastor remembered preaching about Roger's death as an early graduation, Roger not having had the opportunity to finish all of his schoolwork in this life.

Several weeks later, when Father Kroll returned from his vacation trip, he received a more complete report about the condition of Roger's body from Leon Bock, the director of the Bock Funeral Home, who was also the county coroner at the time. Leon Bock told Father Kroll that "all of Roger's bones were broken." Carol remembered that Father Kroll gave this information to Vern and to herself. But Carol said that she understood that all of the broken bones came from Roger being run over by the Sebeck car, the second car. No other information was given to her about how Roger was mutilated and killed.

Years later, Father John Kroll told a parishioner at Brennyville, a neighboring town of Foley, that he was very upset with the sheriffs for not completing the investigation into Roger's death. This parishioner reported, "Father Kroll said that he personally would get Mack for the death of Roger before he [Father Kroll] died." Father Kroll did not "get Mack."

THE WHISPERING BEGINS

The story of Roger's castration escaped from someone who had insider information. This happened between Sunday, the day when Roger was killed, and Wednesday, the day of his funeral. People discovered that it was a word and a story that could not be shared in a normal way. They felt a need to whisper it to one another.

When people heard the word *castration*, their bodies shuddered and their minds wanted to fade into a different direction. As the story of castration was being whispered around, the story of Roger's death became increasingly enfeebled with each telling. Abhorrence for the word and the reality supported the shift in the story of Roger to "some kind of beating" and a traffic fatality. Nonetheless, weird whisperings kept the story of castration from disappearing completely, even if very few could take the extra step of imagining how and why it happened.

WHISPERINGS AT THE FOLEY HIGH SCHOOL

Roger was a senior at Foley High School and was not active in extra-curricular activities. After school he worked several jobs for spending money. His classmates knew Roger and some of them, apparently, heard about the sexual lesson being planned for Roger at the Kitten Club that Saturday night and arranged to be on hand to watch. At least one carload of classmate gawkers were at the club that night, and it is possible they were lurking in the cornfield shadows watching what happened to Roger. When the bloody mutilation and stabbing commenced, they would have scurried for cover to their cars and carried their weird whisperings to their homes.

Many of Roger's classmates gathered at the school for a class play rehearsal on Sunday afternoon, October 6, 1957, about twelve hours after Roger's murder. One of Roger's classmates in the play related the unusual behavior of her classmates: "All my classmates were gathered together. All were grieving greatly; there was real sadness in the whole group. Some did not want to talk about it at all. There was a strange reluctance present in the group about wanting to talk about the death of Roger, unlike other deaths of peers. For good reason.

"Usually kids want to talk about the details, want to hear exactly what went on, want to hear something articulated so that they can relate to the trauma settling in on them. But this death was different; it seemed that the majority of the kids did not want to talk about it. There were a lot of scared kids at the school after that. It seemed that lots of them saw something, but no one would talk about the details."

This same classmate said, "At a play practice on Monday or Tuesday, but before the funeral on Wednesday, a group of classmates were talking about the death of Roger, and I overheard their conversation. I was not part of that group and possibly did not hear everything that was said. But what I heard stunned me, and it stayed with me throughout my whole life. I heard the kids say, 'Roger was stabbed and then dragged through the cornfield and thrown upon the road.' It was also said that later someone found the path where Roger was dragged to the road. They found the place where there was a lot of blood, and the path led from there to the road."

In these whisperings, Roger's castration and sexual mutilation were not included with the other stories of violence. Or, this part of the story was being whispered so circumspectly that only those in the group who were leaning in close could hear the unmentionable secret. If some of these classmates saw the stabbings, they also saw the sexual mutilation that preceded the stabbing. If they only heard about the stabbings from others, then it was possible that the castration was already stripped from the story, or it was shared as a confidential piece that could not be repeated.

There were a number of other stories shared in interviews that revealed what was happening in the school after Roger's death. Several women said that Darlene "cried and cried in school, and no one could comfort her." And Darlene herself said that her experience at the Kitten Club was so terrible that she was going to have to leave Foley as soon as possible.

A classmate said, "The talk around school and town immediately after the death of Roger was that Mack was responsible. He was a hothead, a hard drinker, and an older man who pushed his weight around." She went on to say, "I was severely traumatized by Roger's death for a long time. I would cry and cry in school. They even got a counselor for me."

After hearing some of the details about Roger's sexual mutilation and murder, she said, "I am very angry that someone who was important to me had to endure such suffering."

Another classmate of Roger said, "My friend sat right in front of me in class and cried all the time and was so terribly upset about Roger's death. There was no way to help her. Now I wonder if she was at the Kitten Club that night and saw something that made her so upset."

A classmate of the three girls in the Foley youth, all juniors that year, shared her experience of what happened at school: "I heard in school on Monday that Roger had been killed. I lived out in the country and did not have the direct line with the news of Foley. They announced in the school that some kids would be taken out of class or study hall to be questioned by the police. I know that Darlene, Cindy, and Terrie were taken out of class to be questioned by the police. Lots of kids were crying in the school. All of this was happening on Monday and Tuesday, even before the funeral on Wednesday morning. There was all of this activity, and then absolutely nothing was said to us about what happened to Roger."

A guy in Roger's class said, "After Roger's death, it was common talk among us that some of the big football types in our class who were in the 'A group' drove to the Kitten Club that night and saw what happened to Roger. But we did not know this for sure. This had a big impact on us for the rest of our senior year."

The story of castration had crept into Foley High School. It was a story that even tough teenagers could not handle well. It was a story that had to be guarded carefully. Some classmates and other students knew about it for sure. Some of the students walking the halls, sitting in the same classrooms, or playing on the same teams were involved or close to the scene. The senior class considered Roger "well-liked and friendly." But as their murdered classmate, he was also a troubling presence for many. The unspoken reality of castration left its mark on the senior class.

WHISPERINGS AT THE BOCK FUNERAL HOME IN FOLEY

Four local newspapers reported that Roger died en route to the Princeton Hospital. However, the Princeton Hospital has no record in its archives for receiving the body of Roger C. Vaillancourt or for holding it for any period of time. Mr. Scheffel, deputy coroner and ambulance driver, knew that Roger was already dead, and it's likely that he took Roger's body directly to the Scheffel Funeral Home. Orville Scheffel, director of the Scheffel Funeral Home, would have noted the multiple stab wounds and the missing genitals.

On Sunday morning, Vern Vaillancourt instructed Leon Bock, director of the Bock Funeral Home, or Mark Zawacki, his assistant director, to transport the body of Roger back to Foley. In the telephone conversations between these two funeral home directors and Vern, the fact of Roger's castration, multiple stab wounds, corncob in rectum, and cornstalk in the throat must have been shared.

By Sunday noon, or shortly thereafter, the body was at the Bock Funeral Home. Vern would have been called in to identify the body and to see the results of the violence done to Roger. It can be assumed that during this initial meeting Vern asked the funeral home staff to keep confidential the information about Roger's sexual mutilation and stabbings.

Leon Bock promised to keep the secret. He would have told Vern that the various police departments had to be informed. It was up to Vern to deal with the police about how they would handle this information. There has been no report uncovered thus far that Leon Bock broke the secret with anyone about the castration of Roger.

The Bock Funeral Home was not a cloistered convent on an isolated island in the middle of Lake of the Woods. It was a semi-public facility in the center of Foley, staffed by its owner and director, Leon Bock (deceased), by his assistant director, Mark Zawacki (deceased), and by a part-time assistant, still living. Either Mark Zawacki or the part-time assistant in the first few days shared the condition of Roger's body with at least one other person beyond the confines of the funeral home. The secret was out.

During a research interview, this part-time assistant shared the following: "Mark Zawacki took care of the body of Roger and prepared it for viewing. Later, Mark told a friend of his, who told me, 'This was a terrible murder. Roger suffered great pain and panic. There were multiple stab wounds in the body.'" This information came directly from inside the Bock Funeral Home. This information was not part of some story floating around Foley. This memory has provided a rock-solid foundation for the many stories.

This kind of clear and accurate information about the condition of Roger's body was available in Foley before the funeral on Wednesday. It was a godsend that the secret got out in this way, even though eventually it caused great trauma for many, especially for Roger's mother and siblings. The other holders of the secret might never have shared this truth. From one source it flamed through Foley like a prairie fire on the loose.

Vern Vaillancourt had declared this information confidential. Leon Bock had agreed to keep it secret until the police decided what to do about it. In spite of their best efforts, by Sunday afternoon, the secret was flying around Foley and the local area in its weird whispering way.

It was still not clear if this information was truth or unfounded rumor. But the rumor mill continued to operate, lacking the clarity and proof that it needed from an official statement. As a result, it became the buzz word at bars, bazaars, and backyard parties.

After the initial exposure to the full story behind Roger's murder, the community settled into a more comfortable way of telling his story. The story of castration was simply left in the background.

The research into the story of Roger was almost one year old before someone who had the information revealed that Roger had been castrated. Many stories included the cornstalk in the throat and the corncob in the rectum. Many people related the stabbings. Many people said that Roger ended up on the road and was run over by one or two cars. Some said that Roger had been beaten up badly in the cornfield and then thrown on the road to be run over by someone's car.

A classmate and friend of Roger served as a pallbearer and offered his story. He wanted to be careful and exact in the memories he shared of Roger and his death. He said, "The stories in school between Roger's death on Sunday and the funeral on Wednesday included the details about corncobs in Roger's throat and rectum and about stab wounds found on his body. The story about his penis being cut off might have been given to me later; I cannot be sure. Also I learned later that someone had seen the place in the cornfield where Roger was killed. There was a big area where the corn was knocked down and then there was a drag mark or a crawl mark from there to the road."

This same friend told a story about how he tried to break through the weird whisperings surrounding Roger's death. He said, "On the day of Roger's funeral, I and the other pallbearers were sitting in the waiting area just inside the Bock Funeral Home, waiting for the prayers, the closing of the casket, and the trip to the church. During this little session, I asked Leon Bock, who was standing nearby, if he saw any stab wounds on the body of Roger. Leon looked at me with a strange kind of look and said, 'I didn't see any stab wounds.' I remember that as being an ambiguous response. I expected Leon to have said something like, 'Absolutely not,' when asked if he saw any stab wounds. I was surprised by his somewhat hesitant denial and the strange look on his face."

Finally, Ann's sister broke the logjam in the story of Roger. She was a good friend of Roger, one of his scooter friends. Her boyfriend prevented her from going to the Kitten Club that night. She has felt guilty for the past forty-eight years because she was not there to help Roger out of his hot spot, whatever it was. She put the full blame on Mack for taking Roger out of the Kitten Club and into the cornfield. She said, "Then something terrible happened in that cornfield. I cannot understand why the police never found a place where there were blood spots in that cornfield."

Then this woman, very frail in health but wiry and spunky, said, "I have always wondered why the police never found Roger's body parts." The three-hour interview was coming to an end when she blurted out "body parts." The interview wrapup was halted. Her mention of "body parts" was followed immediately by the question, "Do you mean to say that Roger's genitals were cut off?" She said, "Yes, that is what happened. That is what was being said after the funeral." With her flailing arms she tried to create a cave to crawl into and hide. Rubbing her head and her shoulders, she shook herself and said, "Saying this makes my skin crawl."

Ann's sister was clear and convinced that Mack was the one who castrated Roger. She continued, "It seems so strange that this big cocky navy man would want to take advantage of a small, vulnerable, nice young boy. Mack was the type that was not afraid of anyone and felt like he could do whatever he wanted to do."

WHISPERINGS AT THE KITTEN CLUB

The Kitten Club disappeared sometime in the 1970s to make room for the new northbound lanes of Highway 169. One of the great dance halls in central Minnesota was buried in a deep hole under the road. The younger generations have never heard of the Kitten Club, but older folks can still tell great stories about it.

Al and Leona Lemke were the last owners of the Kitten Club before the property was purchased by the State of Minnesota. They owned and operated the Kitten Club in 1957. Al is deceased. Leona is still alive. Leona was discovered while doing research in the archives of the *Mille Lacs County Times* on the story of Roger. A member of Leona's family works for the newspaper and suggested that Leona has a good memory and would welcome a visit.

Leona has impaired vocal cords and can no longer speak. She can communicate well with various sounds, with a writing pad, and with her whole person. The purpose of the first visit was to plumb the depths of Leona's memory about the possibility of a different castration story involving Mack in the cornfield next to the Kitten Club two to four years earlier than that of Roger. Leona did not want to be distracted by this other story. She wanted to tell what she knew about the story of Roger.

Leona reached for her writing pad. She opened it to a page where she had written large, jagged letters, jumbled together, that had to be studied and deciphered. Gradually, the word *castrated* took shape on the page. Apparently, the family member at the newspaper office had told Leona about the original story of Roger that had been researched in her archives. Leona pointed to her words on the page, written several times, that "the boy from Foley was castrated." When pressed for information about the other story, Leona wrote once again on the page: "castrated that boy from Foley." When asked if she could remember another story of someone being stabbed in the cornfield earlier, she looked upward to the ceiling in frustration, then she shook her head sideways to say, "No."

The stubborn researcher, still bent on a different story, could not grasp at first the truth that had been scribbled on a writing pad five times by this voiceless woman who was a direct link to the time and the place of Roger's death.

After Leona saw that she had finally communicated the truth about "the boy from Foley was castrated," her tears began to flow. She had held this heavy story for almost half a century. Now she could hand it over. She mixed her cries with laughter. Leona was relieved.

After a pause, the questions began.

Question: "Did the police come to the Kitten Club after the death of Roger to ask any questions?"

Leona: "Yes."

Question: "When did the police come? On Sunday?"

Leona: "No."

"On Monday?"

Leona: "Yes."

Question: "Were both you and your husband present when the police came?"

Leona: "No." Leona wrote on her pad, "Al was gone then."

She wrote, "The Kitten Club was not involved."

"You mean to say that someone took the boy out of the Kitten Club and into the cornfield and did this to him there?"

Leona gestured, "Yes."

Question: "Were you working that night?"

Leona: "Yes."

Question: "Did you see or hear anything about Roger that night?"

Leona: "No."

"There were always many people crowded into this great dance hall, correct?"

Leona: "Yes."

The questions continued: "Who was the police officer who came to the Kitten Club on Monday morning, October 7, 1957, to ask questions? Was it one of the state patrol officers?"

Leona: "No."

"Was it Sheriff Hewert Siemers of Benton County?"

Leona: "No."

"Was it Sheriff Bruce Milton of Mille Lacs County?"

Leona: "No."

"Was it Deputy Sheriff Al Wilhelm of Mille Lacs County?"

Leona: "No!"

"Was it another deputy sheriff of Mille Lacs County?"

Leona: "Yes."

Before the next visit with Leona, it was established that Mille Lacs County had another deputy sheriff in its employment in October 1957. It was Deputy Sheriff James Russell Johnson. J.R. Johnson died in the line of duty on June 12, 1959. (Johnson was a passenger in a car driven by Sheriff Bruce Milton, driving from Onamia to Princeton to participate in a police action near Princeton arranged by Deputy Al Wilhelm. Close to Princeton, their car spun out of control; the passenger side was struck broadside by another car, killing J.R. Johnson.)

By a process of elimination, it was established that Deputy J.R. Johnson was the police officer who visited the Kitten Club on Monday morning, October 7, 1957, to ask questions about Roger's. He was the one who told Leona that the boy from Foley was castrated. He might have mentioned other gruesome details about Roger's death, but they were not remembered. Deputy Johnson was probably told by Sheriff Milton not to tell a soul. But the deputy could not help but share what was so troubling.

This information was tested with retired Sheriff Al Wilhelm, the successor of Sheriff Bruce Milton. Wilhelm was a part-time deputy for Mille Lacs County in 1957. He served as sheriff from 1963 to 1974. Al Wilhelm could not accept the possibility that Deputy Sheriff Johnson came to the Kitten Club and told Leona Lemke that Roger Vaillancourt had been castrated. Al said that if that had happened, he would have been told this information by Sheriff Milton or at least by Deputy J.R. Johnson. Al said, "Leona probably heard the stories that floated around Foley surrounding the death of Roger and somehow appropriated these stories as her own and made up this story about a visit by the deputy sheriff."

From the very beginning, Leona Lemke's story seemed truthful and in harmony with the accumulating and converging evidence and stories about Roger. The opinion of the retired sheriff suggested that the research project needed to obtain additional verification about the castration story.

Tearfully, Leona said that she attended the wake service for the "boy from Foley." Leona would have been totally unattached to the family of Roger and their son's death near the Kitten Club. Because the deputy sheriff introduced this story to Leona, she traveled from Long Siding to Foley for Roger's wake service as a mother concerned for another mother mourning the death of her son. Recently after hearing this story, Carol Vaillancourt and her daughter arranged to visit Leona. When Carol appeared in the doorway of Leona's room, both women wept.

WHISPERINGS AROUND FOLEY

Many people shared their own stories about Roger's death. Most would start by saying, "Well, I never heard the whole story, but this is what I know."

Carol Vaillancourt's understanding at the beginning of the research: "The *St. Cloud Times* said that they beat him up. Dewey would not help Roger during these fights, and he just let him walk away from the Kitten Club after the beatings. Then he stumbled onto the highway where he was hit by two cars and got killed this way."

A pallbearer: "Dewey was the person who beat up Roger that night."

A Foley couple: "Roger was beat up badly at the Kitten Club and left in the cornfield; then Roger crawled up on to the highway, getting killed by one or more cars. We heard that Roger ground off the skin on his fingers while crawling to get to the road."

A Foley woman: "There was a big fight at the Kitten Club that involved Roger and the rest of the Foley group. This Foley group took Roger out into the cornfield and beat him up badly. They left Roger there in the cornfield and came home. Roger was still very much alive supposedly, but beaten up. Then Roger walked or crawled out to the road and was run over by one or several cars and eventually died. There was some story about possible stabbings, but I discounted that, thinking that they were surface wounds. Roger got to the road where he suffered his final tragedy. Most of the Foley youth were involved in the beating of Roger in the cornfield."

From Roger's extended family: "Roger was walking home from the Kitten Club. He was beat up, cut with a broken beer bottle, and then run over several times by the carload of kids that beat him up."

From Roger's siblings at the beginning of the research: "Roger was stabbed in the Kitten Club by one person. Then Roger ran out of the Kitten Club and into the cornfield nearby to escape being stabbed again. Then Roger came out of the cornfield to come back to the Kitten Club, because he was afraid of bleeding to death in the cornfield. Roger was walking on Highway 169 when he was hit by the car, which stopped and found Roger badly bruised all over his face and upper body. These folks called the police and ambulance. Roger died on the way to the hospital." When asked if they had heard about two cars being involved, they said, "That is what we heard too, but had forgotten that piece till now. We heard that the first car actually ran over Roger twice or several times to make sure that Roger would die."

From Vern's cousins, the family of Sheriff Milton: "We understood the story in this way: Roger was at the Kitten Club as an underage person. He got himself totally drunk. There was some kind of confrontation, apparently over a girl. Roger felt rejected and ended up throwing himself in front of a car on the highway. The other youth present and aware of what happened refused to talk about what happened. So the story left behind was that Roger's death was really a suicide caused by severe intoxication and some kind of confrontation in which Roger was the loser."

A woman in Foley: "The stories told about a number of Foley youth together in the cornfield where Roger was beaten to death."

A Foley man whose father was a part-time Foley police officer: "I remember my father saying that there was mud in the cornfield where Roger was found and a lot of women's high-heel marks in the area where Roger was stabbed and where he was left for dead. My father always said that Roger definitely was stabbed."

A classmate: "Roger's death at the Kitten Club was the big topic in town for quite a while. I remember that there were two stories about the death of Roger. One, he wandered onto the highway and got hit by two cars. Two, he was murdered. The word around town after the death of Roger was that Dewey was the one who killed him."

A Foley couple: "The story we heard was that corncobs were shoved down his throat and up his rectum and that an ear was cut off. Then Roger dragged himself out of the cornfield and onto the road and then got hit by a hit-and-run driver and then by a second car."

A classmate: "I had heard stories about the possible murder of Roger, but I never had many details. I heard that there was some encounter in the cornfield. A piece of Roger's ear was cut off and found later in the cornfield. After the fight, Roger crawled to the highway, where he was actually killed. After the death, someone supposedly found Roger's wallet and a penknife, along with the piece of Roger's ear."

A Foley man: "I heard a story from Roger's friend at the Brennyville Bazaar on Sunday afternoon, October 6, 1957, that corncobs had been shoved down Roger's throat and up his rectum. Later, I heard from someone else about the mutilation and stabbing and that the group left Roger at that spot in the cornfield for dead. But then he crawled to the road and was run over by one or by two cars. The names associated with the death of Roger were Mack and Darlene. The motive for the murder: Roger and the others got drunk; they went out into the cornfield to have a good time and something went wrong."

A fragment from a Foley man: "I remember people talking in the bars some time after the death of Roger that he had a couple of fingers cut off."

A man from the county who was dating a girl who lived next to Roger's uncle south of the railroad tracks in Foley: "The girl's family had no telephone. So we used the Vaillancourt's phone to call each other. This gave the Vaillancourts the opportunity to share some of their thoughts and feelings, including about the death of Roger. Each time, these older folks would cry when they talked about Roger. I hesitated to bring up the topic. They told me several times, 'Roger choked to death on a cob of corn, which was down his throat, when he was found on the highway.' This detail always suggested to me that Roger had been murdered."

A Foley woman: "Sometime later, after the death of Roger, I heard that Dewey was the person who caused the death of Roger."

A Foley couple: "The community of Foley convicted Mack of the death of Roger right away. And ever since that time, we have had a low regard for him."

An Oak Park man: "I heard of a confrontation at the Kitten Club between Mack and Roger, and then all of a sudden, Roger was dead on the road."

Another Oak Park man: "Roger Vaillancourt was dead before he hit the road, and there was a corncob stuck down his throat."

A classmate: "Roger's appearance in the coffin indicated that he had suffered a terrible death. Roger could not be recognized in the body on display in the funeral home."

A cousin: "I remember that it was said in school that one of Roger's ears was cut off. They showed his body at the wake service, but there was a red netting over his body." When asked if she heard about a corncob shoved down his throat, she said, "It was a cornstalk."

Roger's mother was asked if there was red netting draped over Roger at the wake service and if she saw that Roger's left ear had been cut off. She said, "There was no red netting over Roger. I did not see the ear cut off. But I did not look that closely. I remember seeing a brother-in-law go up to the casket and lean over to look at the other side of Roger's head. Now I wish that I had looked to see for myself. No one was telling me anything."

AT THE VAILLANCOURT HOME

Only one person in the Vaillancourt household knew that Roger had been castrated. Vern learned this truth about his son on Sunday morning, either by a telephone call from Orville Scheffel, the funeral director in Princeton, or by a personal meeting with Leon Bock at his funeral home in Foley, where Vern saw the massive wounds on Roger's body. Vern shared nothing of this with his family.

Vern had a lot of contacts around town. He was well-liked and friendly with the city cops and with the sheriffs of Benton and Mille Lacs counties. He spent his Sundays sitting and chatting with folks at the B & B Gas Station in central Foley. He liked to take his friends and their wives out to dinner, but Carol was never included. As an alcoholic, he spent a lot of time at bars drinking and had several women partners on the side. He lived a separate life from his family. Usually he did not go to church with them.

Most people outside of his home considered Vern a normal hardworking family man who occasionally had too much to drink. Some folks believed his slanderous stories about his wife. Sheriff Siemers knew that his friend, Vern, was an abusive husband. Several times, he visited Carol to encourage her and to help her. Father Kroll consoled her at times about the sufferings of her life and marriage with Vern. The owner of a trucking company employing Vern visited Carol and puzzled over the family's poverty, knowing the kind of income Vern received. At that time, no one intervened to save a victim of violent spousal abuse.

Vern's friends would have been shocked to learn about the violence in his home. Twice, he told Carol that he was going to kill her. She lived in constant fear and panic in their bedroom, in their home, and in their car. Once, she escaped from their car when it stopped at a light on Highway 23, when it seemed to Carol that the threat to kill was ready to be fulfilled. She jumped out of the car and ran for her life, was picked up by another driver, and was taken to the police, who took her home. The violence never stopped.

Between Sunday morning, October 6, and the funeral on Wednesday morning, Vern was a busy man. He had secret meetings away from home with the authorities, with influential folks of Foley, and with special friends. He met with two sheriffs, both of whom were good friends, one being his first cousin. He met with the Foley City Police. He met with state patrol officers. He met with Leon Bock.

Vern went to the home of one of Roger's friends to ask him to select the pallbearers. While this classmate performed this difficult duty of lining up the other five pallbearers for his dead friend, Vern and the boy's father were secluded for a long time in secret conversation. Vern made all of the arrangements with the funeral home, never including Carol in the plans.

Two stories have suggested, strangely, that the authorities needed Vern's permission for additional investigations in this unexplained death. The family remembers that after the funeral, a police officer came to the house on two separate occasions to get permission from Vern to exhume the body of Roger for further investigation. On both occasions, Vern firmly rejected the request. Also, a friend of Roger, who has been well informed about other parts of the story, has been convinced that the police came to the Vaillancourt home on two separate occasions before the funeral to get permission from Vern to perform an autopsy on Roger's body. This friend said that Vern firmly rejected both attempts for an autopsy. The second proposition is most likely the true story.

On Tuesday, Vern dug the grave for Roger. Many people told the story that Vern's family was too poor to have someone else do this work, so Vern himself, with the help of a friend and Roger's younger brother, dug the grave. It was a cloudy autumn day. The whole process took three to four hours. They needed to borrow large pieces of plywood from the trucking company that Vern worked for to hold up the wet walls of Roger's grave. Vern was already a sickly man at this time, unaware of the tuberculosis sapping his strength and straining his heart. His heart attack two years later revealed his critical condition. Vern died six years after Roger and is buried several rows away from him in the St. John's Catholic Cemetery in Foley.

Carol stood next to the casket both nights of the wake service. Her children attended on Tuesday evening. The two sheriffs, Hewart Siemers and Bruce Milton, and their wives signed the book. Three Foley police officers, Jack Lloyd, Ted Tobias, and Don Parent, and their wives also signed.

Dewey and Pete signed the register book in one place, Darlene and Terrie in another. Not present, or at least not signed in, were Cindy, Ann, Shirley, and, of course, Mack, who was back at work for the mining company two hundred miles north of Foley. His girlfriend, Mattie, signed the book.

Roger's Billfold

Roger's billfold kept appearing in various stories.

The billfold's first appearance was in a story remembered by one of Roger's classmates. He said that he had heard the story about the possible murder of Roger but never got many details. "However," he said, "I did hear after the death that someone found Roger's wallet in the cornfield." According to his story, a penknife and a piece of Roger's ear was found along with the wallet. If a wallet was found in the cornfield, it belonged to someone else who was on the scene, as a later story proved that Roger's billfold was not left behind.

The billfold's second appearance was in the story of Mr. Sebeck, whose car was the second vehicle on the scene on Highway 169. Mr. Sebeck reported, "As far as I can remember, the ambulance took Roger away before any state patrol officer arrived on the scene; they took him to the hospital right away. I heard later that Roger took his wallet out of his pocket and told that person to give it to his dad. I do not remember how I know this, but I remember hearing this." As reported earlier, Roger died on the road before the ambulance driver, Mr. Scheffel, arrived. Roger could not have given his wallet to anyone. It was possible that State Patrol Officer Phil Dahlberg took Roger's billfold out of his pants pocket and gave it to Mr. Scheffel to give to Roger's father. Mr. Sebeck might have witnessed Officer Dahlberg giving Roger's billfold to Scheffel and remembered the story incorrectly. In any case, Roger's billfold would not disappear from the story.

The billfold's third appearance was in the story of Mattie's brother-in-law. He told a side story that has remained mysterious and indirectly involved Roger's billfold. He said, "Roger had a lot of money on him at the Kitten Club." Someone told him this not long after Roger's death, but he cannot remember who that someone was. This mysterious person also said that he was at the Kitten Club that night and saw a bunch of guys around Roger, and Roger had a lot of money on him.

The billfold's fourth appearance occurred on October 16, 2004. Eighty storytellers were invited to come together to hear how their fragments of the story of Roger connected with other fragments to reveal a converging story. These storytellers had been promised that they would be kept informed about the research progress. Two weeks before this event, Roger's mother remembered that Vern's younger brother had brought Roger's billfold to the Vaillancourt home on Sunday, October 6, 1957, the same day that Roger was killed. This younger brother attended the storytellers' gathering.

After the three-hour session with the storytellers, Vern's brother was asked if he remembered bringing Roger's billfold to the Vaillancourt home on Sunday, the day of Roger's death. His first response was, "No, I cannot remember that." After a respectful pause and time to remember, he said, "No, I brought the billfold to Vern on Monday. He had called me and told me to stop at the Scheffel Funeral Home in Princeton and pick up Roger's billfold on my way up to Foley on Monday."

It was surprising that the billfold would have been at the funeral home in Princeton. Vern's brother explained that apparently the body of Roger was taken there first by the ambulance service of Princeton, and then the body was transferred to the funeral home in Foley.

Then Vern's brother offered a brief statement that buried all the weird whisperings of forty-eight years. He said, "The director of the Scheffel Funeral Home told me that Roger had been castrated." Many storytellers were still in the room, but only a few heard this extraordinary revelation. This memory of Vern's brother was the truth that was needed to put to rest all the doubts and questions. He had held this secret for all of these years because Vern had asked him to do so. Like everyone else, he did not have the rest of the story available to understand how the castration could have happened or that it was clearly connected to other gruesome violence against Roger and, most importantly, that it was connected to the murder. He held on to this information for the sake of the family.

Vern's brother was asked if Vern knew on Monday that Roger had been castrated. He said, "Yes, Vern knew this fact." He was asked if Vern clarified whether Roger's castration included both testicles and penis. He said, "No, Vern never said anything about that." Vern's brother understood that the castration happened as part of a fight at the Kitten Club or in the cornfield, and that later Roger wandered on to the road and was hit by several cars, causing his death. Apparently, the multiple stab wounds on Roger's body never surfaced as part of the story or were never understood as an effort by someone to murder Roger.

Roger's mother saw the billfold being handed over to Vern. Vern looked through the billfold. He took out the money and put it into his pocket. He gave the empty billfold to Carol. Later Carol found a condom hidden in one of the pockets of the billfold, a memory recalled only recently. Carol believes that Darlene could have given the condom to Roger before his second night at the Kitten Club. The billfold was kept for years in a small box of Roger's things.

CHAPTER TWELVE

THE MOTIVES

How did Roger become the center of so much attention? How did Roger become the focus of angry people? In the summer of 1957, why did Roger, "a very nice, quiet young man, small of stature, never in the middle of what was going on at the time, but rather at the edge of activities" (according to a classmate's image), become the center of a premeditated plot that ended with his sexual mutilation and murder? How did Roger end up in the crosshairs of stalking enemies?

After the tragedy, many people did not want to accept the possibility that Roger was killed on purpose. It was easier to "surmise," as Sheriff Milton said, that Roger's death was the result of "a beating at the Kitten Club." The Foley youth, if involved, were able to keep their role hidden. They said over and over, "It was a fight. Roger ran into the cornfield, stumbled on to the road, was hit by a car, and killed. End of story." The newspapers fumbled and made their story official. The Foley youth convinced enough people that it was a spontaneous happening.

Roger's extended family ended up with a demeaning variation of the group's scam: "Roger was drinking too much, lost a fight over a girlfriend, ran into the cornfield, and then in an act of suicidal despair threw himself on the road and was run over by a car." A classmate blamed everything on Roger: "Maybe he had small man syndrome and needed to prove to himself that he could play the game in the big-time world." The Foley youth's alleged plan disappeared from the story.

A kind and gentle old man in Foley, who remembered taking Roger deer hunting the previous year, knew part of the truth when he said, "Roger died because this group of Foley youth took him out into the cornfield to initiate him, and something got out of hand." Somehow he knew this piece of the truth. He could not fit this piece into the bigger picture—i.e., the possibility that there was a plan.

Roger's mutilation and murder became a simple accident, another traffic fatality, even though the ghastly truth danced wildly in the heads of many. Roger's father, Vern, squirmed. Sheriffs and city police fell in line. Four newspapers fell in line. Civic and church leaders fell in line. Everyone fell in line. The invented story became the official story. Sir Walter Scott's words could never have been truer: "Oh what a tangled web we weave, when first we practice to deceive."[5]

Indeed, the story of Roger's death became a tangled mess. Many people found themselves on the sidelines, mesmerized.

ROGER AS THE WHITE KNIGHT

Roger's fateful journey to his untimely death started as a vocation to be a white knight, called to be the protector of several women in his life. His first call to duty was in his early teens when Roger, as the oldest male child, became the protector of his mother in his family's home. Roger's father was alcoholic and abusive toward his wife. The spousal abuse was not just sporadic or verbal. It was pervasive, physical, and violent.

As Roger grew in awareness and strength, he found himself laden with the unnatural role of trying to protect his mother against his father. It has not become clear how Roger handled this duty or if he ever challenged his father about his behavior. What is known is that teenaged Roger felt a heavy burden to protect his mother. He suffered a sense of failure because as a son he was inhibited from following through on his felt duty.

Several of Roger's friends spoke of his inner strength, that he never backed down, even against an overpowering force. This instinct was

---

[5] Sir Walter Scott, *Marmion: A Tale of Flodden Field* (1812).

developed inside his home where Roger had to submit to the stronger force of his father. He played out in his mind every other circumstance in which he would never back down in his role as a protector of women. Roger was small, but he grew to be tall in his knightly armor, ever ready for his noble duty.

In the summer of 1957, Roger was called to duty again. Roger's cousin, Dennis Leason, died at the bridge south of Ronneby. (The details of this death were described in chapter five.) Sheriff Siemers decided that the death was an accident. Many relatives, neighbors, Foley residents, and farmers were convinced at the time that Mack caused that death. A few weeks later, Mack was a groomsman in a wedding for his sister, taking the place previously scheduled for Dennis Leason. One of the bridesmaids was another cousin of Roger.

After this wedding, Mack pursued a romantic relationship with this cousin of Roger, which lasted for some weeks during the summer of 1957. It was a harassing cat-and-mouse chase, with Mack "never catching on that 'no' meant 'no,'" according to this cousin. Finally, by mid or late summer, she was able to ditch Mack.

During this dating chase, Roger was on the alert because of his protective calling. Likely Roger had heard the rumors that Mack killed his cousin Dennis Leason at the bridge and was ready to provide full protection to another cousin who was being chased by Mack. It was likely that Roger gave Mack a stern warning not to cause any harm to his cousin and that he would be keeping a close eye on him. Roger would not back down. He was called by instinct and training to offer his protection to this special woman in his family against Mack, who was rumored to be the murderer of his cousin Dennis.

Mack was no lightweight in these matters. If rumors are true, he would not have stood for anyone blocking his way. Is it possible that by mid summer, Mack was looking for a way to deal with "the Roger problem" in the way that would give Mack his biggest sexual kick? Was Roger in Mack's crosshairs?

During this same time in the summer of 1957, Roger was again called to duty to protect a young woman in his neighborhood, Darlene, who was one year younger than Roger and in whose home he spent a lot of time. As was said before, one of Roger's best friends was Darlene's brother, who had joined the marines. The plan was that Roger would join his friend in the marines after graduating the following year.

Roger promised his best friend that he would protect his sister and was committed to protecting Darlene from the feverish pursuit of ardent admirers, a thankless task in a small-town pool full of hungry sharks. But Darlene was not an easy girl to protect. She was drifting away from her family and beginning to run with the wild group in town. She described the problem faced by Roger, the protector: "Roger did not run with this crowd that I associated with going to dances. Dances were the major social happenings at that time. I remember going to all the dance halls in the area with my group, but Roger was not part of that group. Drinking was part of this social scene and part of the dancing group. But Roger was not into this kind of life."

Roger had a genuine fondness for Darlene and a real concern for her safety. A good friend of Roger said, "Roger would talk to my husband about Darlene and how he was concerned for her, more like a brother. But clearly, Roger seemed to like her too."

Darlene told a story that remained an unsolved mystery during dozens of interviews with others. Her story generated much speculation with the introduction of the "red alert factor." Darlene seemed genuinely puzzled by the reason for or danger behind the "red alert." At first, the question was focused on the danger to Roger. Who was chasing Roger? Why was Roger feeling threatened, creating a need for him to keep Darlene away from himself and his own danger in town? But now the issue seems focused on Roger's protecting Darlene. Did Roger know that a predatory man in town was preying on Darlene? This could have been the dangerous "red alert" and why Roger ended several scooter rides telling Darlene, "Go in your house and stay there; do not come downtown tonight; don't be around me in town."

Several of Roger's friends had no doubt about the "red alert." They said, "It had to have been Mack." Mack may have been bristling from Roger's brusque shielding of his cousin, which happened a bit earlier in the summer of 1957. If so, in the later part of summer, Mack may have been on his own alert to find the right time to sexually mutilate this white knight of Foley. Could Mack's taunting of Roger to get at Darlene have been a conniving ruse to get Roger worked up and vulnerable?

Good friends of Roger said, "We heard that Mack was at odds with Roger that night [at the Kitten Club], and we think that Darlene was the reason for the conflict; Roger was being protective of Darlene, and Mack wanted to get connected to Darlene." These friends seemed to have some clarity about this triangular piece of the entangled mess, but they could not see the story behind the story—namely, what Mack was possibly up to.

This was only one part of the complicated story leading to Roger's death. Roger's vocation as protector of special women in his life may have brought Mack into the story. Mack was not part of the Foley youth, did not party with them, and never went to the Kitten Club with them, except that one night. Mack was a lone wolf, not running with the pack.

Several weeks before his death, Roger rode his yellow scooter to his great uncle's farm several miles north of Ronneby. According to the testimony of someone who was a teenager in this family at that time, Roger spent most of that day on this farm hiding from someone who was threatening to kill him. At about 5:00 PM, Roger told his great uncle that he needed to return to his home. His great uncle asked him, "Are you sure you are going to be safe now, that no one will try to kill you?" Roger said, "I will be okay now." Roger's relative overheard this conversation.

Two of Roger's classmates felt sure that Mack was following them on several occasions, perhaps thinking mistakenly that Roger was with them. A storm was gathering. The dark clouds and sounds of thunder were looming.

THE WHITE KNIGHT BEFRIENDS DEWEY

The summer of 1957 was a season of change for Roger. He was working several jobs. Astride his yellow scooter, he was giving rides to dozens of friends to all corners of the county. The protector of women was on duty, intense about his defense for his cousin and Darlene, dogged about never backing down, all the while allegedly dodging the wily maneuvers of Mack.

It was also a time for Roger to take those uncertain steps across the threshold of innocence into the dark world of the wild ones in town, also known as the Foley youth. It is likely that on one of his scooter rides, Roger decided that he was going to deal with his shyness with girls. For a short while, Roger was the sweetheart boy at the Rainbow Café. Before long, his innocence seemed to become a problem for the core members.

The Foley youth belonged to Dewey. He was the instigator, architect, the big daddy champ; he was the dark knight of this Foley wilderness. Perhaps he needed this fringe group as a bragging place for his sexual exploits and victories. The group gathered around Dewey and gave him due respect.

People noticed when Roger began a friendship with Dewey in the summer of 1957. It was a strange fellowship. They knew about Dewey's proclivities and wondered why Roger would hang out with him. Someone close to the wild ones said, "I remember that Roger was some kind of friend to Dewey and Cindy." Another within the circle said, "Dewey was one of Roger's best friends." She went on to say, "People talked about Dewey and Roger being together." Quiet, shy "town kid" Roger chumming with Foley's finest strutting charmer!

Roger's siblings remembered their father trying desperately to keep Roger away from Dewey, without success. Roger was drawn to him and to his fringe group. Roger didn't need another friend; he had dozens of them. Roger was looking for something else. He was not seeking the turbulent waters stirred up so easily by Dewey. Roger needed a friend, maybe a fatherly friend, to ease him into mature things that seemed beyond his grasp.

We cannot say for sure what happened between these new friends. But we can take a good guess. Dewey would have bragged to Roger about his many triumphs with girls and women, scoring on almost every try. Then Roger would have stepped over his fears and shared with Dewey his sexual innocence and shyness around girls. Dewey would have taken Roger to a woman in town to "teach him a lesson." But Roger wouldn't have been able to perform, to score, to participate in sex on demand like his friend could. Roger would have gone back to Dewey embarrassed and vulnerable and shared his deep sense of shame and failure.

The white knight and the dark knight were strange friends. Dewey himself could have been Roger's first sexual encounter, a friendly surrender to the close at hand—no big deal for Dewey; a staggering awakening for Roger, "teaching him a lesson" in the raw. But Dewey might not have wanted to be saddled with Roger; he had other trails to follow and finer treasures to claim. Perhaps Dewey asked Pete to "teach Roger a lesson" in the joys of bisexual fun.

THE WHITE KNIGHT GETS A GUARDIAN ANGEL

Pete was a wholesome man who radiated goodness to everyone, and he was a true bisexual. Ann said that at the time of Roger's death, "Pete had a crush on a couple of gals, one being Cindy; at the same time, he was sexually intimate with Bill Fox, an openly gay man in the Foley area." Pete's goodness made him the guardian angel of the Foley youth. Roger needed a guardian angel and the goodness of Pete.

Pete was different from the rest in the wild group. He focused on sharing his goodness. Roger would have welcomed the calming spirit of Pete. Roger was still searching to get beyond his shyness with girls and his fear of sex. This good, quiet, bisexual man, ten years older, could have been the guardian angel to open up the sexual mysteries for quiet, shy, younger Roger. Their personalities were a comfortable match. Both were innately good. Both were guardian angels for others.

As conjectured earlier, Pete would have taken Roger in his yellow Buick to a secluded spot far from the eyes of Foley. It was meant to be a private experience, but neither one would have considered it a total secret. It was more like a gift, a way of sharing in the wild group. Soon enough, Roger or Pete would have exposed their experience to someone at the Rainbow. In this tiny moment, the goodness of these two men would have been squished and squashed in the dirt on the barroom floor. The rest of the story of Roger began at this moment. His innocence would have been shattered. He would have stood naked in the eyes of the Foley youth and became helpless in the crosshairs of hateful eyes.

The group would have whispered and told the tale to one another. The sweetheart boy would have been teased and taunted and told what to do to keep his story off the streets. Roger would have wanted to turn tail and run, but he would have been tied to them, not free to kiss them goodbye. They would have had fun with him. And big trouble would have been brooding in the bosom of a woman scorned.

The Angel of Passion Craves the Abyss

Cindy was a young woman aflame with passion and madness for love. She was sixteen years old in the summer of 1957, but already an experienced woman. Other women of the group expressed awe at Cindy's gift for keeping two or three older men tilted in her direction at the same time.

According to storytellers, Cindy dated several older men with a purpose. She was willing to suffer the precarious balance in the sexual sphere in order to achieve her goal. She daringly endured this delirious sway between joy and grief, tension and release, between heaven and hell, to escape her family's poverty and brokenness and Foley's rejection. Her hopes and dreams were centered on Pete, the chosen one. He was eleven years older, but the finest pick in the corral. Cindy only needed a little more time. Nothing and no one would stand in her way.

If the story of Roger and Pete's sexual encounter were true, Cindy may have been stunned to discover that her "savior" might be bisexual. She may have been furious that "hurting Roger," as she called him, enticed Pete away from her and their promising future together. For Cindy, Roger may have been more than a hurting person. He may have been a spoiler of dreams, her dreams. Was Roger caught now in the crosshairs of Cindy's crazed eyes?

Was the friendly world of the Foley youth flying apart? If Cindy found her dreams exposed as empty and misguided and felt laughed at for having had a sexual relationship with a bisexual, she may have blamed Roger for making her look like a fool among her friends at the Rainbow. She may have sent Pete spinning with her biting, bitter words. He would have been stunned by her fierce anger and, in his goodness, not known what to do with such wild intensity. Pete would have stepped back from Cindy, knowing that their fine relationship was finished because of an innocent intimate moment with Roger.

Perhaps Cindy was not finished yet. She may have taken after her brother, Dewey, for undermining her love life and ruining her future. She may have fumed at him for his foolish friendship with this shy, scared kid. She may have accused him of jeopardizing the group by recklessly connecting her own partner with this troublesome pest. If so, the rest of the group may have stood apart, waiting for the angel of passion to simmer down. They would have begun to wonder what to do about "the Roger problem."

Did Cindy become the driving force to do something about the problem? Did she give Dewey due warning to deal with it, teach Roger a lesson, get him straightened out with sex, or scare him away from the Foley youth forever? Was she craving revenge?

CHAPTER THIRTEEN

THE SECRET PLAN

If the speculation about Cindy's motives were true, Dewey would have known that he had stirred up his sister's wrath and would have had to find a way out of the mess he had created. He may have seen himself as the master of a secret plan, a plan to take care of "the Roger problem." Each member of his group would have to play a role without knowing the role of the others and without knowing the whole story. He would have to set the stage, pull the curtain, and let the play begin. In teaching Roger a lesson about sex, Dewey may have thought that it would solve Roger's problem for good and help Dewey ride out the storm with his sister.

It would have been madness for Dewey to think that he could play with the Foley youth and with Roger's sexuality in this explicit way without unleashing incalculable chaos. But perhaps Dewey was so enmeshed with his own sexuality that he could not think beyond his own modest possession, giving no thought to ending up with a crime of sexual assault.

The challenge for Dewey would have been to teach Roger a lesson about sex so that Roger was no longer afraid of girls and could do his own scoring. The goal seemed simple enough. The problem would have been finding a lesson that worked. Perhaps it was decided that the girls and the guys of the Foley youth would teach Roger his lesson at the Kitten Club with each one knowing only part of the plan. The lesson that may have been concocted: get Roger drunk, taunt him to hit on girls, guys throw up their guard, Roger fights for what he wants and thus routs his fear of sex with girls. Roger, the protector of women, finds his own girlfriend and leaves his problem behind.

Roger was aware of something in the works. Did he sense a new resolve in Cindy? Perhaps Dewey made it clear to Roger that he would be going with the group to the Kitten Club, if he wanted to keep secret his experience with Pete. Roger himself told one of his friends, "I will be going to the Kitten Club to learn how to dance, because learning how to do this is going to help me get established with some girl." The goal was clear to Roger. He would have been afraid to fathom what else was being conceived.

In three different conversations with Cindy while researching the story of Roger, she asked, "Have you been able to come up with more details about what actually happened?" When she heard that the mission was to find out what really caused the murder of Roger, she smiled strangely and said, "Well, you have your work cut out for you!"

Convoking a Cast of Characters

It has been possible to peer through the cracks and crevices of people's stories to sketch the outline of a version of Roger's story and the secret plan. All the key players in this version who are still alive shared stories that included elements of truth, but more importantly, upheld their story, which seemed to be hiding the real thing. As it turned out, both the elements of truth and their invented stories were helpful in exposing a story behind the story.

Roger was escorted to the Kitten Club by the Foley youth on two separate occasions. The first night at the Kitten Club was at least one month before the deadly night of October 5, 1957. In this version of the story, the first night turned out to be a warm-up, a kind of dress rehearsal for the second, the real thing. The cast of characters assembled for the first night at the Kitten Club can be described, sometimes using their own words.

Dewey was remembered as "being a couple" with two gals of the group, Ann and Darlene. Their own memories of their shared date were part truth and part self-protection. Ann said that her parents called Dewey "a snake in the grass" and tried their best to break up this relationship.

Terrie also reported that Darlene was dating Dewey at that time. Darlene said that she was warned by Dewey's own family, "Stay away from him because he is no good." Then she said as a curious hindsight, "I never knew what they meant." Then she pointed the finger, "Dewey could very well have been involved in what went wrong for Roger." Not to be forgotten was Shirley, who was Dewey's live-in girlfriend at the time, living with him at his mother's home on weekends.

"Pete had a crush on a couple of gals at that time," reported Ann. His primary date was Cindy. But Ann wanted it understood that the gay man, Bill Fox, was also part of the story. In other words, Cindy and Bill Fox were competitors for Pete.

Terrie offered her own tidbit on the group's complex sexual untidiness: "Cindy dated a number of older guys and sometimes several at the same time." Unfortunately, no one in the interviews brought to light Terrie's dating patterns at this time. She herself gave the impression that she was just going along for the ride, an unlikely situation.

As the story goes, all of these characters were present for the first round at the Kitten Club to teach Roger a lesson in sex. There were three guys (Dewey, Pete, and Roger) and five gals (Cindy, Darlene, Ann, Terrie, and Shirley). All of them seemed entwined with each other in some way, with Dewey as the captain of the fleet and Cindy as the driving wind. The powerful undertow shaping the impending disaster seemed to be spelled out clearly by Ann: "Dewey was concerned for Cindy, his sister, and for Pete."

It seemed that Pete would never have gone along with or tolerated any kind of hurtful action planned against Roger. Numbers of people asserted that the goodness of Pete could not have been corrupted knowingly. His participation in this affair suggested the forceful control taken by Cindy and Dewey. They would have pressured him to be there for Roger's lesson. They may have threatened to make public his sexual encounter with Roger or convinced him that nothing bad was going to happen to Roger.

One important person not yet appearing in this cast of characters was Mack. He had not yet taken up his role with the Foley youth. He was already in the story of Roger, lurking and trailing him and waiting for the right moment. Dewey had not yet recruited him, or Mack had not yet forced himself into the group to take advantage of their scheme to deal with "the Roger problem." At the time of Roger's first night at the Kitten Club, these two forces were still involved in separate maneuvers.

Coaxing and Cajoling Shy Roger

Roger would have found himself cornered. He would have had no way out but to go with the flow. He would have had to submit to Dewey's threat. At the same time, he may have been hopeful that he could find the freedom within to begin to dance, to get close to a girl, and to put his hidden fears to rest. Roger gave the Kitten Club a whirl.

A few of the group said that they were amazed that Roger was with them at the Kitten Club. They were sharing a truth. Roger was a newcomer at the Kitten Club, and it was his first time with them there.

Darlene puzzled, "Who would have asked Roger to come along to the Kitten Club?" Ann said, "I felt it was strange for Roger to be at the Kitten Club at all." Terrie added, "Roger did not hang out with me and my friends." Cindy was willing to open the door a bit: "Roger did not fit into our social group very well. He was more shy and more reserved than the rest of us. But he would join us occasionally. I am not sure if Roger went along to other dance halls or went to the Kitten Club earlier than that night of October 5, 1957. But Roger would be part of our group only some of the time."

Was Dewey in charge of getting Roger to the Kitten Club on both occasions and making sure that Roger would not back out? A threat to dump Roger's sexual experience with Pete on the streets of Foley, or to tell his father, may have been a sufficient shove for Roger to have no second thoughts.

Roger spent the Saturday, before his first night at the Kitten Club, with good friends, a husband and wife team, helping them grub their new farmland, cutting down trees, removing stumps and rocks, and preparing the land for plowing and planting. It was a good day of hard work with friends and good conversation. Now they treasure this memory of Roger.

Several times they said: "Roger was a very good kid, a very nice boy. We liked him a lot, and he was never in any kind of trouble in town."

Roger came home from his work, gobbled down a quick supper, showered, and dressed for a night out. One of Roger's sisters remembered that night: "Roger was standing in the kitchen area and begging his father for permission to go to the dance at the Kitten Club. Vern said, 'No, no, no.' Roger begged and begged. Finally, Vern said, 'Okay, but only if you're home by midnight.' Then Roger went to the car and got Dewey to come to the house and promise Vern that they would meet the curfew. Dewey poked his head into the house and promised to have Roger back by midnight. I remember seeing Dewey for that instant, the first time seeing him. I remember his dark, greasy full head of hair. I remember his noisy car sputtering in front of our house. I remember very clearly Dewey saying, 'No problem; home by midnight.'"

We do not know what happened at the Kitten Club on Roger's first night there with the Foley youth. What we know for sure is that the first night was followed by a second night when Roger had no chance for dancing at all. Supposedly, the second night would get serious about "the Roger problem"; the second night would teach Roger his lesson.

Hopefully, Roger was able to get out on the dance floor on that first night at the club. He was eager but inexperienced. He was shy and maybe too sober. If there was a plan for Roger to get wild, hit on someone's date, trigger a duel, overlook his shyness, and end up in the arms of a girlfriend, it failed. Dewey had him home by midnight. Nothing happened to deal with "the Roger problem."

COMBINING THE RECKLESS AND THE CRUEL

Between Roger's first and second nights at the Kitten Club, it seems as though separate plans were spawned and converged. More people wanted to teach Roger a lesson. It became a colliding chase on the irreversible highway to evil. There were at least three separate plans that were exceedingly reckless. There was a fourth that could only be called premeditated murder. During the intervening weeks, the four plans became connected. It was not clear how much the individuals involved were aware of these connections. Some might have been willfully ignorant. Some blindly out of touch. Others were plotting together. Most would not have been concerned about the potential for evil in this convergence of the cruel and the reckless.

This version of the story maintains Dewey as the master planner, who needed to heal the rupture with his sister. He was not as confident as before about finding a plan to fix Roger. His standing with his sister and the group, and his reputation as the sex king of Foley, was on the line. He organized another night at the Kitten Club for Roger and the group. For the second effort, it was crucial for Roger to be recklessly drunk and maybe drugged. He reckoned that Roger would have to be boosted over his shyness with girls. "Hurting Roger" must be ready to dance to Dewey's devilish dirge. Dewey would have decided that the next time at the Kitten Club, one of the girls of the group would have real sex with Roger.

Somehow, it seems, the secret of Roger's sexual debut with Pete was leaked to others outside of the group. It was being passed around like a naughty toy for a nervous laugh and an uneasy chuckle. A few of his classmates in school got the word. Roger was aware and became a very edgy young man. These classmates also heard about Dewey's plan to heal Roger at the Kitten Club. They held this as a secret for the chosen few. They wanted to be there when their shy classmate took his thrilling plunge.

One of Roger's good friends, a girl from the neighborhood, who took many scooter rides with him, shared a story about this edginess: "About two weeks before the death of Roger, my boyfriend and I were at the Foley movie theater. My boyfriend was not in the lobby at the time. Roger came in and walked up to me and was ready to say something to me that seemed to be weighing heavy on him. But before he could get a word out, my boyfriend came back, and Roger turned around and walked away. I have always felt that Roger had something to share with me that was very important. I feel badly that the circumstances were such that Roger was not able to share what was on his mind."

Another girl, who was a sophomore in September 1957 and two years younger than Roger, told about her experience being in the same typing class. Her story suggested that Roger was making some clumsy efforts to overcome his shyness, just a few weeks or a few days before his death. He was under a lot of pressure to change his image, his feelings, his inner self, and save his good name.

While Roger was trying desperately to break new ground in his personal life, he no longer felt safe or comfortable around his wilder friends. He stayed away from the home of Dewey and Cindy. Pete stayed away from Roger. Roger stayed away from the Rainbow Café. Roger offered no more scooter rides to Darlene. Roger was tense but tamed, fearing the wildness of his frivolous friends. He felt more isolated and alone than ever before in his young life.

The next rendezvous at the Kitten Club was set for Saturday, October 5, 1957. The Foley youth were supposedly better prepared to teach Roger a lesson about real sex and get him over his silly shyness with girls. During this second round, the lesson for Roger would be the real thing with one of the girls. Dewey would have selected Darlene as the most promising paramour in the group. Darlene was sixteen years old at this time and one of the three or four regular dates of domineering Dewey, who was twenty-three years old.

Dewey's assignment for Darlene would not have sat well with her. She was Roger's neighbor and friend, and not yet aware of Roger's new squeamishness toward her. Yet if she wanted to keep Dewey as her date, help Cindy and the wild group settle down, and help save "hurting Roger" from his bumbling embarrassment, she would have had to do her part. According to this theory, she decided to share her burden and get help from someone who seemed never to be afraid of anyone or anything; she opened the door to Mack. Supposedly, he had been prowling around her for several months, looking for the right moment to pounce, offering her his finest charm, best behavior, and tall handsomeness, and pushing past Roger's protective custody and care for her. Was this a foolish mistake that had deadly consequences for Roger and heartbreaking sadness for many, many people?

Roger's mother offered a memory that brought this hidden piece of the story into the light. One day in the middle of a conversation about something else, Carol suddenly remembered, "My sister told me soon after the death of Roger that Darlene had told Mack to beat up Roger. And I think that is the truth." When asked how her sister might have heard this part of the story, Carol said, "One of the girls who was at the

Kitten Club that night told my sister about this." Did this story originate from one of the girls who was in the cornfield? It was shared with Roger's aunt within a few weeks after the funeral and shared soon afterward with Roger's mother. It was stored in Carol's memory for forty-eight years and was suddenly made available in the middle of a conversation about some other matter.

This story was remarkable and revealing, but it needed some interpretation. The story revealed that one of the girls who had been at the Kitten Club and possibly in the cornfield needed to talk to someone else about the traumatic ordeal of Roger's mutilation and murder. The girl who needed to talk might have been Cindy or Ann or Terrie. The conversation happened shortly after Roger's funeral. The girl confided to Carol's sister a small piece of the story. This one member, who was part of a group experience, pointed the finger at another (Darlene) as the accused, the scapegoat who was blamed for everything that went wrong. Usually when finger pointing happens, some truth of a real story hidden behind an invented story is surfacing.

If indeed the real story is surfacing, what are the possible elements of truth? First, Darlene initiated one of the three reckless plans to teach Roger a lesson. She did this either on her own initiative or after discussing it with one or several of the other girls. Second, Darlene and Mack became partners in this particular plan. She approached Mack and opened the door to him and invited him into the group to teach Roger a lesson. Third, telling Mack "to beat up Roger" needed to be reinterpreted. Darlene would not have instigated any kind of physical violence against Roger. The group's issue with Roger was not something calling for a "beating" but rather a "lesson" in sex. The term *beat up* in this small story might have been lifted from the initial story. After Roger's murder, they talked about Roger being "beat up." Also this wording was used in the stories floating around Foley about why Roger suffered bodily violence. *Beating* was also the term used in several newspaper articles to describe the initial violence forced on Roger before he ended up on the road and was run over.

The corrected version of this story told by Carol might be, "My sister told me soon after the death of Roger that Darlene told Mack to teach Roger a lesson." Presumably, Darlene was oblivious to Mack's history.

In this way, Mack could have become an insider in the plans for the second night at the Kitten Club for Roger. Darlene would have surprised Dewey with this news. These two guys knew each other around Foley like two bulls in the same cow yard. In the summer months of 1957, they bumped into each other occasionally at the Rainbow and the Parkway. They pawed the ground and snorted but maintained a respectful distance. They did not hang out together lest their meanness kick off an unnecessary brawl of bullies.

Dewey would have approached Mack to talk about his plan for Roger's lesson. Dewey may have found himself dominated and his plan for Roger taken over by Mack. Did the master of the secret plan find himself shoved around and sidelined by a greater force? Perhaps even Dewey felt the circle of fear tightening around him.

In the first interview with Cindy, she was not able to stick to the story when she started to speak ever so carefully about Mack. "I remember Mack in terms of a mysterious 'fear factor.' But then it is not really 'fear' either. I cannot identify and put into words my deep, hidden feelings towards Mack." Cindy was the only one who told about "some conflict between Dewey and Mack," which "happened before our night at the Kitten Club." It was a very important piece of the story. It was possible that she did "not remember what the conflict was about," as she said. But perhaps telling what the conflict was about would have revealed too much..

It's not likely that Cindy was an uninformed weak bystander frittering away in the wings. She was Dewey's sister. She would have known everything that Dewey knew about the story of Roger and about this conflict between Dewey and Mack.

In their interviews, the rest of the Foley youth professed that they knew nothing about Mack's takeover. In their stories, they stayed as far away from Mack as possible. Dewey, Terrie, and, for most of her interview, Darlene said that they did not know him at all. Dewey could not remember him being there at the Kitten Club. Cindy, Ann, and, at the end of her interview, Darlene did not know why he was in the car or at the Kitten Club with them. But is it possible that all of them were fully informed about the takeover and were fascinated about a much bigger happening at the Kitten Club than they could have pulled off by themselves?

COVERING STRANGE AND SCARY TRACKS

Mack was too smart to have been a two-bit player in the staging of masterful deceptions. He seemed to be a skilled master of deceit who knew how to cover his dirty tracks. After being invited into the group's plan by Darlene and after locking horns with Dewey, Mack would have considered how he could carry out his own plan for Roger and then leave the mess in the group's lap.

Mack knew Roger's father as a rough and tough man like himself. They knew each other's bragging stories from sitting together at various bars in Foley and surrounding towns. Mack told his finest tales from his years in the navy. Vern shared stories from his years as an over-the-road truck driver. Vern was a hard and heavy drinker. Mack was a careful and calculating drinker who wanted to be in control all the time.

Mack would have been confident about how Vern would react after hearing that his son had had a sexual experience with Pete and learning about the group's plan to teach Roger a lesson in sex. Perhaps Mack wanted Vern to know this much of the plan and that he had offered to help the group with their lesson on their next trip to the Kitten Club with Roger. This exchange would have happened one or two weeks before Saturday, October 5, 1957. That would allow enough time for Vern to go through the predictable cycle of denial, confusion, abhorrence, anger, rage, and passion to eradicate this sickening scourge from his family.

Mack would have been pleased with how he set up Vern and shared the story. Vern would have been enraged and not known what to do first or next. Mack might have convinced Vern to let him help the group help Roger get over his problem of shyness with girls. Vern would have agreed and given his blessing to Mack and to the wild group to do whatever it took, even though he despised Dewey and his clan. Vern might have promised to hold off in doing anything else.

Vern would have blazed with hostile feelings that no amount of alcohol could temper. He had never dealt with anything like this before. He was used to taking violent action against anything that he felt strongly about. Supposedly being bonded to silence with others taking control in his family, he shared this story with no one, not even his wife. But he needed to explode, to strike out, to take control, to hurl his fury into the despicable darkness.

Volatile and alcoholic, Vern could not contain himself or hold a secret. In the week before Roger's second outing to the Kitten Club, Vern would have confronted his son about this story. He would have cursed Roger with all his fatherly abhorrence for anything that was even a loose relative to homosexuality. Roger would have tried to explain that his only problem was being too shy with girls. Vern could not listen to his son. He could not understand such a gray state of affairs. Angrily, he may have told Roger to go to the Kitten Club with the Foley youth, learn his lesson well, and come back home cleaned up, ready to be a man.

Roger's mother had an open, compassionate relationship with Roger and with her other children. They humored and enjoyed each other and suffered and survived together. Carol trusted that Roger would be able to speak to her about anything troubling his young life. Roger's story of being shamed into silence goes against the mother's sense of her son. When asked if she knew whether Roger's friends in the group treated him badly in any way before the night at the Kitten Club, she said, "If that were so, Roger would have said something to me." The wound suffered by Roger was deeper than words could tell and beyond the reach of normal communication. Roger could not talk to his mother about this sexual whirlwind.

Suddenly it was Saturday, October 5, 1957. Roger spent some time that morning bowling in the alley with his four-year-old brother. Then Roger worked at the Baskfield Shoe Shop for the rest of the day. Vern was nervous and different around the house. He didn't have his usual drinks that Saturday. Carol remembers Roger's last night at home in this way: "Roger came home from work and ate a quick meal. I made hamburgers for that meal, and also apple pie. I remember Roger asking, 'How come you didn't make my favorite, lemon pie?' [Carol had explained that she always did her baking on Saturdays.] Roger ate the apple pie quickly and then he had to leave to get to the gathering place, which was the family home of Dewey and Cindy, about a quarter-mile away. Roger's uncle on my side of the family was there for dinner and offered to drop off Roger at the gathering place. Vern's younger brother was also there for supper.

"Vern was also there that evening for supper. Vern had no objection to Roger going to the Kitten Club that night, and there was no curfew expectation given." When asked what Vern's spirit was like that evening, Carol said, "Vern was more quiet and peaceful than usual. Also he had not been drinking like he usually did on Saturdays. And Vern had no comment about other people being around for supper."

CHAPTER FOURTEEN

SHY INVESTIGATORS

An astute observer of local Foley affairs made her own effort to find out the truth about Roger's death. She said, "At the time of Roger's death, I heard that his body was greatly mutilated. I knew all the details of the story: corncobs, genitals cut off, ear cut off, and stab wounds. Once after the funeral, I asked the chief of police of Foley, Jack Lloyd, about the murder of Roger. Mr. Lloyd waited until we were outside of the grocery store and then told me, 'When the eyes of Roger were pressed opened, there was a look of grimaced terror in his dead eyes.' I will never forget those words.

"When I asked other questions, the chief did not want to talk further. At that time, I accepted that. Today, I would not accept that kind of response. I do not know what the sheriff's department knew about the case; I never pursued the story with them."

Darlene said that she conducted a little investigation of her own and went to a friend to find out about the police cover-up. Her friend most likely was Don Parent (deceased), who changed jobs from deputy with the Foley police department to guard at the St. Cloud Reformatory not long after Roger's death. Don Parent had told others in Foley, "After Roger was killed, I tried to find out the truth about his death. I could get nowhere, in spite of all the stories floating around Foley. Chief Lloyd continued to say that Roger was killed by a car, 'and that is the whole story.'" Darlene was clear about what she experienced. In her little investigation, she wanted to find out what the authorities knew, and if they knew who was on the scene.

Darlene reported, "This police cover-up has always bothered me. Sometime after the death, I talked to a very good friend who worked at the St. Cloud Reformatory, asking him why nobody told them anything about who was involved in Roger's death. This friend said to me, 'You will never, never know, Darlene, because it was one of those investigations that was closed down. The ones who were involved you will never know. Nothing will ever be done about it.'" When asked to guess at what was behind these comments about the cover-up, she said, "Maybe the Mob was involved, somebody with high pull who could cover-up everything."

A MUDDLED INVESTIGATION OF THE FOLEY YOUTH

The wild ones wanted to create the impression in their interviews that the police work was absent or cursory at best. Terrie said, "I certainly was never questioned by any sheriff. And I do not think that any of the other Foley youth at the Kitten Club that night were questioned by any sheriff. I find it difficult to understand that the two sheriffs did not follow up on an investigation and come up with a better explanation about the death of Roger."

As reported earlier, Ann said that the investigation was one little conversation through the screen door: "A cop came to our house on one of the days after the death. He talked to me through the front screen door, never came into the house. I told him that I didn't know anything. There was never any other police work with me." Her sister observed this police interview; she said, "I tried to get Ann to tell me what happened to Roger at the Kitten Club, but Ann would not say anything, just cry. On Monday, one of the cops of Foley, either Ted Tobias or Jack Lloyd, came to our house and talked to Ann, but apparently got no information from her. During all of these years, she has never shared with me what happened. She simply refused to talk about it."

Darlene did not reveal anything about being questioned by police. Cindy was asked to comment about the police investigation but would say nothing. Dewey was anxious to share a small piece of the investigation: "On Sunday morning, a state patrol officer and Foley Chief of Police Jack

Lloyd came to our house to check out the car that I had driven to the Kitten Club. They checked it out and found nothing wrong, no blood on the car, and left satisfied, as far as I understood."

Mack admitted to being questioned. He said, "I was questioned by the police on one of the days after the death of Roger just like everyone else from Foley was questioned. Then I thought that my part in the story was done with. But a week later, I drove back down to Foley and heard that someone had accused me of knifing Roger. I heard about this accusation several times during the month after that, and that was the last that anything had ever been mentioned to me about this until the phone call last night asking for an interview. I haven't thought about that incident since that month after the death of Roger."

A person in Foley who was close to the families of the young people involved said, "There was an extensive investigation of all the Foley youth who had been at the Kitten Club that night. I remember it as a fact. All of these kids were interviewed a lot by authorities. This investigation went on for a couple of months. It was a big scandal in town for a long time. It seemed that all of these kids had gotten together and had come up with the same story that they kept repeating over and over to the various investigators, until they gave up, not being able to come up with any good evidence about how Roger actually died."

INVESTIGATION AND COVER-UP SIDE BY SIDE

The most common memory of the storytellers was that the investigation lasted about a month. Students in school and people in town, some knowing the gruesome details and most having heard the stories of brutality, waited one week after another for an official report. Four local newspapers carried badly researched stories during the first week after Roger's death. Two weeks later, on October 24, 1957, the *St. Cloud Times* reported that an investigation would lead to arrests soon. That was the last official notice of any investigation.

In the *St. Cloud Times* article, Sheriff Bruce Milton of Mille Lacs County stuck to the false story that Roger had "died of injuries suffered when he was hit by a car and dragged several feet," even though he knew the full story. He told the *Times* that "his office did not, at this point, know definitely that a beating took place but was only 'surmising.'" He told the reporter that if there was a beating, for which there might be arrests, the truth remains that "the youth did not die of injuries resulting from the suspected beating." The sheriff was sticking to the official report that "Orville T. Schuffel, [sic] Assistant County Coroner, [had] ruled the death accidental."

Sheriff Milton also debunked the story that two cars were involved. The newspaper said that "authorities [namely, state patrol officers] first surmised that [Roger] had been hit a few minutes earlier by a hit-and-run motorist. However, Sheriff Milton told the *Times* today that he did not think there was a first car. He speculated that the boy had stumbled and fell on the highway after two-and-a-half hours at a nearby dance hall that night."

The paper continued, "Milton said his office is progressing in the investigation and plans to make arrests in connection with the sale of intoxicating liquors to minors and the suspected beating, but he did not know when and how many."

The troubling factor in this newspaper report was Sheriff Milton's apparent intention to retain the misleading information in the public story. He had seen the body of Roger. If not, Sheriff Siemers and Chief Jack Lloyd had seen the body. These two sheriffs and the chief had close communication with each other, with Leon Bock, and with Vern. They knew the truth that someone had murdered Roger. They knew that, after the castration and multiple stabbings, a first car either intentionally crushed Roger or was a hit-and-run accident that "broke every bone in Roger's body," as reported by Leon Bock.

Sheriff Milton told the reporter that he was planning to make arrests. The arrests would be for minor offenses of a "suspected beating" and for the "sale of intoxicating liquors to minors" when capital crimes had been committed. The apparent truth in the background of this newspaper report was that Sheriff Milton was planning to do nothing about the sexual mutilation and murder of his cousin's son. After this article was printed on October 24, 1957, the story of Roger disappeared on the official level. No further action was taken. No further action was ever intended.

Many storytellers remembered how the cover-up gradually wreaked havoc in their lives. In the first week after Roger's death, they handled the horrific stories of Roger's mutilation and death. The wake services and the funeral and the newspaper articles, even though incomplete and confusing, helped them to take the first steps in dealing with the trauma. The second week was accepted as a time for the authorities to do their work.

The third week included the article in the *St. Cloud Times*, which promised some arrests but gave no indication that Roger's death would be explained and that someone would be arrested for his castration and murder. The fourth week was quiet, no word from any law enforcement office. A number of folks said that it became a "big hush-hush thing." People began to feel frustrated that the authorities were not on top of things. Then weeks piled on weeks without a word. Gradually, people began to realize that something had gone terribly wrong. The weeks became months, and the months became years.

INVESTIGATION SIDELINED

The son of Mr. Sebeck shared what his father experienced on Monday, October 7, 1957, in Milaca: "My father's car was minimally involved in what happened to Roger. My father went to the authorities in Milaca to find out what kind of legal problem he was involved in and to obtain some legal help. He was looking for a public defender attorney, because our family had very little money. Dad had written the two testimonials on that Monday, which were witnessed by some police or court officials.

"When Dad asked the prosecuting attorney what he should do, the prosecutor told him, 'Keep your mouth shut, and everything will be taken care of. Go home and don't do anything.' So Dad did exactly that. A week or so later, he received from the State of Minnesota a notice that his driver's license was suspended for thirteen months. It was not true that Dad lost his driver's license because of no car insurance. He had insurance, and that is noted on the police report.

"This strange action on the part of the state without any explanation and with no other legal action taken was never explained to our family. There was never any lawsuit filed. There was only silence after the initial events and exchanges. It was felt to be a strange result. I had to drive my father to and from work in Milaca for those thirteen months. This whole experience shook up my father for a long time."

The successor of that prosecuting attorney has explained that it was possible in those days for the prosecutor to make an independent judgment about a case and to personally decide that it was not worth further legal action. That might have been a sufficient explanation for what Mr. Sebeck experienced. However, the words remembered by the Sebeck family have suggested something more: "Keep your mouth shut, and everything will be taken care of. Go home and don't do anything."

Roger's siblings and several storytellers remembered that a police officer made two separate attempts to obtain Vern's permission for further examination of Roger's body. These stories suggested that at least one officer of the law, possibly Sheriff Siemers, wanted more information. (It is not clear if the law allowed a citizen to block an autopsy, or other investigations, in an unexplained death.)

Roger's sister has a clear memory: "My father refused to sign a permit that would have allowed the sheriff's department to investigate the crime of Roger's death. The police came several times, and Vern would not give in."

A classmate remembered, "There was an effort on the part of the sheriff's office to get permission from Vern to do an autopsy before the burial. Vern refused to give permission for that autopsy."

The part-time assistant to Mark Zawacki at the Bock Funeral Home said, "There was no doubt in Mark's mind that Roger was murdered. Mark said that the police wanted to send the body to the University of Minnesota's forensic department. That would have happened, but Vern Vaillancourt refused to give permission to exhume the body of Roger."

MORE STORIES

One of Roger's classmates and a very good friend left high school in his sophomore year and got a job on the oar boats in the Great Lakes. He was on a boat when his mother sent a telegraph message to call home for an emergency. When he got to shore to telephone home, his mother told him that Roger had been murdered. She was also the mother of Cindy and Dewey.

Roger's friend told his story: "When I got home from the Great Lakes that year, I began to hear some of the stories that were going around about Roger's mysterious death. I organized a little group of friends who did our own little investigation. Nothing came of this effort. It was so sad to hear that Roger was focused on for some dumb reason." This friend could not elaborate on the "dumb reason."

Another story came from Vern's sister's family. As a truck driver hauling to the Twin Cities, Vern often stopped and stayed over at his sister's place. This sister is deceased. Her family reported that she and Vern often talked about Roger's mysterious death. One of the stories told by Vern was that "the girls that were in the car felt such guilt over time that they eventually went to the sheriff [Siemers] and told him the whole story. At that point, the county [Benton County] was supposed to have been unable to afford to prosecute the men. Uncle Vern was told that the county would prosecute if he himself could pay for it, which he was unable to do. This sister of Vern was convinced of this part of the story, because she believed that this caused Uncle Vern the greatest heartache and eventually led to his death."

No evidence has surfaced that Cindy, Darlene, Terrie, and Ann ever confessed to playing a role in the murder of Roger. As the girls in the car, they are the only ones who could confirm this story to be true or false. If there were no truth to Vern's story about the girls and if he told this false story to his sister, the questions to be asked would be: Why did Vern make up this story, and what was he trying to gain from it, or what would this fabricated story mean to Vern?

If it was a true story that these "girls … eventually went to the sheriff [Siemers] and told him the whole story," the question to be asked would be: Why did Sheriff Siemers refuse to accept their confession and to take the legal actions required?

The likeliest option was that this story was a fabrication created by Vern for his own purposes.

THE WILD ONES MAKE A PACT

A cousin and good friend of Roger recalled, "I heard that these Foley youth had gotten together after the death and funeral of Roger and made a pact that they would never tell anyone about what they had experienced at the Kitten Club that night. I could never figure out why they would feel a need for a pact if they were not involved in the death of Roger."

When Cindy was asked a direct question about the existence of a pact, she said, "I cannot remember anything about a pact." As nimbly as possible, she did not deny the fact of the pact. Later, she almost crawled out from under the veil of secrecy when she divulged the heavy burden suffered by herself and her group: "After the death of Roger, there was a long-standing unease among all of us that there was something more than Roger being hit by a car. I cannot recall if there was any clarity about the motive for his death. The official story that Roger was killed on the highway by two cars running over him was not accepted as true."

On another occasion, both Cindy and Dewey heard that parts of a secret story of Roger's mutilation and murder were no longer covered up. They heard that someone had shared the story about how their whole group, bloodied and muddied from the cornfield at the Kitten Club, had gathered at their mother's home to wash their clothes, to bathe, and to wash their hair to get Roger's blood out. They were shocked. They denied any knowledge of or participation in such an event. Then Cindy played the cover-up theme, which Dewey chimed in on, "I do not feel any guilt about anything in regards to this past event, no guilt at all."

Dewey and Cindy's mother is deceased. Before she died, she told her story to two friends, a husband and wife, now deceased, and this couple told her story to their children, who shared it in an interview: "Dewey and Cindy were in the cornfield and present when Roger was stabbed."

Shirley carried the burden of Roger's story as well as she could until she died in 2000. Her husband said that she never talked about any details. But she was not totally silent either. He said about his wife, "Shirley never gave me the details about what happened to Roger in the cornfield. But several times she said to me, 'What happened to this boy was the most terrible, terrible experience of my life … it was a shame what they did to that boy … Dewey and Cindy were with me when I experienced it.'"

SHY INVESTIGATION WOUNDED MANY

One of Roger's siblings expressed the family's dismay after hearing the story of Roger's mutilation and murder and learning about the complicity of the authorities in the cover-up: "How could they! How could they do that? It was obvious that our family did not have money to press the case. But the two sheriffs were closely connected to our family. Sheriff Hewart Siemers of Benton County was a close friend of the Vaillancourts. Sheriff Bruce Milton of Mille Lacs County was a first cousin to my father. How could these two public officials drop this case?"

The wife of Sheriff Milton offered a positive explanation for her husband's professional conduct: "Both sheriffs, Bruce and Hewart Siemers, tried to run down the story, but there were no witnesses. There was nothing more that they could do. Bruce and Hewart were good friends with each other and with Vern. Vern was the oldest Vaillancourt child, and they all lived around the same area and got to know each other. Later, Bruce was challenged by one of Vern's sisters, who wrote him a nasty letter and accused him of not doing enough to solve the case. Bruce knew that that part of the Vaillancourt family had turned against him. Bruce was also upset that the case was not solved."

Roger's uncle (deceased) on his mother's side expressed to a friend his mournful sadness about the cover-up. This friend described this uncle as "one of those wholesome, happy guys who would give you a full arm wave whenever you drove past his place." But with Roger's death and cover-up, things changed. She said, "Once, after a dinner at his place, we were standing outside, and the topic of Roger's death came up. He responded with a mournful moan, 'Oh, there is nothing that we can do about it.' This mournful feeling stayed with me as an indication of what happens when a murder remains so mysterious and covered up as Roger's."

One of Roger's cousins said, "Occasionally I would ask Sheriff Siemers what he knew about Roger's death. Hewart always seemed to give the impression that he knew something but that he could not say anything."

An astute observer of local Foley affairs who has worked with the Minnesota Bureau of Apprehension on various cases said, "The police flubbed on their job in pursuing the culprits in the murder of Roger. I know that the death of Roger changed the life of Roger's parents and had a big impact on many people. I have learned that many law enforcement people are very detached about the small lives lost, and they are not interested in the little people who are victims of crime and whose families do not have the means to push for results."

Members of a family who lived north of Oak Park have vivid memories of Father John Kroll's anger at the sheriffs. Several of them reported the same story: "Father John Kroll, pastor in Foley, was very angry that the sheriffs did not follow through on their investigation into the death of Roger and bring this matter to justice. We remember hearing about this from our own pastor, Father Aloysius Kroll at St. Elizabeth parish in Brennyville, a cousin to Father John Kroll. Because of his anger at the sheriffs, Father John Kroll was determined to live long enough to see that justice would be done about the death of Roger."

A classmate of Roger, who classified himself as a member of the alienated group in Foley as a youth and who was often in trouble with the law, remembered Sheriff Siemers as a fair-minded public servant. He said, "Sheriff Hewart Siemers was a noble guy. I believe that if Sheriff Siemers came to the conclusion that it was nobler to cover-up the story of Roger's death for some larger good, that would be understandable by me."

A man in Milaca knew early on that Roger had been murdered. He was twenty-five years old when he heard Leon Bock, the funeral director of Foley, talk about the stab wounds on Roger's body. This man was standing with a group on the back steps of a church near Milaca, during a funeral, because there were no more seats in the church. This man said, "Leon Bock was talking loud so I couldn't hear the sermon for my friend, and I was frustrated. All of us there heard Leon Bock say, 'You should have seen the number of stab wounds that this kid [Roger] had on his body under his clothing.'"

CHAPTER FIFTEEN

Cover-Up
Speculations

Any cover-up of great human trauma creates a fertile field. A cover-up challenges the human imagination to find the hidden story, the mysterious link, the missing piece that makes some sense out of the insufferable. Speculation fulfills a real need. It can be very helpful. It can also get out of hand. In the human story, it is unstoppable.

Avoiding Trauma by Avoiding Speculation

Roger's immediate family has been forced to live with his murder for forty-eight years without any clear explanation. The cover-up has been devastating for them. Whenever gruesome details were remembered or brought up, they had no way to deal with them. All they could do was suffer the pain again in darkness. In the absence of any clarity or light, they avoided conversation about Roger.

One of the hurtful results of the cover-up was the shunning of Roger's family by others. Often when the story of Roger surfaced, shunning happened. People in the circle stepped back, went silent, darted for cover. The family avoided this shunning by keeping the story of Roger under wraps.

It was not easy for some in the family to get beyond this avoidance routine. The first interview with one of Roger's siblings resulted in this response: "We do not want this story told, because it would be hurtful to our mother, who is elderly and has health problems. If she found out that this story was being told, she could become depressed.

"Our mother has never talked about Roger's death with us, except to give a sigh or a slight comment if someone would bring it up, giving every indication that she does not want to talk about this experience. She does not want her family to talk to her about Roger's death.

"Our mother keeps a copy of a newspaper article about the death of Roger in the Foley High School Yearbook in which Roger was memorialized. Maybe she has other items in that yearbook. But she will not show that yearbook or the newspaper article to anyone in the family or to anyone else."

When asked if the stories of Roger's mysterious death were known to the family, the response was, "Oh, there were all kinds of stories. There was even a story that he was shot. But why bring up all of this since we will never know anything for sure?"

Another sibling was ready to talk about Roger and quick to arrange an interview with Roger's mother, Carol. The first topic that Carol needed to share was her experience of Vern's violence and abuse. It was an overwhelming story, and the story of Roger was buried beneath it. It was not possible to get to the story of Roger without first digging through these other layers of trauma. Once done, it was possible for Carol, in the second interview, to let Roger's story come to the surface.

When asked how she felt about not knowing why this happened to Roger, Carol said humbly, "I probably did not want to know." When asked about the story that the police sought permission from Vern for some kind of follow-up investigation, which was denied, Carol said, "I never heard of that before. If that happened, then Vern never told me about that." As the story unfolded, it turned out that Vern kept most of the information about Roger's death away from Carol.

Roger's mother learned about the story during the research process. As this began, one of her children said, "Mother has been open to new adventures recently. I believe something has been preparing her for this venture." Once the research started, Carol insisted, "I want to know all."

Others, not in the family, also struggled with the effects of the massive cover-up. One of Roger's best friends said that he spent much of his life since 1957 trying to put this story to rest. He said, "I thought about it a lot, but have really not talked to others about Roger's death. I can say that I didn't want to know about it, and I did want to know about it. Only recently have I been able to think kind thoughts about Dewey."

A compassionate woman in Foley was saddened to relate how the cover-up touched herself and her family. She said, "My husband [deceased] followed a strict rule with our family: No one was allowed to share rumors or gossip unless we knew we had accurate truth and that sharing it would be helpful. We heard about the many stories floating around after Roger's death. There was no way to establish their truthfulness. So my husband refused to have these stories talked about in our home. As a result, we were not as helpful to Roger's family as we could have been, and I am not able to be as helpful now with the story of Roger as I would like to be."

Many people were surprised, even shocked, to hear that Roger's story had been rediscovered and was being researched. They asked repeatedly, "How did you hear about it? Who told you about it? What are you going to do with it?" They were at the same time pleased and worried, encouraging and cautious, favorable and fearful. The cover-up was still highly toxic. Most wanted to get out from under it, but many were afraid of what new suffering would have to be endured.

Speculation: Use of Drugs and Drug Running

The use of drugs and drug trafficking was a major speculation spawned early by the cover-up. During the research process, most people denied that illegal drugs were a factor in Foley in the late 1950s. They understood that the drug of choice in the 1950s was alcohol and that many were overusing it and causing huge problems for themselves and their families. They were sure that the so-called hard drugs were not yet on the scene. A minority of folks, however, who worked with law enforcement or made it their business to know the undercurrents of public life, asserted that there was a growing market for hard drugs in the local area.

The cover-up of Roger's mutilation and murder often suggested to people that there was a greater, more sinister force controlling this event and the authorities responsible. Drug addiction, big money, shady deals, out-of-town connections, control of local market, pay-offs and percentage cuts, recruiting new users, witnessing drug deals, bizarre behavior, and dangerous exposure to drugged crazies offered plausible explanations for the inexplicable madness taken out on Roger and the apparent control of the local authorities. The atrocity itself seemed to require a force of evil greater than small-town Foley could produce on its own.

The possibility of drugs on the streets of Foley was answered when an article in the *St. Cloud Times* in 1951 spoke about the availability of hard drugs in the St. Cloud Reformatory. If inmates could get drugs, Foley citizens could do the same. An astute observer of the Foley scene said, "The 1950s were the era for the beginning of drug use by kids in the Foley area. Heavy rumors persisted that Roger's death was drug related. The Kitten Club was famous as a place where drugs could be gotten. I believe that if it were possible to identify who introduced drugs into the Foley area, it would be possible to find an answer about who killed Roger. I graduated from high school in 1951. I was seeing drugs in Foley in 1951."

A couple in Foley who did some socializing with Roger in the bowling alley and on his scooter said, "We have some faint memories about drugs being considered as a possible cause, that Roger was buying or selling drugs or couldn't come up with the money. But these are just faint memories."

A classmate said, "I heard that Roger owed money to someone and was not able to pay up and thus got himself into trouble with someone, which might have caused his death. If this story were true, it might suggest that Roger could have been using or dealing in drugs. But I have no knowledge about where this piece of the story came from or what it really meant. It was possible that this piece of the story could easily have been made up later to explain why the investigation into Roger's death was never completed and made public. In other words, drug money was a bigger challenge for Sheriff Siemers than he was able to handle."

Drugs in Foley in 1957 were a fact. Drug use or drug dealing by Roger was a faint memory, a loose connection with money owed, or a heavy rumor that Roger's death was drug related. A cousin and close friend said, "I never saw Roger under the influence of drugs—that is, glassy-eyed and strange-looking." A student in the same typing class with

Roger in September 1957 saw him kicked out twice in that month for smarting off to the teacher. She said that there seemed to be a personality change in Roger after the summer of 1957 while he was running with the Foley youth. She speculated that his strutting and making younger girls uncomfortable suggested a personality change caused by using drugs. She said, "There was a noticeable change in Roger at the beginning of his senior year; other students noticed it too."

The stories of Roger using or dealing in drugs have been speculative. There has been no solid evidence to place him in that world. Some stories about hard drugs having a role in Roger's death and its cover-up were connected to Mack. His connection to the drug world has been reported more often and more convincingly. Mack was seen occasionally with Roger at a lunch break in the Rainbow Café. But there was no story suggesting that Mack was pushing drugs to Roger.

Roger's cousin and close friend suggested that it was possible that Mack was bringing drugs into Foley. He said, "I saw Roger talking to Mack in the Rainbow Café. It might have been just a casual connection. Roger was in the café during his lunch break on a Saturday. Mack was sitting at the bar drinking a beer, sitting about ten feet in from the door and watching everyone coming into the place. Roger came in and sat three to four feet from Mack and ordered his sandwich. They were chatting. This probably happened in the latter part of that summer of 1957. Mack had a strange look in his eyes all the time. I stayed away from him. It was possible that Roger witnessed some drug dealing by Mack which put him in danger."

A neighbor to Mack in the Foley area, who had a career in law enforcement, said without equivocation, "Mack was dealing in drugs, bringing drugs from the big cities to Foley in the 1950s. He always had new clothes, a new car, and was bringing expensive gifts to his parents. Everyone wondered where he was getting his money from. Most of the other youth and young adults did not want anything to do with him because he would get so wild due to the drugs that he was using."

Mack was kicked out of Foley High School in his sophomore year, 1951–1952. His parents got him into the navy in the spring of 1954. For two and a half years, he operated on his own. Folks in Foley reported that during this time Mack was running with hoodlums who were not from

Foley. He was in constant trouble with the law, and often his parents had to bail him out. It could have been during this time period that Mack developed drug connections. He could have kept these connections fresh during his regular leaves from the navy until he was discharged. He lived in the Foley area during the summer of 1957, until he landed a job with a northern mining company in the middle of August of that year, six to seven weeks before the deadly night at the Kitten Club.

Mack's neighbor, with a career in law enforcement, studied the history of gangs and their criminal history. He said, "In the 1950s, the gangs were motorcycle gangs, called hoodlums. They were rowdy, drug-dealing, and fighting all the time. They preceded the gangs of the 1960s, such as the Jutes in St. Cloud, which were more advanced. In the 1950s, some of the wilder people from the bad parts of places like Anoka attended dances at the Kitten Club. It would be common for an Anoka motorcycle gang to be operating in the areas of Princeton, Milaca, and Foley.

"In the 1950s, local law enforcement departments did not have the funds or the expertise to deal with gangs, such as these motorcycle hoodlums. Local police and sheriffs backed away from them. These gangs were organized enough to buy off sheriffs in those days; that was a very common thing at that time. They were trying to function like the Mobs of the big cities. They took care of 'business.'

"Both Sheriff Siemers and Sheriff Milton could easily have been bought off by the gangs. These motorcycle hoodlums were dealing in coke and heroin at that time, bringing these drugs in from the big cities and trying to develop their own markets. Mack could have developed his own interest and tendencies toward drug dealing. He grew up close to the Oak Park and Foley bootlegging world. As a youngster, he would have heard about the tolerant or corrupt local law enforcement. Mack was known as a lazy young man who detested physical labor. It made sense for him to look for a way to give himself a motorcycle ride on the fast lane to success without having to work."

Research has not been able to locate any friend, fellow hoodlum, or informed observer of Mack in his mid-teen years. Several interviews were attempted by telephone, but not surprisingly, subjects were shut down immediately after the name of Mack was mentioned.

One story added lots of detail and color to the speculation that drugs and gangs were involved in Roger's death. It was the story known as the "Anoka connection." A cousin and good friend of Roger was known in Foley as one of the pool sharks. He told his own story: "One day, some guys from Princeton arrived in Foley looking for the best pool player in town. I was playing cards at the Rainbow Café and was not interested at that time in playing pool. These Princeton guys would not leave without playing me. So I went to the pool hall and beat all four of them, one after another.

"After I beat them, we became good friends and continued to play each other between 1958 and 1960. They came to Foley often to play pool. On one of those days, I brought up the topic of my cousin Roger being killed at the Kitten Club a few years back. When I said this, they went into some kind of shock and clammed up and would not say anything about what they were thinking. I asked them directly, 'Did you hear about Buck [Roger's nickname] Vaillancourt getting killed?' Finally, they broke down and said that they had heard that he got run over by a couple of cars. I said to them, 'There was a lot more to it than that.' I asked them if they had heard that there had been some fighting in the Kitten Club that night. Then they would say no more.

"A year or two later, these Princeton guys came to Foley again. This time, one of them said that they had been to a party in Anoka earlier. Everyone had been drinking, and some loose talk slipped out. He said, 'We were pretty close to his killers.' He would not give any names or say any more about what he knew. I was left with the clear impression that some guys from Anoka were involved in the killing of Roger Vaillancourt. But this man never gave me any more information."

This same man, formerly of Princeton, was interviewed. He had no memory of any such conversation with Roger's cousin. The "Anoka connection" has remained a mystery. Is it possible that some of Mack's hoodlum friends from earlier years met him at the Kitten Club that night and were observers of the violence enacted against Roger? Mack had been two hundred miles north of the Kitten Club for six to seven weeks at his new job. Perhaps Mack was dealing in drugs on the side with these hoodlums the night Roger died.

The "Anoka connection" could still play a role. It might refer to the "three or four guys" standing outside of the Kitten Club door in Mack's story, when he told how Roger ran off into the cornfield after Roger challenged the big navy man to a fight. Mack had said in his interview, "There were three or four guys drinking beer right outside of the door who saw this whole thing." The "Anoka connection" has not been integrated into the story of Roger. So far, it has not justified any major change in understanding what happened. This story has represented another example of how the cover-up has spawned dozens of speculations. All kinds of people have tried to make sense out of the unsolved mutilation and murder of Roger.

Another speculation about drug dealing suggested that Mack and Vern Vaillancourt might have been partners in this kind of crime. Vern was an over-the-road truck driver, who occasionally made trips to Chicago. One of Roger's siblings was asked if there was some kind of drug business going on between Mack and Vern. The response was, "I have wondered about that in the past. Vern would hang out at the Brown Hotel in Chicago, a prominent whorehouse at that time. Some of his salary money was spent there. Did some of the money go into drugs? That was certainly possible."

The speculation of possible criminal complicity between Mack and Vern opened up lamentable scenarios. Did Roger witness some drug dealing between his father and Mack that put Roger in danger? If this speculation has merit, did Mack act alone, or did he and Roger's father act together in dealing with "the Roger problem"? No evidence has appeared to corroborate this story.

Several group members suggested that Mack added some drug to Roger's alcoholic drink in the car on the way to the Kitten Club or at the club. They speculated that Roger got totally drunk too fast. Ann's sister said, "The story goes that Roger kept falling down on the floor, slipping under the table, looking like a rubber chicken, like a rag doll."

Almost all of the speculations about drug use and drug dealing have maintained that Roger was not a user. He was drinking alcohol and sometimes too much during the last months of his life. Darlene said, "I would be willing to bet my life that Roger was never on drugs."

Most storytellers never speculated that trafficking in hard drugs could have been behind the cover-up. However, a few people with solid information about drugs in Foley in the late 1950s have believed strongly that the drug factor offered viable explanations for the mutilation and murder of Roger and subsequent cover-up by the authorities. One reason for the drug option was people's perception of Mack and his capacity for dirty business. Drug money also created possible connections between Mack, Vern, and the sheriffs. In the midst of these speculations, Roger remained basically clean of any rumors of drugs or drug running.

SPECULATION: A SEXUAL ISSUE OR SEXUAL SCANDAL

From the beginning, the stories associated with Roger's mutilation and murder had suggested that some sexual scandal might have caused the cover-up. Most storytellers were reluctant to initiate this topic. Once introduced, some were willing to share their long-simmering feelings that some sexual issue was buried in the story, even though they were at a loss to know the details.

The primary sexual issue raised by storytellers, once the door had been opened, was the question of Roger's sexual orientation. Was Roger gay? (In the 1950s, *homosexual* or *homo* or other derogatory terms would have been used. The term *gay* was initiated later.) A number asked the question. Nobody had any information to say that he was. When Roger's cousin and good friend was asked if Roger gave any indication of having homosexual tendencies, he said, "Absolutely none." He explained his perception of Roger's sexual issues as a problem of "coming of age." He said, "Roger wanted more in life than he had. He was at a crossroads for growing up. He wanted to get more into women. He had aspirations for Darlene or Cindy. But Roger with girls seemed like a ten-year-old boy on May Day."

The classmate who remembered "Roger's pretty eyes" went on to describe Roger's personality as quiet and meek. At the end of her description, she suddenly asked, "Do you think Roger was gay?" It was pointed out that Roger had many friends who were girls and many friends who were boys, but apparently he never had a girlfriend. It was suggested that Roger might have been slow in getting in touch with his sexuality or simply shy with girls. The classmate agreed that this could have been the case with Roger.

One storyteller introduced a story with possible gay sexual undertones. She said, "I have a faint memory of some mysterious connection between Mack, Eddie Deppa [deceased], and Roger. I do not know what this connection was all about, and I do not know how I know this. It is just in my memory." Another said, "At that time, Eddie Deppa was thought to be an active homosexual."

Edmund "Eddie" J. Deppa was three or four years older than Roger. He was closer in age to Mack. Eddie died in 2003 after spending most of his adult life in three Minnesota prisons: the Stillwater State Prison, the St. Cloud Reformatory, and the Lino Lakes Detention Center. A guard at the St. Cloud Reformatory remembered Eddie as often sickly during his time there. Eddie was inclined to theft and other misdemeanors during his teenage years. He was a loner, living on the fringe, without many friends.

Roger's mother remembered that Eddie and Roger were friends. When asked if Eddie ever visited Roger at the Vaillancourt home, Carol said, "No, Eddie always had Roger come over to his house, which was south of the tracks in Foley. Roger was just a good friend of Eddie."

When Eddie was in the St. Cloud Reformatory, sometime in the early 1980s, Eddie called Carol and asked her to come and visit him in prison. Carol visited Eddie on a Sunday afternoon for about a half-hour. When asked what Eddie wanted to talk about, Carol said, "Just ordinary things." When asked if Eddie spoke about Roger, Carol said, "Eddie never mentioned Roger's name." Carol thought that, as a friend of Roger, Eddie simply wanted to "show his concern for me, the mother of his friend."

Later on, after Eddie was out of prison, he called Carol and asked if he could come to her home for a visit. Carol informed her daughter about the appointment. The daughter was at Carol's home waiting for Eddie to show up, just to provide the normal protection for her mother during the visit of an ex-con. Before Eddie came, he called again and was told by Carol that her daughter was with her at that time. Eddie never showed up for his visit. Carol said that Eddie never visited her after that. If Eddie had something to share about "the mysterious connection" between Mack, Roger, and himself, that piece of the story was lost.

It was possible that Eddie and Roger were just good friends. Roger was not a loner like Eddie, but Roger seemed to have a heart for folks on the fringe. A Foley couple confirmed this friendship: "We knew that Roger and Eddie were friends, but we did not know what kind of friends they were. Roger was a town kid, and Eddie was a town kid, and they were together at times."

They explained, "Back then, we did not have conversations about gay sexuality, but we were aware of this sexual difference in the community. It would not surprise us that Eddie was gay. Eddie could easily have been a gay person or could easily have gone either way."

A classmate of Roger said, "Eddie was a leather jacket, greasy scumball kind of guy. We were aware that Eddie used to come to school at times and pick up a girlfriend."

The story about a "mysterious connection" between Roger, Eddie Deppa, and Mack has not been clarified. It has seemed like an odd set of relationships. A sexual element could be hidden in the story. If Mack was sexually involved with Roger and Eddie Deppa in the summer of 1957, or only with Eddie Deppa, who shared this information with Roger, Mack could have compelling reasons for making a four-hundred-mile round trip to and from Foley on the weekend of October 5–6, 1957, to take care of business.

As reported earlier, storytellers described Mack as "violently anti-gay." At the same time, stories indicated that he had a compulsive attraction to males, a compulsion that he supposedly covered up with violent repulsion by castrating the one to whom he was attracted. If Mack was attracted to Roger and/or Eddie Deppa and the stories are true, castration was the predictable next step.

In addition, Mack had a need, in both his memory and storytelling, to ride very close to the cutting edge of his knife. He did not hide from his evil. He embraced it as the work of God. This closeness could have been lurking in this memory of Mack when he said, "I met Roger one time before that night at the Kitten Club, but I do not remember exactly the circumstances. I am quite sure it was some festive party event." As Mack recalled that "festive party event," his eyes rolled into his familiar faraway, glazed look.

The gay sexual factor was given another speculative spin by Dewey and Cindy during their second interview. A number of other speculations for the cover-up were reviewed with them. Who needed protection? Were there big-time drug dealers threatening the authorities? Were there payoffs? Was someone, still unnamed, present and involved in Roger's death who caused the authorities to cover up the story? Was there a family scandal that was best buried in the grave, as one of Vern's comments indicated? Was there a sexuality issue that caused shame or threatened danger to some significant people in the area? Dewey and Cindy listened to these speculations but refused to comment about any of them.

Next, the gay sexual speculation was reviewed with them. Was Roger enticed by someone into a gay sex experience? Did Roger experiment with gay sex with someone? If this happened, did someone panic that Roger could not keep the secret and therefore had to die? This time, Dewey and Cindy broke their stony silence. Both came alive and said that there had been some gay sexual activity in Foley back then. Then Dewey said something strange: "There was some connection between Bill Fox and Vern Vaillancourt after Roger's death." When asked to say more about this connection, Dewey said he could not remember anything else about this memory.

Dewey blurted out his statement apparently without forethought. His inability or refusal to remember anything else about this connection left serious questions unanswered. His comment was made in the context of a brief conversation about some gay sexual activity that might have contributed to Roger's mutilation and murder and the cover-up. The context for the comment seemed important. Was Vern paid hush money by Bill Fox to keep some gay sexual event under cover? Did Bill Fox, as an intimate friend of Pete, cover the bribery demands of Vern to keep Pete from being exposed in Foley as the bisexual who possibly had a single sexual experience with Roger, which sent Cindy into revenge orbit? These speculations have remained unresolved.

It was not unthinkable, however, for Dewey to attempt to throw dust in the air to throw off track any thoughts about his own connection to Roger's death. Dewey had spent a lifetime covering his tracks in this manner. Or, was it possible that the comment was a spontaneous remark that exposed some truth that has remained unexplained?

The speculation about Roger possibly being gay or having a caring heart for gay and bisexual people on the fringe has remained a mystery.

There has been no solid information about Roger's sexual orientation or sexual attractions. The perception among Roger's family and friends has been that his orientation was heterosexual. Only one perception about Roger's sexuality has become relatively certain: Roger was shy about girls, and his shyness motivated him to join the Foley youth. It has seemed apparent that the group and Mack treated Roger as someone with homosexual inclinations. Their perceptions and their alleged actions created the questions and speculations about Roger's sexuality.

SPECULATION: INFLUENTIAL PEOPLE MANIPULATE RESULTS

For forty-eight years, many have wondered if an influential family in Foley took control of the story of Roger to protect one of its own. Before the social upheaval and leveling of the 1960s, the culture, communications, and institutions of small towns like Foley were controlled by a few wealthy, influential families. With behind-the-scenes adroitness, these few families kept their hands on the controls. They decided the big questions. With professional confidence, they gave the thumbs-up or thumbs-down on how the scramble for life proceeded. Folks at the bottom could not fathom such mysteries. Folks in the middle despised such mischief. Those who hungered for just a taste of the power of the few parleyed for friendly deals.

One of Foley's current seniors was a newcomer back then. She described her experience: "The history of Foley showed a tendency for the wealthy and influential people to be easily inclined to cover up their problems and manipulate the system to their advantage. A couple of families tried to run the show. They considered themselves better than the rest and treated me as someone not up to their standards. As a result, I developed a kind of fear of these families and their social clubs in town. I decided to focus my energies on the church."

This was the social atmosphere in Foley in 1957 when a cover-up took control of the story of Roger after his sexual mutilation and murder. When the cover-up ensued, those aware of the workings of the social strata were not surprised that a few professionals or a few influential folk might have given the thumbs-up on the cover-up. Some understood very well and were outraged. For years, they have tried to imagine and speculate which "first class" family had something to hide and commanded the cover-up.

One of Roger's classmates wondered, "The idea of two sheriffs from two different counties, Foley's police chief, and a funeral director, who was also the coroner, closing the investigation makes one think that a prominent family or a very close friend was involved. There has to be a connection between them somehow. Were they motivated by the larger good of the community? I doubt it."

A family member of Pete has been greatly puzzled by the apparent fact that the authorities of several counties and towns concurred in a major cover-up of this investigation. She said, "Such a massive cover-up seems so unreal, but apparently it happened. None of the families of the participants at the Kitten Club and in the cornfield were 'first class' families in Foley; all of them were considered 'second class' or even 'third class' families. None of them had any power or influence or money to buy off all of these people. All of these authorities would have been delighted to put all of these 'Foley youth' in jail for this murder, if this was all there was to the story. One thing that would make sense out of all this cover-up would be if one of the authorities' own were involved."

So far, research has not established a solid story that a son or daughter of one of the wealthy or influential families was a participant in the sexual assault, mutilation, and murder of Roger. Stories have suggested, however, that one or several carloads of Roger's classmates went to the Kitten Club that night to observe the sexual lesson to be given to Roger. These stories have floated in Roger's class and in Foley for forty-eight years. Speculation about which classmates were the curiosity seekers that night has surfaced names, with hopes that one of them would come forward with helpful information. The role of "classmate gawker" would be understandable; the role of cover-up caretaker would not.

SPECULATION: A MENACING INDIVIDUAL OR GROUP TARGETED ROGER

Some people preferred a simpler speculation, avoiding the complicated complicity of authorities, the Mob, influential families, or messy sexual insinuations. They did not like the heaviness of many people possibly being involved. They targeted their blame on one person who alone targeted violence on Roger.

Ann's sister typified this approach. She targeted the whole story on Mack. When asked to explain why Mack would have done such violence against Roger, she said simply, "There are those kinds of people out there." When asked later to say more about what possibly could have motivated Mack, she said again, "There are those kinds of bullies out there."

The trail taken to find that "dangerous someone" who created the "red alert" for Roger in the summer of 1957, according to Darlene, wound through many stories and speculations. The speculation about the "dangerous someone" has led a combination of Mack and Darlene, the latter apparently not knowing that she was part of the problem. As the story goes, Roger was her assigned protector and knew that he was being targeted by Mack. Roger was trying to defuse the explosive threat by keeping his protective role for Darlene at a low profile. So she was to stay in her house and keep away from him in town.

Occasionally, other storytellers included this speculation in their repertoire of explanations about Roger's death and cover-up. One of Roger's uncles said, "I believe that Roger had seen something that put him in danger." This kind of simple statement attempted to say too much and did not offer new clarity, but created more mystery. It had also the smell of a copycat phenomenon.

One speculation was not copied at all. It was totally unique, never hinted at by anyone else. A classmate and "best friend" of Roger reported this story: "There was even a rumor going around that Roger was killed by mistake. Dewey was supposed to have been the target, but Roger got killed instead. To some, Roger looked like Dewey. Shirley of the Gilman area was a girlfriend of Dewey for a while. She was madly in love with Dewey. She was adopted by some family in the Duelm area but kept her name. Her name was part of that rumored story that somehow Roger was killed by mistake when Dewey was actually the target of whomever was out to do some harm."

One explanation of this rumored story was that Shirley's family was so upset that she was "madly in love with Dewey" that they decided to save her from "that idiot." They knew that Dewey was hosting a handful of regular girlfriends at the time with extras on the side. Another explanation suggested that one of the families whose younger daughter allegedly had been impregnated by Dewey were seeking revenge, and they ended up killing Roger by mistake instead of the Don Juan of Foley.

SPECULATION: ROGER'S YOUTHFUL
MISTAKES CAUSED HIS PROBLEMS

For many, the story of Roger lacked clarity because of the gruesome realities of sexual assault and sexual mutilation. There also was some doubt in the air whether Roger was actually murdered or died as a result of one or two cars running over him. These realities were hidden in the cover-up. As a result, some folks speculated that Roger's youthful mistakes were sufficient explanation for the "beating" at the Kitten club and his death on the road. This unfortunate speculation blamed Roger for all the violence committed against him.

These speculations were not intentionally malicious, but they were suspiciously shallow. They almost seemed concocted to contribute to the cover-up.

There was no doubt that Roger made some serious youthful mistakes in the last year of his life, especially in the summer of 1957, between his junior and senior years in high school. First mistake: He tried to run with the Foley youth, which regularly mixed alcohol and sexual activity. Second: As the protector of several women, he challenged Mack not to defile his charges. Third: He drank excessive amounts of alcohol at times, which released forceful aggressiveness. Fourth: He decided that he needed to be sexually active before his time. Fifth: He accepted Dewey as his mentor in these mature affairs. Sixth: He allowed his father's abusive violence to take control of his young life. Seventh: Roger drifted away from his many good friends who could have helped him in his personal struggles.

To blame Roger's youthful mistakes for the grievous violent crimes committed against him is inexcusable. A fair speculation about this matter would suggest the following: If Roger drank too much alcohol at the Kitten Club, ordinary people would have taken care of him for the time being and taken him home at the end of the evening; if Roger was fighting over one or several girlfriends who were dates of other men, ordinary people would have dealt with that in a normal way.

A member of Roger's extended family on Sheriff Milton's side represented another speculation that Roger's mistakes caused his death: "The understanding of what happened went something like this: Roger was at the Kitten Club as an underage person. He got himself totally drunk. There was some kind of confrontation, apparently over a girl. Roger felt rejected and ended up throwing himself in front of a car on the highway. The other youth present and aware of what happened refused to talk about what happened. So the story left behind was that Roger's death was really a suicide caused by severe intoxication and some kind of confrontation in which Roger was the loser."

This relative continued, "So the story goes that the two sheriffs must have met with Vern, and together they decided not to go public with this story because it would be an unnecessary embarrassment for the family. In those days, that kind of action could be taken by the authorities."

This cousin admitted that this story was never shared with Carol or with the other members of Roger's immediate family. It was asserted, however, that this was the story passed around within Roger's extended family. A number of inquiries were made with other members of this extended family. They denied that they had heard this version of the story.

This speculation about the cover-up made its own huge mistake because it was willing to blame the massive violence against Roger on his youthful mistakes. This speculation was not willing to place the blame where it belonged. As a result, sexual assault and mutilation became a "beating." Multiple stab wounds and murderous car crushing became a suicide, "caused by severe intoxication and some kind of confrontation in which Roger was the loser."

These huge mistakes in this speculation are unfortunate. Setting aside all of the gruesome stories and settling on suicide, stemming from a confrontation, has pleaded for a reasonable explanation. This explanation was given in the second part of the speculation—namely, "the story goes that the two sheriffs must have met with Vern and together they decided not go public with this story because it would be an unnecessary embarrassment for the family."

Finally, it seems as though the cover-up has offered a bit of truth. Perhaps the cover-up was not fathered to protect the family of Roger from "an unnecessary embarrassment," but to protect Roger's father from "an unnecessary embarrassment."

CHAPTER SIXTEEN

THE TRUTH BEHIND
THE COVER-UP?

The story of Roger was not the story of Vern, but Vern's story had an immense impact on his eldest child.

LaVerne Vaillancourt was the oldest of twelve children, a family of six boys and six girls. He was born on August 29, 1917. He died on December 6, 1963, at the age of forty-six, six years and two months after Roger's death. He was buried several rows away from Roger's grave in St. John's Catholic Cemetery in Foley.

Vern was not successful in taming the life forces within him. He lived with serious unresolved and unidentified anger about some old hurts or weaknesses. His anger was turned against himself with the abuse of alcohol, turned against his wife with physical abuse, and turned against his eldest son with frequent outbursts. He was promiscuous away from home as an over-the-road truck driver and with several women in the Foley area. Vern's anger and rage, his untamed sexuality, his misuse of over-the-counter drugs for staying awake on the road, his possible use of illegal hard drugs, and his serious hidden health problems mixed together to cause grave instability for Vern in the weeks before Roger's murder.

Roger's cousin and good friend offered his perception of the father-son relationship: "Vern was an abusive father. Roger would go from being lighthearted to being real sullen, when his father was around or would call Roger into the house. There would be noisy exchanges. Roger would come out and be very sullen. He would only share a light complaint about what his father had said or done, not a heavy complaint. Roger would get irate, but he never really vented his deeper feelings.

"Roger was so fast and strong. When Roger was called into the house by Vern and after a lot of hollering, Roger would come out and say, 'Dad is at it again,' and then clam up and never say what he was feeling. Roger did not fear his father at all. Roger was strong enough physically and fast enough that he was not afraid. He was more afraid about using his strength against his father. He was very fast with his hands. When Roger encountered his dad's abusive behavior, Roger would not become 'moody-moody' but would no longer carry on the lighthearted conversation that we were used to. It was probably some kind of depression."

After hearing the recovered story of Roger, one of his classmates speculated, "Was Roger's father really his biological father? What was done to Roger was horrific. How could a father be so cold-blooded regarding the death of his son, even if he was a nasty man himself? How could he not care what happened to his son? Was he bought off? Why was he afraid about his wife finding out what really happened?"

One of Sheriff Siemers' sons expressed something similar: "Vern was a strange man. He never wanted to pursue the case of Roger's death. Vern kept saying, 'He is gone; it's a bad deal; there is nothing that can bring him back; nothing to do about it now.' I found that so strange. If Roger had been my son, there would have been nothing in the world that would have prevented me from finding out what happened to my son, and who did this terrible thing to him. Vern was different. Yes, he had his problems with alcohol and he was abusive to his wife and family, but not wanting to find the truth was strange."

Something changed with Vern between Roger's first and second night at the Kitten Club. On the first night, Vern did not want to give Roger permission to go to the Kitten Club with Dewey and his wild gang. Roger's family remembered that Vern did not want Roger associating at all with Dewey. This was true for many parents in Foley. Four or five weeks later, Vern had a very different reaction. When Roger was getting ready to leave for his second night at the Kitten Club, Vern had nothing to say—no objection, no curfew. Carol remembered that "Vern was more quiet and peaceful than usual. I remember that he had not been drinking like he usually did on Saturdays. Also, Vern had no negative comment about other people being around for supper."

It would seem that Vern was aware of something in the works for Roger. Was he anticipating that something would happen to Roger that night at the Kitten Club while Roger was with Dewey and the other wild ones? Was Vern sitting on a secret?

Five or six hours later, the police came to the Vaillancourt house to inform Vern and Carol that Roger had been killed on the road north of the Kitten Club. Vern didn't say anything to Carol during the rides to and from the crime scene. Then the rest of the events of that Sunday rolled on. Vern and Carol went to St. John's Rectory before the 6:00 AM Mass to inform Father Kroll about Roger's death, where they were scolded severely. They went home and returned for the 8:00 AM Mass, where they were scolded in church. Vern went to church with his family, which was unusual. After Mass, they visited several close relatives in Foley and told them the news.

Later in the morning, Vern and Leon Bock arranged for the transfer of Roger's body from the Scheffel Funeral Home in Princeton to the Bock Funeral Home in Foley. Without Carol's knowledge, Vern allegedly went to the funeral home, identified Roger and saw his body castrated and stabbed, heard about the cornstalk and corncob, and saw how badly mangled his son's body was. Vern called or told his younger brother, Roger's uncle, to pick up Roger's billfold at the funeral home in Princeton when coming to Foley on Monday from the Twin Cities.

Carol does not remember the two sheriffs or other authorities coming to the house on Sunday. Vern met with them at another location and said nothing to Carol about these discussions.

It has not been easy for people close to these events to remember with clarity the little pieces of information that were later made available to them. At first, members of the Siemers family could remember their father answering their questions about Roger's death by saying, "Don't know, and that's all there is." Sheriff Siemers used those same words over and over with many folks. Sheriff Milton did the same.

One member of the Siemers family said that he remembered Vern telling his father several times, "Leave it alone. We don't want any more trouble."

Recently, after hearing the recovered story of Roger, the sheriff's son was able to remember more clearly what he heard from his father: "My father, Sheriff Siemers, told me and my brothers what he knew, but then he told us to keep our mouths shut."

When asked to clarify this memory, this son said, "When my father went to Vern right after the death of Roger, Vern told the sheriff, 'You leave this damn thing asleep.' My father told my brothers and myself that Vern hollered at him to make his point … a very unpleasant experience."

Vern's words to Sheriff Siemers, now remembered, revealed a hidden story behind the cover-up. Vern's words, "You leave this damn thing asleep," needed to be probed. This original statement was different than Vern's later words to the sheriffs, as reported, "Leave it alone. We don't want any more trouble." Also, Vern was saying more than what Sheriff Milton's son speculated was the conversation between Vern and the two sheriffs: "The two sheriffs must have met with Vern and together they decided not to go public with this story because it would be an unnecessary embarrassment for the family."

It was a sad and sorry day when it became apparent that Vern Vaillancourt was the primary reason for the cover-up. Vern himself forced the cover-up on the sheriffs. These two law officers were close to Vern as first cousin and good family friend. Apparently, they could not step away from this relationship to hold their own and do their duty. Vern ended up with control over the authorities, the investigation, and the cruel results of a massive cover-up. Vern's need to control left a legacy of shunning of Roger's family and of deep sadness and endless heartaches.

Why did Vern's words have so much power? What was "this damn thing" that needed to be kept "asleep"? Vern would not have referred to Roger or his murder as "this damn thing." It is possible that Vern could have referred to Roger's castration as "this damn thing." But the physical fact of castration, while difficult to speak about, was not an insurmountable fact. Also castration itself was insufficient to merit such forcefulness with the sheriffs that Vern was able to wrest full control away from them.

Vern could have been thinking about the sexual mutilation behind the reality of castration and the corncob. But even this ghastly evil could not by itself have had such power. Sexual mutilation coupled with murder would have generated a father's rage, even with all of his personal deficiencies, if some other factor had not crippled his capacity for demanding justice.

Vern could have been thinking about the possibility that his son might have been homosexually inclined. Roger's possible sexual experiment with bisexual Pete could have fueled Vern's anger, whether Vern's perceptions of Roger's sexuality were correct or mistaken. Vern could have feared great embarrassment, if and when this sexual problem would have become public as part of an investigation. But Roger's sexuality was not Vern's problem. He could have expressed his abhorrence and stepped away from it easily enough.

Something more powerful was behind Vern's words about "this damn thing." This power came from Vern's discovery that he was implicated in the crimes against his own son. Vern was concerned about his own precarious and compromising situation. His personal predicament compelled him to yell at Sheriff Siemers.

Vern's role in what happened to Roger had to be patched together from pieces of the story. First of all, Vern's fast response to Sheriff Siemers has to be explained. A father dealing with the mutilation and murder of his son could not have responded so quickly to the sheriff by saying, "You leave this damn thing asleep," without a lot of anxious foreboding and forethought. Vern's response came too fast.

Retracing Vern's tracks, it can be said that Vern's anxiety-driven thinking began when the police awakened him and Carol in the night. His total silence during the car rides to and from the death scene suggested that Vern was both in shock and scheming. His private meetings on Sunday, before the funeral, with Leon Bock, the two sheriffs, and Police Chief Lloyd at a location away from the Vaillancourt home revealed someone determined secretly to take control of the investigation and its results. Vern's apparent success at committing the authorities to silence and secrecy about the gruesome realities of Roger's death proved that Vern was in charge.

Once under the control of Vern, the authorities were forced to follow through. Sheriff Milton would have accepted the task to explain to the prosecutor in Milaca the need to sideline the case against Mr. Sebeck.

Two weeks later, Sheriff Milton handled the cover-up with the *St. Cloud Times* with their follow-up article on October 24, 1957. The officers who conducted the investigation of the wild ones and Mack had to have been coached to tread lightly and wrap it up after a sufficient public effort.

The hard question to be asked is: What was Vern's prior knowledge and involvement in the sexual assault, mutilation, and murder of his son?

The first set of tracks was found in the story that Roger's mother remembered. The tracks were not clear but suggested a direction to follow. This story was reported earlier. Carol said, "My sister told me soon after the death of Roger that Darlene had told Mack to beat up Roger. And I think that is the truth." When asked how her sister heard this piece of information, Carol said, "One of the girls who had been at the Kitten Club told her about this."

This memory came from the days or weeks right after Roger's death. It was a memory of one of the girls in the group. It became important in the story. Darlene was a friend of Roger, and it could be assumed that she would not have asked Mack "to beat up Roger." But did she ask him instead to "teach Roger a lesson" or "help the group teach Roger a lesson"? This wording would make sense within the larger story. From this point in the research, "teaching Roger a lesson" became a guiding light in the darkness.

Later on, this same wording reappeared in a memory that came directly from Vern's mouth, shared with his sister and her husband. In the years after Roger's death, Vern often stopped at his sister's place in the Twin Cities after unloading his truck. Vern had long conversations with his sister and her husband over many cups of coffee. Both his sister and her husband are deceased.

The niece and grandniece of Vern's sister remembered a conversation that was very helpful. Four women visited a family member who was sick. The niece and grandniece said, "After the visit, we stopped to eat on the way home. [Vern's sister] was telling us of the many times that Vern had stopped and talked to her and her husband. Vern needed to express his grief at the suffering that Roger had gone through. Vern's sister said that the people who did this to Roger were trying to teach him a lesson."

It was clear to the niece and grandniece that this information, coming directly from Vern, was considered highly secret, never to be shared with any other members of their family, the extended family, or with Vern's family. Vern felt a need to control this information. Why was this small piece of information so dangerous, offensive, troublesome, or toxic that it needed to be controlled? The hidden truth seemed to be that Vern needed to conceal the revealing fact that he knew about this "lesson" before Roger was mutilated and murdered in the midst of that lesson.

What was Vern's grief that he needed to share with his sister and her husband under the cloak of secrecy? As a father, Vern would have experienced grief for the suffering endured by Roger during his night of grimaced terror. But Vern's real grief was for his own sufferings coming from his still mysterious involvement in the sexual assault, the sexual mutilation, and the murder of his son. Vern could not even tell his own sister and her husband the true reason for his need to express his grief. Vern was locked in a solitary cell with his secret.

Could Vern have learned that Roger was supposed to have been taught a lesson after his death? Not likely. The Foley youth's story after the death was that Roger was drunk, fighting, running into the cornfield and getting a beating, and ending up on the road by himself to be killed by two cars. Mack and the wild ones would not have talked to the police or to Vern about teaching Roger a lesson after the death.

The grandniece said that she heard Vern's story a second time in this way: "Roger's friends intended to teach him a lesson because he was allegedly flirting with their girlfriends and they weren't happy about it."

The story of Roger shared by many storytellers had always suggested a heavy sexual element at work at the Kitten Club that night. Vern's reference to a "lesson" suggested a sexual purpose. This "flirting" as the reason for the sexual lesson could not be accurate. There were three other men in the group at the Kitten Club: Dewey, Pete, and Mack. Mack's girlfriend was Mattie, who was at her parents' home that night. Besides, Mack was an oddball with the group that night. He hadn't socialized with them before.

Pete and Cindy had been a couple. Cindy said that there had never been any connection between Roger and her. The story of Roger suggested instead that Cindy and Pete had a falling-out over some sexual experience between Pete and Roger.

Darlene was a couple with Dewey at this time. Roger flirting with Darlene made no sense to her in her interview. She said that she and Roger were like brother and sister, never anything else between them. They were scooter friends, not romantic friends.

None of the group ever hinted that there had been a plan to "teach Roger a lesson." However, admitting that much would have put them into the fiery circle where Roger was sexually assaulted, before he was sexually mutilated and murdered. Teaching Roger his lesson would have happened in the Kitten Club and in the parking lot, as the story has been told. It would have happened before the entire group went into the cornfield. It could therefore be assumed that at least some of the wild ones would not have gone into the cornfield if the entire group had not participated already in the lesson.

Roger flirting with other men's girlfriends was a perfect cover-up story used by Vern and by many others. They said that the flirting caused the fighting, the beating, and the rest of the bloody story. Roger's flirting meant that the beating was a spontaneous result, that there was no premeditated plan, no lesson planned for Roger. The fact that Vern told his sister and her husband that Roger's "friends" planned this lesson for him suggests that Vern knew that the "flirting" story was untrue and a cover-up of the premeditated sexual lesson.

It seems that Vern knew about a sexual lesson for Roger before the second night at the Kitten Club. However, it has not been established how much Vern was involved in the plan. In the absence of information, to the contrary, it should be assumed that Vern did not play a lead role as initiator, master planner, group organizer, or enforcer. Vern's role in the plan would have been as supporter to the others, giving his blessing to what they intended to do for Roger.

If Vern had given his support to the lesson that led to Roger's death, his role had placed him in great jeopardy. At least one person would have known about his involvement. It was probably unclear to Vern exactly how much his complicity contributed to the actual violence against Roger. He would have lived with the dread of being exposed by anyone who knew of his role. He would have lived with the distress of not knowing how much his role contributed to the mutilation and murder of his son. He would have had to live always alert to keep his cover-up intact and to keep "this damn thing asleep."

Roger's family understood that Vern's attitude about Dewey changed after Roger's death. Before his death, Roger was not supposed to associate with Dewey. After Roger's death, no one in the family was allowed to go close to Dewey. Also, Vern restricted any family contact with Darlene. Vern's younger brother remembered that Vern, who was very sick with tuberculosis and a weakening heart, had said, "Before I die, I will have to kill Dewey." Did Dewey know too much about Vern's role in Roger's death? Perhaps the cover-up still had its deadly potential.

During her interview, Darlene hinted at a troublesome connection between Vern and Mack. Her story was a patchwork of pieces, scrambled memories, and strivings for truth. Perhaps she wanted to say that Vern and Mack got together in some way before Roger's death. She would have had trouble doing that because in the interview she kept insisting that she could not remember Mack. But his name slipped into her conversation whenever she was more spontaneous. When telling one of her stories, she added a strange tidbit: "Vern and Mack went back to find Roger." When asked if she meant to say "Vern and Mack," she said, "I cannot remember if Mack was in Pete's car when we returned from the Kitten Club. Anyhow, I went to bed."

It was difficult to decipher exactly what Darlene intended to say with her statement. It seemed she was inventing a story. The intended invented story was not important. What was important was the spontaneous slip in saying, "Vern and Mack went back to find Roger." When questioned about this, she quickly deleted the name of Mack as someone she could hardly remember. But Darlene left the clear impression that in her mind Vern and Mack were connected in what happened to Roger.

The sheriffs and Chief Lloyd heard Vern loud and clear, "You leave this damn thing asleep." But did they know Vern's motivation for the cover-up, Vern's support for Roger's lesson? Did Vern share with them his personal precarious predicament? Would Vern have been able to convince them to drop the investigation based only on his forceful demand? Or did Vern risk sharing his vulnerable, wounded, humiliating mistake? These questions have remained unanswered.

What will the authorities do today once they have understood the staggering evil done to Roger forty-eight years ago? How will they assess their predecessors? What will they think of Vern's very own and very effective cover-up?

Cindy seemed to be begging for someone to explain the story of Roger to the authorities. Three times in interviews she asked, "Why haven't you turned over to the authorities the information that you have received about this possible murder?" She wanted to maintain the great chasm between herself and Roger. Yet she was asking, almost pleading, that someone should do what she could not. Hopefully, Cindy's prayerful wish has been struggling to the surface in the souls of Dewey, Darlene, Ann, and Terrie, and especially in the soul of Mack.

CHAPTER SEVENTEEN

KNIFING IN THE SOUL

Each living member of the wild group revealed a real and specific fear of Mack when telling their versions of the story of Roger. Each one's memory was scarred by a troubling trauma and a personal history of trying not to remember. Each strove mightily over the years to keep far away from this mysterious man who seems to have had such an impact on their lives. Has their shared fear bonded them for forty-eight years?

Many people have wondered how it would have been possible for eight people to keep such a heavy secret for so many years. If the story is true, seven of them allowed Mack to keep them confined to a cornfield closet without risking even a little peep. It seemed improbable. How could one man create such terror?

It has been said that controlling fear and appalling shame could have merged to make the improbable happen in the story of Roger. Possibly self-protection played a role, since each member of the group could have assumed being an accessory to a crime that had no statutory limitation. Maybe fear of Mack also served as a funeral pall over the naked, mutilated body of Roger, keeping Roger under wraps, out of sight.

In the final moments of her interview, Darlene heard that Mack would be interviewed soon in his home out west. This comment instantly created acute panic for Darlene. She pleaded that her name would never be used with Mack or that he would not be told anything about her or where she was living. She was promised that her name and the names of the others in her group would not be used with Mack. Darlene and the others did not owe a lifetime of posttraumatic stress disorder to Mack. It seems that fear of Mack still hounds the wild group, that he has left his scent on each of them, and that the wolf and the group are locked in an odd embrace.

Neither Mack nor any member of the wild group told the story of what happened to Roger in the cornfield that night. The story was recovered from a hundred different sources and then restored to wholeness. Pieces are still missing; gaps appear; and parts might be assembled in the wrong places.

A key link for learning the true story of Roger is capturing the stories of the people who were in the cornfield and uncovering how they lived for forty-eight years with their memories of that murderous night. If the Foley youth were involved and present in that cornfield, they have kept well the secret of the actual events, but they cannot have lived well in their hearts and minds. Psychic pain can be buried deep, but eventually it betrays itself.

DEWEY

Dewey has hung tight and survived by remembering very little. Very careful selective memory has worked for him. "I do not remember" and "I cannot remember anything" were repeated in the interview again and again. This strategy worked for Dewey before his mild stroke. It has worked even better since. He remembered only those tidbits that have kept him at a safe distance from any violence against Roger. He remembered the cornfield and Roger running into it, and then he said, "I remember leaving the Kitten Club without Roger and driving home and going to bed not knowing what happened to Roger."

When the stories of Terrie, Darlene, and Ann were related about Roger fighting and being out of control, Dewey quickly remembered that. The mild stroke was exposed as causing little or no impairment. When told again about the story of Mack showing off his knife in the booth, Dewey snapped nervously, "I cannot remember anything that happened in the dance hall that night."

When Dewey heard the details about the sexual mutilation of Roger, including a cornstalk in the throat, a corncob in the rectum, and genitals cut off, his whole body shook convulsively for a few seconds. Was Dewey revealing how he handled the PTSD panic factor?

CINDY

Many stories have pointed to Cindy as one of the main people involved with Roger's death in the cornfield. The tellers of these tales have not been able to unscramble the complicated intermingling of real and invented stories. They have had no way of learning the whole story. They just know this part is true: Cindy was the driving force behind Dewey and the rest of the group in whatever they did to contribute to the brutal death of Roger. Cindy has had to live with this knowledge and with her own unique psychic pain.

Cindy participated in two lengthy interviews about the story of Roger. In both cases, she was highly poised and operated at the level of extreme alertness. She has finely honed her skills for cautious comments. She revealed her instincts for penetrating watchfulness, deflecting inquiries with deft distractions to irrelevant topics. She seldom relied on the common tactic of "I cannot remember anything about that." Normally she was prepared with a smooth answer that revealed only what she was willing to share. Her alert mind and psyche probably has meant sharp psychic pain with her memories. She has been able to lean on her brother, Dewey, for occasional support. Someone who knows the family well said, "Cindy has been very close to one of her brothers, namely Dewey, probably because they have shared a very traumatic and shameful experience that bonds them in a code of secrecy."

While Dewey seemed to be afraid to remember anything about Mack or even to recognize him in a picture, Cindy stepped vigilantly forward. As reported earlier, Cindy remembered Mack in terms of "a mysterious fear factor, but not really fear either. I cannot identify and put into words my deep, hidden feelings toward Mack. He was some kind of oddball guy who created fear around him. He was around town but not part of our social group."

Cindy was willing to remember Mack. But she did not remember his alleged threat to kill. At the time of her interview, one question was whether she had heard the same threat by Mack in the car leaving the Kitten Club as reported earlier by Ann. A threat that came immediately after a knifing experience could not possibly have been forgotten. Often a painful memory becomes sharper as time goes on.

Nonetheless Cindy answered the question: "I do not remember at all any statement by Mack that he left Roger dead in the cornfield. Nor do I remember Mack making a threat that the same thing would happen to anyone who opened her mouth. If I had heard that threat, I certainly would have remembered that all of these years." Perhaps her last statement, slightly reconfigured, has represented the truth of her psychic pain: She heard the threat; she has remembered it all of these years; and each remembering has included graphic images of what happened.

During the second interview, the story of the castration of Roger was shared with Dewey and Cindy sitting together. At the moment when they heard the word *castration*, the bodies of both Dewey and Cindy shook convulsively at the same time for a moment. It was painful to watch.

In several telephone calls setting up the interviews, Cindy asked, "Have you found out any other pieces of information of the story?" She wanted to appear helpful but revealed a compelling curiosity. When she heard that a number of people in the Foley area have been convinced that her brother, Dewey, murdered Roger, she groaned sadly, "Oh, that is such a heavy burden." Did her sad groan also resonate with her own "heavy burden" as one of the main people allegedly involved with Roger's death in the cornfield?

ANN

As the story of Roger was just starting to come together a few years back, Ann's older sister called Ann and asked if she was open for an interview. The older sister had been a good friend of Roger and one of his scooter riders. She herself had hoped to join the group at the Kitten Club that night, but her boyfriend would not go for it. She felt guilty all these years that her younger sister was there and she was not, when Roger needed her stable support. Ann had never told her anything about what happened to her friend that night. This time, Ann surprised her sister: "I am willing to tell everything that I know about that night at the Kitten Club." It seemed like a breakthrough opportunity. Finally, someone who had been on the scene was willing to tell all.

Ann's revelations about Mack started with her sister's first telephone call asking her to participate in an interview. Ann tentatively tiptoed to the truth. Her sister said, "For the first time, Ann explained to me that Mack took Roger out and did something to him. When it was done, Mack gathered together the rest of the Foley youth outside and threatened them if they would ever say anything to anyone."

During the interview, Ann made a second effort to share information about Mack. She told stories that set up Mack and kept herself in the clear. She found it helpful to make the murder appear as a spontaneous, non-premeditated event. Nothing was said about the group's premeditated plan for a lesson in sex. She stated that there was no connection between this madman and the group. She said, "I had no sense that Mack was setting up Roger for this violent result."

Next came a murder scene and motive that kept her safe. She said, "Darlene and Cindy took Roger to the car. It was said that Roger was not in the car when Mack went out to the car looking for him." After another round of dancing, she found four people standing by the booth "looking at some kind of a hunting knife." She said, "It was closing time at 1:00 AM. I found standing by the booth Mack, Pete, Dewey, and Cindy. Mack had a knife lying on the booth. Mack said, 'Roger woke up and was going to walk home, but I showed Roger that he was not going to walk home.' When the evening ended, all of us went out to the car. We found the back seat empty and the door was open and there was no Roger."

Ann was asked to review the details of this revealing story. She clarified, "When Mack came back to the booth, after his trip out to the car and the cornfield, he had a knife. Mack said that Roger was not in the car and that the door was open. He said that Roger was not going to walk home and get him in trouble."

Ann added her own interpretation about the motive for this spontaneous murder. She said, "Mack was on probation for some criminal activity. If he were caught buying liquor for a minor, he would have been in serious trouble with the law. If Roger would have tried walking home drunk, Mack could have been caught with a violation. Mack said that he had to kill Roger to prevent this trouble from happening."

Ann's third story to expose Mack unfolded in the car shortly after leaving the Kitten Club. This story was more explicit and included the threat to kill. "When we were driving out of the parking lot of the Kitten

Club, we could see a number of police cars, with lights flashing, stopping traffic. So we drove straight ahead through Long Siding to take back roads home to Foley." Her story included exact details, suggesting that she had thought about it many times over forty-eight years, revealing the possibility of psychic pain.

She continued, "When we got away from the Kitten Club, Mack said, 'I left Roger dead in the cornfield.' Mack was riding on the passenger side next to Pete, who was driving; the three girls were in the back seat. Mack said that he believed he left Roger dead, and he said, 'If anyone of you opens your mouth, you will get the same thing.' We understood what Mack was saying—namely, cops were on the road, Roger was dead, and we knew that we would be dead." This story closely associated Roger's death and the threat of death for "anyone of you who opens your mouth … There was no need for Mack to reinforce his threat later on. We knew from the way Mack was and the way the threat was made that we were not going to open our mouths."

Ann tried to tell more of the truth to her older sister in a second telephone conversation after the interview. In the first version, she told her sister that Mack "took Roger out and did something to him." Then he gathered together the Foley youth outside and threatened them. In this second version, Ann said a bit more to her sister: "Mack did something terrible to Roger and told this to the group while standing around in the parking lot at the end of the night at the Kitten Club." She finally admitted to her sister that she was aware all along of the terrible things done to Roger.

DARLENE

Darlene agreed to talk about Roger, but only for ten minutes. She was terrified about accepting a telephone call. It took coaching from a sister and Terrie. At the end of a two-hour interview, she confessed, "I had decided that I was not going to talk about these old memories which I had put to rest a long time ago. I was afraid of bringing them up again." She did very well in telling her version of the story of Roger. In the process, she shared her own wrestling with psychic pain from the knifing of Roger.

Darlene spent a lot of energy during the interview and during the past forty-eight years leaning against the floodgates of fear of Mack. His name she did not recognize. His face she could not fathom. Darlene said, "I do not remember Mack. I cannot picture him." Her denials sounded like a stranglehold was clamped around her neck.

Halfway through the interview, Darlene said, "I can faintly see him sitting there as we talk more about him." Her words suggested that Mack was like a vision appearing through a mist, long forgotten. But her fear of him had to be throttled down to a hum to keep him from thrashing her peace of mind and spirit. After he was out in the open, she treated Mack like a misplaced mannequin with no real role to play.

She could not remember or visualize Mack until the story arrived at the edge of the cornfield. Then she said that his presence was starting to come back. But she continued to talk about "the guys" as being only Dewey and Pete. She actually left the Kitten Club in the car driven by Pete, with Mack sitting in the front seat. Yet she could not remember him in the car or remember his threat to kill anyone who opened her mouth.

When they arrived back in Foley, according to her story, Pete dropped her off at her home. At this point in her interview, she blurted out a strange comment: "Vern and Mack went back to find Roger." Suddenly Mack, who was still a phantom presence for Darlene, was unexpectedly associated with Vern. When asked to explain this new piece of information, Darlene ducked the question by saying, "I cannot remember if Mack was in the car with Pete when we returned from the Kitten Club." This strange comment coming from Darlene connecting Mack and Vern has remained unexplained.

After this stumble, Darlene said, "I went to bed. On Sunday morning after the first Mass, my mother came upstairs and woke me up and told me what had been announced at the first Mass—namely, that Roger had been run over on the road by the Kitten Club and was dead."

When she heard that a visit to the home of Mack was coming up soon, the floodgates of fear collapsed. Darlene blew the lid on her self-control and commenced a full-blown panic attack. Mack was no longer an unreal childhood monster tucked away in the shadows of a storage closet. She began her plea for anonymity and protection. She regretted accepting an interview. She was sorry that she had said too much. This explosion of acute anxiety revealed more of the true story than the rest of her cautious conversation. She wanted to take back whatever she had said so far, most of which was a harmless story.

Darlene expressed her great fears, "I have deep fears and concerns about exposing this story once again, because names and situations can be brought out and create a dangerous situation for other people. I am very frightened about this possibility for myself. I have been afraid of Mack all of my life. I have succeeded in putting him out of my mind. I have found it too scary to talk much about him."

Humbly and exhausted with fear, she said, "I talked a lot more than I had planned." Then she said something about her true memories of the knifing of Roger: "I had decided not to talk to anyone about my gruesome memories, because of what happened and the way Roger died."

TERRIE

It appeared that Terrie had not carried a particularly heavy burden over the years. Yet she seemed deeply relieved that recovering the story of Roger might bring about some healing. She said that she got out of Foley right after high school, because it was a small town running on a rumor mill.

The night Roger died, Terrie had a "split second" sighting of "some weapon" lying on the other booth used by the Foley youth across the aisle. It seemed as though she wanted to say something about the weapon, but perhaps she did not want to re-experience the psychic pain connected with the knifing of Roger. So she said, "Maybe it was a gun lying on the booth; I am not absolutely sure what it was. I remember being very scared; it scared the devil out of me." If Terrie were present during the knifing of Roger, the memory of a gun being used to kill Roger would have been easier to take.

Terrie could not disguise her surprise when she heard that a newspaper article had said that Roger died in the ambulance on the way to the Princeton hospital. This report was mistaken. Actually, Roger died on the highway after the cornfield ordeal but before he was taken away by the ambulance. Nonetheless, Terrie's eyes sprung open wide when she heard that Roger was still alive after she and the others left the scene. Her surprised look suggested fear that Roger might have been able to tell someone what had happened to him.

Recovering the story of Roger has generated some healing already. Terrie said that she was pleased that this effort was being made.

PETE

Two of the Foley youth who allegedly experienced the knifing of Roger suffer from psychic pain no longer. If Pete and Shirley were at the Kitten Club and in the cornfield that night and experienced the knifing of Roger up close, both carried this burden secretly and took it to their graves.

Pete left the Foley area a few years after these events, living in the Twin Cities for some years. Later he returned and took up farming, married and raised a family, and, from all appearances, prospered. He was highly respected as a husband, father, businessman, and member of the local community. He died in 1999. If he were living today, Pete would have shared the whole truth. He was that kind of a man.

His spouse said that the two of them married as mature older folks and never probed the secrets of their separate pasts. She said that Pete was totally faithful during their married life. He continued to be the prince of goodness, almost too good at times. They shared everything in common and communicated easily with each other, but they never talked about Roger's death.

She shared this story in the first interview: "Pete did not share with me his deepest, darkest burden—that is, whatever he knew about the death of Roger. He carried that burden with him to the grave. I never asked him about the death of Roger, even though I thought about it often. Both of us knew that it was a taboo topic in our relationship. I was probably afraid what I might find out, not that he had done something to hurt someone, but that he did not tell the authorities what he knew about that event. I now regret that I never took the initiative to ask him what he knew."

After hearing how the story of Roger was recovered, Pete's beloved spouse said, "This theory about the story of Roger seems to be true. The recovered pieces of the story tied together in this way make sense to me. It now seems likely that my husband, Pete, was in the cornfield with the rest of the group and witnessed the murder of Roger, even though this goes against the logic of everything else that I know about him, a man who wouldn't hurt a flea. His surgeries for stomach ulcers five years after the death of Roger probably resulted from these painful memories."

SHIRLEY

Shirley was a wounded person most of her life. But she was no weakling. She was able to dance with the likes of her boyfriend, Dewey. At times, she was psychologically challenged. Dewey and Cindy's mother accepted Shirley into her home with kindness. Shirley spent many weekends with this family. She did not have the stamina to be a member of the wild group. But she traveled, danced, and partied with them.

Shortly after the shocking experience of Roger's terrible murder, Shirley left Dewey and the town of Foley to find a new life. She found an understanding man whom she married, and they moved to another state. She died on January 21, 2000, in a hospice center after a long ordeal with cancer. During her time of dying, she was assisted by two priests, the chaplain of the hospice center and the pastor of a local parish. Her husband explained, "Neither priest could help my wife find peace with whatever she was troubled about in her life. She struggled with her religion right up to the end and couldn't accept dying because she could not find any peace. She remained very troubled in spite of all the efforts of the two priests to help her."

After hearing how Roger was mutilated and killed, Shirley's husband said, "Now I can understand why my wife was so deeply troubled during her time of dying. She was completely close-mouthed about this horrible experience throughout our married life. I am terribly dismayed and sad that she had to carry this burden for all of those years, because of fear or because of being an accessory to the crime of murder." He promised to go through all the boxes of her personal things to see if she left any information or clues about what happened back then. Later he reported he found nothing at all.

Her husband said that she never told him exactly the details of how Roger was killed. He did not have in hand the larger story in order to evaluate the incalculable significance of her few comments. This is the story told by Shirley's husband: "She told me that she had been with the group at the Kitten Club when Roger was killed. She never said that she had witnessed the death of Roger. But she said that this experience was the most horrible experience of her life and that she couldn't talk about it." The husband said, "I never tried to pry into the secrets of this 'most horrible experience.' She said that she had been at the Kitten Club and was dancing, and this horrible experience happened after the dancing. She knew this guy, Roger, who was killed. She said that this horrible experience left her in a state of shock for a long time."

In addition to these revealing comments, Shirley told her husband, "Both Dewey and Cindy were there to experience this horrible experience with me." Her husband said that Shirley quit seeing Dewey shortly after Roger's death. He said that he and Shirley began to see each other in the latter part of 1958 or early 1959 and were married in 1960. At the time, both were working in the Princeton area.

Her husband, her sister, and her brother said that Shirley was a very close-mouthed person during her life. However, it seems Shirley tried to divulge considerable information about Roger's death with her few comments of exasperation to her husband. In characterizing "this most horrible experience" as a "shame" event, "shame" suggested sexual brutality. Perhaps she was talking about Mack's threat to kill anyone who said anything about what they had seen in the cornfield when she told her husband that she "could not talk about this most horrible experience." Does her comment also suggest that Mack succeeded in making her and her whole group directly involved in the brutal castration and slaying of Roger so that they would be silenced as accessories to the crime of murder for the rest of their lives?

MACK AND MATTIE

It seems as though only one person has been totally free of any troubled, painful memories. Mack has suffered no trial or turmoil in his life from Roger's death. During his interview, he said that after the first month he had never given the death of Roger a second thought.

Mattie, on the other hand, seems to have suffered just knowing about the story of Roger, even though she was not at the Kitten Club or in the cornfield to experience the knifing personally. She was at home that night, waiting for Mack. Early in the interview she complained deeply, "Why can't these people leave these terrible things of the past alone; why do they have to bring this stuff up again and again?" A good neighbor who had been invited to be present for this exchange offered this response, "As humans we love the trash; just look at the news; we have a hard time to let go of the trash."

During the interview, Mack offered an apparently redeeming confession: "God must have a sense of humor to save a man like me." This appealing statement has to be placed next to one of his standard boasts: "I am so saved by the Lord that I could kill someone and no one could do anything against me."

It seems as though both Mack and Mattie have been on the run spiritually, running from one organized religion to another and then to their final spiritual destination: "We do not belong to any church now and never will again. We meet in groups twice a week to study the Bible and learn together about the Living Word of God who has saved us." One interpretation of their spiritual chase suggested that Mack and Mattie have been yearning desperately for liberation from their own disastrous lives.

In spite of his cocky spiritual confidence, Mack was caught off-guard with the sudden request for an interview about the story of Roger. His cunning mind did not allow him to refuse the interview. He said at the start, "I was shocked and surprised that this story about Roger's death was still hanging around the Foley area."

A woman in Foley expressed her great sadness that the full truth of Roger's death has not come forth yet. She said, "I can't believe it! I can't believe it! How can they live with their conscience? Don't they want to deal with this before they die?" This woman in Foley is only one member of a much larger local community of prayerful suffering, bonded by the undying pain of Roger, by the psychic pain of those marked with a hunter's knife and Roger's blood, and by the unhealed pain of Roger's family, friends, and a growing number of storytellers.

The crime committed against Roger C. Vaillancourt was monstrous. The escape from just consequences was intolerable. The successful cover-up was scandalous. The healing of such a mammoth open wound will come in due time with the raising of Roger's Cross.

GROUP MENTALITY

The history of religious human sacrifice speaks of a very tight group solidarity that needs to be in place before humans can sacrificially kill one of their own for the sake of the group's deeper communion and the group's survival from their own deadly social conflicts. The group has to be so tight with each other that the only reality experienced is the tight communion itself, the tight bond of body, mind, and spirit. The group's awareness of the victim is squeezed into this tight group feeling so that the victim becomes one with this shared solidarity, which overtakes all other reality.

Thus, absolutely no person in the group is allowed to "sit it out" or to stand by and watch. Human sacrifice becomes impossible if even one is allowed to *see* what is going on. The circle of sacrificial sharing must be absolutely unbroken. All are numbed into a blinding blurriness. Afterward, all involved can say with total honesty that no such terrible thing as a murder happened. The "incident" was not even experienced as a group secret. It just never happened as other people say it did. The sacrificial event was like a black hole in the universe that consumed all reality without emitting any light.

Human sacrifice has been part of human culture from the beginning. The full bloody version has become less frequent. Lesser versions, just short of the act of killing, continue to reappear in the human story. Sometimes the ancient ritual returns. The human sacrifice of a scapegoat victim, if all goes well, is meant to serve a higher purpose, bringing the group to a deeper communion that overrides all chaos and turmoil threatening the life of the community. But nobody in the group is allowed to actually see the victim sacrificed. A new story or myth is developed to blind the group from looking at the murdered victim. And as the story is told and retold, it is meant to keep alive the beneficial effects of the sacrifice for the group. This myth becomes the true story for the group. The myth is never an outright lie. It is a mixture of fragments of truth and invented details creating a new story that uses a special coded language understood by the group. The story of Roger has become one of these myths.[6]

---

[6] These insights about the dynamics of human culture come from the groundbreaking work of Rene Girard and Gil Bailie.

EPILOGUE

The full story of Roger's death is destined to be told. No amount of fear, shame, or willful forgetfulness will be allowed to control the truth any longer. Too many people have decided that it is time to fling open the locked door of the cornfield closet. The myth of Foley will be unveiled for all to see.

It might have been a naïve hope to expect that simply recovering the story of Roger would bring forth the healing truth. That was the hope guiding the research. That was the mission of *Raising Roger's Cross*. It is still a valid hope and a worthy mission. Who knows what the book alone could have accomplished.

In the last weeks before publication, this mission expanded to include: Kare 11 television of Minnesota committing to investigate and produce a quality news feature about Roger's death; the family of Roger requesting that the coroner open an investigation by exhuming Roger's body and performing an autopsy; and the Mille Lacs County Sheriff's Department deciding to prepare for an official investigation of Roger's death after the autopsy. Lately Roger's hand has been on all of these shoulders, guiding them to share in the same mission.

As officials often say, this is an ongoing investigation. *Raising Roger's Cross* is arriving in the midst of all this commotion. It is uncertain how each of these separate efforts will unfold. Each group will do its own work according to its own designs and purposes. The spirit of healing will use every opportunity in **Raising Roger's Cross.**

KITTEN CLUB

The Kitten Club provided great dancing music to the communities of Long Siding, Milaca, Princeton, Foley, and other small towns in the area. The club was four and one-half miles north of Princeton on Highway 169. It had at least four previous owners and other names. In the 1970s, the bar and dance hall found itself in the path of progress, when new northbound lanes created a four-lane highway. Remnants of the Kitten Club were torn off and carted away as relics or rough lumber for other buildings. The rest was buried in a deep hole under Highway 169, just east of Long Siding in central Minnesota.

The Kitten Club has a long history. But today, few people remember it at all. The young clerk at the Long Siding Township Hall across the street has never heard of the Kitten Club. She has worked there for four years. It seems that the records and the memories of the Kitten Club were meant to be buried along with the building to make room for new times and Twin Cities' travelers driving north on their way to lakeshore homes or cabins in the wood. No one notices Long Siding these days, and no one knows that they are driving over the burial place of the Kitten Club.

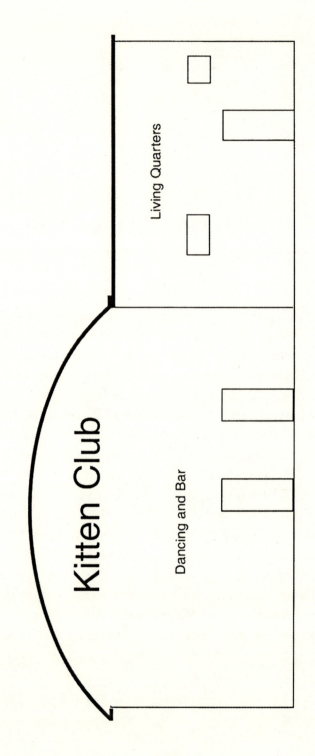

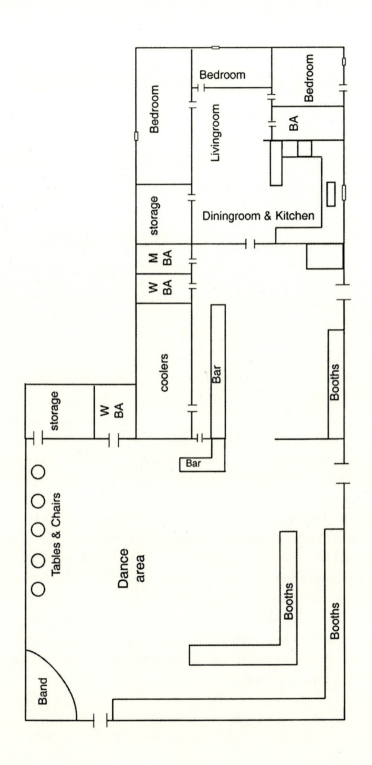

Newspaper Articles

St. Cloud Times

Tuesday, October 8, 1957

Highway patrolmen and Mille Lacs county sheriff's officers were trying to learn if there were any witnesses to the hit-run accident in which Roger C. Vaillancourt, 17, Foley, was injured fatally. Thus far no witnesses had been located, and no inquest was scheduled.

The accident was reported by Norman Sebeck, 43, rural Foreston, Minn., whose car struck the prostrated Vaillancourt on U.S. Highway 169 four miles north of Princeton.

The highway patrol said evidence indicated the youth had been hit a few minutes earlier by a motorist who failed to stop. Vaillancourt, the son of Mr. and Mrs. Vern Vaillancourt of Foley, was still alive when Sebeck stopped another motorist, who summoned patrolmen. Vaillancourt died en route to a Princeton hospital.

Orville T. Schuffel, assistant county coroner, said there was no evidence the Sebeck car had more than struck the injured youth a glancing blow. Sebeck said he didn't see Vaillancourt lying on the highway until his car was on top of him.

St. Cloud Times Obituary

October 9, 1957

Roger Vaillancourt

Roger Vaillancourt, 17-year-old senior at the Foley school and son of Mr. and Mrs. Vern Vaillancourt, Foley, was killed in a car accident four miles north of Princeton at 1 a.m. Sunday.

He was born in Foley July 26, 1940 and had attended the Foley public schools.

Surviving with his parents are the following brothers and sisters: Lana, Richard, Judy and Robert, all at home.

Friends may call after 7 p.m. tonight at the Foley funeral home.

Funeral services will be Wednesday at 9:30 a.m. at St. John's Catholic church with burial in the parish cemetery. Rev. John Kroll will officiate.

Benton County News

Wednesday, October 9, 1957

High School Senior Victim, Hit-Run Driver

Roger C. Vaillancourt, 17-year-old Foley high school senior was the victim of hit-run drivers early Sunday morning on highway 169 about four miles north of Princeton. He is the son of Mr. and Mrs. Vern Vaillancourt of Foley.

The accident occurred about 1:00 a.m. Reporting the accident was Norman Sebeck of rural Foreston, whose car struck the Vaillancourt boy as he was lying on the highway. Sebeck stopped another motorist who summoned the highway patrol and other authorities. The Foley youth was still alive at the time, but died enroute to the Princeton hospital.

According to the report of the State Highway patrol, evidence indicated that Vaillancourt had been hit by some other motorist a few minutes earlier. No witnesses to the accident have been found, but the State patrol and Mille Lacs County authorities are checking into every detail of the case.

Funeral services for Roger Vaillancourt were held at St. John's Catholic church, Wednesday, October 9th at 9:30 a.m. Very Rev. John

Kroll officiated at the funeral mass. Burial was made in the parish cemetery.

Pallbearers were students of Foley High School, Jim DeMarais, Jackie Semrau, Gerald Kampa, Donald Wruck, Jr., Gordon Scherbing and Mike Cheeley.

Members of the Foley High School faculty and the senior class attended the funeral services in a body. The church was filled to capacity.

Roger Vaillancourt was born in Foley on July 26th, 1940. He was to have graduated with this year's senior class. Surviving him are his parents and four brothers and sisters: Lana, Richard, Judy and Robert, all at home.

PRINCETON UNION

Thursday, October 10, 1957

Foley Boy Is Killed On 169 *Estimate Body Dragged 50 Feet By Norman Sebeck's Car Accident 1 a.m. Sunday*

Sunday morning about 1:00 a.m., Norman Sebeck, 43, who lives near Foreston, was driving north on Highway 169. When he was about four miles north of Princeton and a mile north of the Kitten Club, he saw an object lying on the pavement in the east traffic lane. Another car was approaching from the north and he could not turn into the west traffic lane, but he turned his car to straddle the object, which he thought was a dog.

The deputy coroner estimates the body was dragged about 50 feet. When Sebeck alighted from his car, he was horrified to find that the body which he had dragged was that of a boy. It was Roger C. Vaillancourt, 17, of Foley.

Orville T. Scheffel of Princeton, deputy coroner, was immediately summoned and went out with his ambulance. When he arrived, Vaillancourt was not dead but he was badly injured. His left leg and both hips were broken, his neck was broken, his skull fractured, and he was bleeding profusely. Mr. Scheffel started with Vaillancourt back to the Princeton hospital, but the boy died before he reached there.

Vaillancourt had been seen near the Kitten club about midnight or a little later on Saturday night. It is thought that he left there and started to hitchhike home. It is not known why he was in the east traffic lane or why he was on the pavement at all. He should, of course, have been walking on the shoulder. It was at first thought that he might have been struck a glancing blow by another car and thrown to the pavement just before the car driven by Sebeck reached him, but there is no evidence to establish any facts in the case.

Mille Lacs County Times

Thursday, October 10, 1957
Youth Found Seriously Injured on Highway 169

Roger Vaillancourt, 17, of Foley, died enroute to Princeton hospital early Sunday morning after being found lying along highway 169 .6 of a mile north of the Kittenclub.

Norman Sebeck, 43, and his family, of Foreston, were traveling north on Highway 169 about 1 a.m. and his car ran over the body of a man lying on the east side of the pavement. Lights from oncoming cars prevented Mr. Sebeck from noticing Roger on the pavement until he struck his body. The youth was carried a short distance down the pavement by the running gear of the car. Highway patrolmen and Sheriff Bruce Milton were called and the youth was taken to Princeton by ambulance but died before reaching the hospital.

Sheriff Bruce Milton in trying to piece the story together of how Roger happened to be on the pavement reported that a group of Foley young people went to the Kittenclub to dance and when it came time to go home Roger refused to accompany them. The group left for home and the last that was seen of Roger was when he entered a cornfield just north and east of the club. It is thought that Roger might have wandered back onto the highway and was struck by a car before being hit by Sebeck's car, as one of his socks was found some distance to the north of the spot where he was struck the second time. He suffered a fractured skull, a broken jaw, crushed chest and his left leg was badly mangled.

Roger was the son of Mr. and Mrs. Laverne Vaillancourt and was a senior at the Foley high school. He was born in Foley July 26, 1940.

Surviving with his parents are the following brothers and sisters: Lana, Richard, Judy, and Robert, all at home.

ST. CLOUD TIMES

Thursday, October 24, 1957
Sheriff Investigating Death of Foley Youth

Sheriff Bruce Milton of Mille Lacs County is investigating the possibility of a beating and liquor law violations in connection with the accidental traffic death Oct. 6 of a 17-year-old Foley youth.

Milton told *The Times* today there will be arrests made in the alleged incidents which he said were contributing factors in the death of Roger C. Vaillancourt who died of injuries suffered when he was hit by a car and dragged several feet on U.S. Highway 169 four miles north of Princeton. He said his office did not at this point know definitely that a beating took place but was only "surmising".

The sheriff emphasized however, that the cause of death was accidental and that the youth did not die of injuries resulting from the suspected beating. Orville T. Schuffel [sic], assistant county coroner, ruled the death accidental.

Vaillancourt was lying on the highway when he was struck by the car driven by a Foreston farmer.

Authorities first surmised that he had been hit a few minutes earlier by a hit-and-run motorist. However Sheriff Milton told *The Times* today that he did not think there was a first car.

He speculated that the boy had stumbled and fell on the highway after two-and-a-half hours at a nearby dance hall that night.

The youth had been at the dance with a group of other youths and girls ranging in ages from 19 to 26. All were questioned in connection with the incidents which preceded Vaillancourt's death.

Milton said his office is progressing in the investigation and plans to make arrests in connection with the sale of intoxicating liquors to minors and the suspected beating, but he did not know when and how many.

APPENDIX C

OFFICIAL DOCUMENTS

MOTOR VEHICLE ACCIDENT REPORT

Day of Accident: October 6, 1957; Day of week: Sunday; Hour: 1 A.M.

Place where accident occurred: Mille Lacs County; Outside of city limits: 1 mile, north of Long Siding.

Road on which accident occurred: U.S. Highway 169; if not at intersection: 1 mile north of crossroad by Kitten Club.

Vehicles involved: 1; serial number: 21JJE10288; 1951 Chevrolet Sport Coupe; vehicle license no: 1957, Minnesota 4N1922.

Driver: Norman Daniel Sebeck; Address: Route 1, Box 77, Foreston, Minn.; Date of birth: 8-9-1914, male; driver's license 1169802.

Owner: Norman Daniel Sebeck; Address: Route 1, Box 77, Foreston, Minn.; Parts of vehicle damaged: None.

Other Vehicle No. 2: Pedestrian.

Name: Roger Clark Vaillancourt; Address: Foley, Minn; Date of birth: 7-26-40.

Injured Persons: Roger C. Vaillancourt; Address: Foley, Minn.; Pedestrian; Age: 17, male; Did person die: Yes; Were there visible signs of injury such as bleeding, bruises, limping, etc.: Yes; Nature and extent of injuries: broken leg, 2 broken hips, broken neck, brain concussion; Injured taken to: Princeton, Minn.; By: Ambulance.

Insurance: Name of insurance company: Great Northern Insurance Co.; Name of policy holder: Norman Sebeck; Address: Rt. 1, Box 77, Foreston, Minn.

Road surface: Dry; Weather: Clear; Light conditions: Darkness; Kind of Locality: Not built up.

Was there a police officer at the scene: Yes; Name: Dahlberg 232; Department: Highway Patrol.

Witnesses: Bruce _____of Milaca, Minn. Age 23; Bob _____ of Milaca, Minn. Age 21; David _____ of Milaca, Minn. Age 22.

What drivers were going to do before accident: Driver No. 1 was headed: north on Highway 169; Going straight ahead.

What Pedestrian was doing: Laying [sic] in the Highway.

Diagram of accident scene describes the following: Kitten Club is drawn on northeast corner of the intersection of Highway 169 and Long Siding crossroad. Long Siding is drawn on northwest corner of the same intersection. Three small boxes are drawn on the right side of the roadway of Highway 169: the first box is Vehicle No. 1 (Sebeck's car) right before the figure representing the body of Roger, with an arrow pointing north to indicate direction car is traveling; the second box is beyond the body; the third box is pulled the far right side off the road, on the shoulder, with the wording "Parked car on shoulder." The wording point to the figure representing the body is: "one mile from Kitten Club body was laying in highway."

Describe what happened, including any improper driving by drivers (Refer to vehicles by number): Vehicle 1 was driving north on Highway 169. Met a group of cars coming toward me, as the last one past [sic] saw something in the road direct in front of me swerved to avoid hitting it but ran over object. Stopped car immediately past object. Ran back and found a person. Drove vehicle 1 off the highway and stopped another car to go call an ambulance and Highway Patrol.

Signature of person submitting report is required: No signature is given.

(Possible reason for lack of signature: State Patrol Officer Phil Dahlberg finished this report after he released Norman Sebeck between 2:20 and 2:30 AM. For that reason, Officer Dahlberg signed the second testimony written by Norman Sebeck at Milaca on Monday, October 7, 1957. That testimony was witnessed by two police officers of Milaca.)

First Testimony of Norman Sebeck

October 7, 1957
Milaca, MN

I, Norman Sebeck and Family went to my brother-in-law to pick up some roofing paper in St. Francis. We arrived there at 9:00 in the evening and left at 12:15 a.m. Our route home was 56, then to 95 into Princeton, then north on Highway 169. We passed the Kitten Club. About one mile later I approached oncoming cars, dimmed my lights. I was going about 45 miles an hour, when I saw a black and white object laying in the road. At first I thought it was a dog, then the car passed [and] I saw clothing and swerved the car to avoid hitting the object. But I felt 2 bumps as I did. I stopped immediately and went back to see what the object was. I saw that it was a person. I got in my car, moved it off from the highway onto the shoulder. Then went back beyond the person and flagged down a car and asked them if they would go for help and they said they would.

I continued to direct traffic from running over the person again and then others stopped and they helped me. We waited for the ambulance and the highway patrol. The ambulance came and took the boy. Then later the highway patrol came. They asked questions; then let me go home. I arrived home at 2:45 in the morning.

(Signed by Norman Sebeck)

SECOND TESTIMONY OF NORMAN SEBECK

October 7, 1957
Milaca, Minnesota

I, Norman Sebeck, give the following statement without threat or promise of reward and of my own free will. I was coming from St. Francis on my way home to Foreston on Highway 56, 95 and 169. I came past the Kitten Club approximately one mile. I saw this object in the road. At first I thought it was a dog because I saw the black and white. Then as I came closer, I saw the clothes and swerved the car to miss it. The object was laying in the middle of my driving lane facing north and south on his stomach. After oncoming cars had passed, I recognized it was a person and swerved to the left to miss the object. I pushed on the brakes and stopped and went back to make sure what it was. When I saw what it was, I pulled my car off the road onto the shoulder. My wife and 4 children were with me but they were all asleep. This happened at about 1:10 A.M. He was laying with his head toward the north. I had heard two (2) distinct bumps and he was laying close to the same position as when I first saw him. Then I tried to flag a car and the first car stopped and then the car went to get help.

Then it was about 15 minutes before another car stopped. This car stopped so the lights were shining on him. This car went to the Kitten Club to call for help and then came back. They then shined the lights on the boy, which was about 20 minutes after the accident. Someone asked if he was still alive. At this time the boy rolled his head back and forth twice. Someone pulled his shirt back and blood was coming from his mouth. Then the ambulance came and took him away. I waited then until the Highway Patrol arrived at the scene. My approximate speed was 45 M.P.H. The headlights were on low beam and I had 4 rolls of Mica

Paper in the trunk. My wife and 1 child was riding in the front seat and 3 other children were asleep in the back seat. The initial incident happened at approximately 1:00 A.M. but I didn't have a watch.

(Signed by Norman Sebeck and witnessed by two city police officers and State Patrol Officer, Philip Dahlberg.)

CERTIFICATE OF DEATH

(Report on record at the Mille Lacs County Courthouse, number 4-391-3—205.)

Place of death: Mille Lacs County; Township: Princeton; Length of stay in 1b (Princeton): 2 hours. Name of hospital or institution or street address: No. on Highway 169. Is place of death inside corporate limits? No.

Usual residence where deceased lived: State: Minn.; County: Benton; Village: Foley; Address: Foley; Is residence inside corporate limits? Yes; Is residence on a farm? No

Name of deceased: Roger Vaillancourt; date of death: October 6, 1957; Sex: M; Color or Race: Wht; Marital status: never married; date of birth: July 26, 1940; age at last birthday: 17; usual occupation: student; kind of business or industry: school; birthplace: Foley, Minn.; citizen: U.S.

Father's name: Vern Vaillancourt; mother's maiden name: Carol Leason; Spouse's name: none; was deceased ever in U.S. Armed Forces? No; Social Security No.: None; Informant's own signature: Vern Vaillancourt, Foley, Minn.

Cause of death: immediate cause: Fractured Skull & Neck.

Other significant conditions contributing to death but not related to the immediate cause given: Severe Lacerations of Head—Fracture of Left Hip and Left Leg (Femur).

Was autopsy performed? No

Accident, suicide or homicide (specify): Killed by Accident.

Describe how injury occurred: Dragged by car on Highway # 169

Time of injury: 1:10 A.M.; Date: 10/6/57

Injury occurred (while on) Highway # 169, 5 miles north of Princeton; Mille Lacs County; Minnesota.

Date signed: October 6, 1957

Burial or cremation or removal: Burial; October 9, 1957; name of cemetery: St. John's; Location: Foley, Minn.; burial permit issued: October 8, 1957

Dated filed by local Reg.: November 1, 1957; Registrar's signature: Carl Eckdall; Signature of Mortician or Funeral Director: Leon W. Bock, Foley, Minn.; Signature of Sub-Registrar: Leon W. Bock.

PUBLIC RECORDS OF ROGER'S DEATH NOT FOUND

No record at the Benton County Sheriff's Department.
No record at the Mille Lacs County Sheriff's Department.
No record at the Minnesota State Patrol Center in St. Paul.
No record at the Foley Funeral Home.
No record at the Fairview Northland Regional Hospital Archives (Princeton Hospital).
No record of a police investigation.

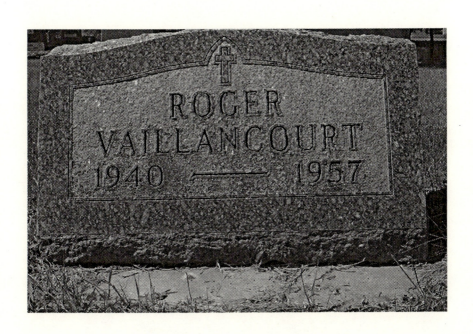

MAY HE REST IN PEACE.

Printed in the United States
41943LVS00003B/219

9 781420 877939